Saarinen Houses

Saarinen Houses

Jari Jetsonen and Sirkkaliisa Jetsonen

Princeton Architectural Press · New York

6	Foreword *Gregory Wittkopp*	14	**YEARS OF COLLABORATION** Gesellius, Lindgren, and Saarinen, 1896–1905 Saarinen and Gesellius, 1905–7
8	Acknowledgments		
10	The Home as a Work of Art	16	**Villa Wuorio** Helsinki, Finland, 1898–1901
		26	**Pulkanranta** Mäntyharju, Finland, 1900–1
		34	**Villa W. Karsten** Helsinki, 1900
		42	**Villa Miniato** Espoo, Finland, 1901–2
		56	**Hvittorp** Kirkkonummi, Finland, 1901–2
		70	**Hvitträsk** Kirkkonummi, 1902
		90	**Summerhouse for A. and E. Lindberg** Vihti, Finland, 1903–5

100	**ELIEL SAARINEN IN FINLAND**	146	**THE AMERICAN YEARS**
	1907–23		Eliel Saarinen, 1923–50
			Eero Saarinen, 1936–61
102	**Villa G. J. Winter**	148	**Saarinen House**
	Taruniemi, Sortavala, Russia, 1908–11		Bloomfield Hills, Michigan, 1928–30
108	**Villa Granagård**	166	**Koebel House**
	Kauniainen, Finland, 1909–10		Grosse Pointe Farms, Michigan, 1937, 1939–40
118	**V. Sjöström Studio**	178	**A. C. Wermuth House**
	Helsinki, 1909–10		Fort Wayne, Indiana, 1941–42
128	**Villa Keirkner**	188	**Loja Saarinen House**
	Helsinki, 1916–18		Bloomfield Hills, Michigan, 1950–51
138	**Row House in Hollantilaisentie Street**	196	**Miller House**
	Helsinki, 1916		Columbus, Indiana, 1953–57

214	The Dwellings We Inhabit
	Susan Saarinen
218	Biographies
220	Selected Works
222	Notes
224	Illustration Credits

Foreword

> It is fundamental that whatever forms a man brings forth through honest work, those forms will not be altogether convincing unless they are a true expression of his life—his emotions, his thoughts, and his aspirations. His art, at best, is a significant testimony of his integrity of mind and spirit, the product of his real personality. No work of art in any field can be considered a work of art unless it reveals the basic nature of the artist himself.
>
> —Eliel Saarinen, quoted by Albert Christ-Janer in 1948

While there are many designs and motifs that echo between the interiors of Hvitträsk, the home Eliel Saarinen built for his family in Finland, and Saarinen House, his later residence at Cranbrook Academy of Art in Bloomfield Hills, Michigan, none are more symbolically potent than the placement of a globe. At Hvitträsk, Saarinen placed a globe on an oak stand he designed in the center of the large hall-like main room, the very heart of their home. Nearly thirty years later in Saarinen House, a second globe rests on a contemporary, asymmetrical base with cantilevered shelves designed by Eliel and Loja Saarinen's son-in-law, J. Robert F. Swanson, and stands in the living room directly on axis with the front door. Here, it immediately commanded the attention of guests who visited the Saarinens in America. In homes that Saarinen conceived as total works of art, where each and every element was either designed or carefully selected by the architect to complement the whole, these two placements of globes and their carefully designed stands symbolize the Saarinens' view of themselves as citizens of the world. As we look back on Saarinen's long and prodigious career, one that lasted more than five decades and spanned two continents, we can see the globe at Hvitträsk as one of aspiration and anticipation and the one at Cranbrook as one of realization and reflection, together encapsulating the breadth of this remarkable career.

While the architect's life and work in Finland is well documented, and monographs exist on many of his individual homes and iconic buildings, Sirkkaliisa Jetsonen and Jari Jetsonen's book is the first to unite his work in both Europe and America into a single volume. Focusing on Eliel's most intimate spaces—the homes that he designed for his own family, relatives, friends, and

(From left to right) J. Robert F. Swanson, Eero Saarinen, and Eliel Saarinen in 1939, standing by the model of the Smithsonian Gallery of Art, with the competition jury. Next to Eliel is jury member Walter Gropius.

valued clients—*Saarinen Houses* not only offers lush portraits of both Hvitträsk and Saarinen House, walking us through them with insightful narratives and compelling photographs, but also places these two iconic houses within much broader contexts. In Finland, the Jetsonens guide us through twelve homes and summerhouses that Eliel, initially with his architectural partners and later alone, created for clients ranging from his parents and his wife Loja's sister to Finland's leading businessmen and professionals. In America, the Jetsonens use Saarinen House, the first of five homes on this side of the Atlantic, to demonstrate Eliel and Loja's supportive partnership as well as to introduce us to the careers of their son Eero and daughter Pipsan Saarinen Swanson and the latter's husband and architect-partner J. Robert F. Swanson. They follow Saarinen House with the home that the Saarinens, together with the Swansons, completed outside Detroit, the Koebel House, and conclude with Eero's recently restored masterwork, the home he designed for Xenia and J. Irwin Miller in Columbus, Indiana. While the histories of these remarkable designers cannot be told without comparable portraits of their public buildings—most notably Eliel's Helsinki Railway Station and Eero's Dulles International Airport Terminal—it is through the homes they designed for themselves and others (a number of which are open to the public) that we may witness the effects of their "integrity of mind and spirit" and glimpse something of their basic natures and personalities.

Gregory Wittkopp, Director
Cranbrook Art Museum and Cranbrook Center for Collections and Research

Acknowledgments

We are grateful to all those whose generous contributions have made this book possible. Special thanks go to the National Council for Architecture and Design in Finland for the support of the research and preparation of the book. We thank the author of the introductory essay, landscape architect Susan Saarinen, for her thoughtful and sensitive contribution, and Gregory Wittkop of the Cranbrook Art Museum for his insightful foreword. We are grateful to editor Nicola Brower of Princeton Architectural Press for having faith in this project.

The greatest thanks, however, go to the owners of the houses who allowed us into their private homes to photograph them and assisted us in finding archival material relating to the buildings, and the representatives of public owners: Veera Lassila, Fregatti Oy, Helsinki; Martti Saarinen, Outi and Pauli Kainulainen, Päivi Helosvuori, Markku Järnefelt, Ilona Puranen, Helsinki; Villa Vuosanta, Helsinki; Pirjo and Markku Jokela, Espoo; Jari Poukka from the Evangelical Lutheran Parishes of Espoo; Pepita Ehrnrooth-Jokinen and Marianna Metsä from the Hvitträsk Museum; Marja-Liisa Mäkelä and Matti Mäkelä, Vihti; Bernt Paqvalén and Lars Paqvalén, Kauniainen; Markku and Stefanie Rentto, Helsinki; Pirkko and Jukka Suvanto, Helsinki; Gregory Wittkopp and Roberta Frey Gilboe from the Cranbrook Art Museum; Miriam C. Nolan and James A. Kelly, Grosse Pointe Farms; Barbara and J. Paul Gentile, Fort Wayne; Stephen R. Dailey, Bloomfield Hills; R. Craig Miller and Bradley C. Brooks from the Indianapolis Museum of Art.

We thank the staff of the Picture Collections of the National Board of Antiquities in Finland, the Helsinki City Museum Picture Collections, and the Manuscripts and Archives Yale University Library for all their help. Special thanks go to curators Elina Standertskjöld, Anna Autio, and Petteri Kummala at the Museum of Finnish Architecture, to the curator at the Cranbrook Center for Collections and Research, Leslie Edwards, and the curator of American Decorative Arts at the Indianapolis Museum of Art, Anne M. Young, all of whom have generously provided help finding written documents, drawings, and old photographs in their archives.

Petri Pajumäki from Adelta Furniture has provided helpful information on Saarinen furniture. Jüri Kokkonen translated the texts of the main chapters.

We are grateful to Eero Saarinen's son Eric and his daughter Susan, and fondly remember how we met on Sirkkaliisa's birthday at a Finnish friend's cocktail party in Los Angeles in 2008. That evening became a real starting point for this book, when Susan kindly promised to recommend us to and help us connect with the owners of houses by the Saarinens in the United States. That was a wonderful birthday present.

Sirkkaliisa and Jari Jetsonen
Helsinki, November 2013

The Home as a Work of Art

> Always design a thing by considering it in its next larger context—a chair in a room, a room in a house, a house in an environment, an environment in a city plan.
>
> —Eliel Saarinen[1]

Eliel Saarinen (1873–1950) and his son, Eero Saarinen (1910–1961), represent not only two architectural generations but also two nations, Finland and the United States. Eliel, born and raised in Finland, established his first practice, a joint office with Herman Gesellius and Armas Lindgren, near Helsinki and soon became the most successful architect of the country, known throughout Europe for his Helsinki railway station (1904–14) and other large-scale projects. In the course of his career, which spanned the first five decades of the twentieth century, his architectural expression developed from early Jugendstil and Finnish national romanticism toward classicism and art deco, the latter seen most famously in Saarinen House (1928–30), his home at the Cranbrook Educational Community in Michigan, whose director he became after his move to the United States in the mid-1920s. Eero, who studied architecture at the Yale School of Architecture, joined his father's practice in the 1930s and would go on to become one of the masters of the International Style. Dedicated to the principles of modern architecture, his work focused on function, structure, and technology. Eliel and Eero's collaboration lasted until Eliel's death in 1950. Their ouvre is characterized by large public works, such as Eliel's railway stations and town halls, and Eero's airport designs. Through important competitions, such as that for the Smithsonian Art Gallery (1939), and through their large-scale corporate works, such as the General Motors Technical Center (1946–56), they greatly influenced the modern American architectural scene.

Father and son were also connected through their interest and love for art. As a young man Eliel wanted to become a painter, and Eero studied sculpture before enrolling at the Yale School of Architecture. In their joint projects they brought together a strong artistic influence and practical problem solving. The homes and dwellings designed by Eliel and Eero Saarinen—together and independently—are based on their belief that a house belongs to its landscape and that its furnishings and details are a part of the building. This concept of total design was first developed by Eliel in Finland, and although the architectural style of the houses designed by Eero in the 1950s is much different from his father's art deco–inspired dwellings, such as Saarinen House, this legacy endured; Eero's Miller House (1953–57) can be seen as a perfect example of a home as a total work of art.

In most cases, the houses by the Saarinens were a result of collaborations, either with colleagues, as in the office of Herman Gesellius, Armas Lindgren, and Eliel Saarinen; with other artists and designers, including members of the family, such as Loja Saarinen and Pipsan Saarinen; or with clients. Many of the clients who commissioned the Saarinens had a strong interest in culture, either by profession or personally. Their houses provided settings for music, art, and design, while also reflecting their way of life. The shared spaces of their homes, where family members spent their time and where guests were received, were more important to them than private areas, and the design of these common rooms reflect this. In Eliel's early houses decorative art played a large role and was integral to the spirit of the interiors, as seen in Hvittorp's (1901–2) painted scenes and grand fireplaces, as well as in the Villa Keirkner (1916–18), which was partly built to exhibit the clients' art collection and was one of Eliel's most sumptuous and luxurious designs. In later houses, interior design took on a similar importance. The Koebel House (1937, 1939–40) features custom-designed interiors, furniture, and lighting.

Carefully executed gardens and landscape design connect the houses with their environments and root them in their locations. Eliel's Finnish villas often have dramatic settings near the sea or a lake, such as Villa Miniato (1901–2), Hvittorp, and Hvitträsk (1902). Among his earlier works the most extensive garden was that of the Villa G. J. Winter (1908–11), whose owner had a particular interest in botany. Eero's Miller House integrates a landscape design by Dan Kiley that continues the architectural concepts in the surrounding landscape in a remarkable way.

Two of the Saarinen family's homes, Hvitträsk in Finland and Saarinen House in Michigan, in particular, crystallized the characteristics of the architects' residential designs, featuring harmonious and cozy rooms and carefully considered details that create a unique mood and a balanced domestic environment. Eliel wrote in *The Search for Form in Art and Architecture* about the importance of individual, personal design in dwellings:

> Moreover, the mission of the home is to provide a moral and ethical ground from which the growing generation may further grow. Honesty of thought and sincerity in work are the inheritances with which the home can and should endow the youth. To that end, all the means must co-operate, and in this respect the form-treatment of the home—if honestly conceived and sincerely executed—is a vital, although perhaps subconscious factor.... We say this to stress the fact that there must exist a spiritual interrelationship between the family and the form-treatment of the home. In other words, it must be understood that the form-treatment of the house should not be just an impersonal and coldly technical combination of various rooms for various purposes, but rather a treatment of form which is capable of bestowing a proper resonance to the human atmosphere in the home. The form-treatment of the home, consequently, is comparable to the body of the violin, which has not only its practical function of supporting the strings, but even more so its musical function of giving the strings their singing tone.[2]

The individuality of Eliel and Eero Saarinen's houses, spanning a period of some sixty years and located on two continents, is clearly apparent in the following pages, but the homes discussed here also have a lot in common. They all blend into their surroundings in a natural, unforced manner. They are approached gradually—coming to the house is like an overture. They reward their inhabitants and guests with inviting nooks, comfortable chairs to sit in, and rooms heated with fireplaces. The views from the windows are mostly of surrounding nature or of a luxuriant garden. As Eero stated in 1959:

> I see architecture not as building alone, but the building in relation to its surroundings, whether nature or man-made surroundings. I believe that the single building must be carefully related to the whole in the outdoor space it creates. In its mass and scale and material it must become an enhancing element in the total environment.[3]

The informal and tranquil vacation homes and residences featured in this book were designed to make living as pleasant as possible. These are houses where beauty is present.

Years of Collaboration

Gesellius, Lindgren, and Saarinen, 1896–1905
Saarinen and Gesellius, 1905–7

Herman Gesellius, Armas Lindgren, and Eliel Saarinen met at the Polytechnic Institute in Helsinki and established their joint office in 1896, while they were still students of architecture. Before long, their studio became one of Finland's leading architectural practices, enjoying success in competitions and taking on commissions of various kinds. The architects received international recognition in 1898 when they won the competition for the Finnish pavilion at the Paris World's Fair. Built in 1900, the pavilion aroused international interest in the primal energy of Finnish architecture and its original forms of expression.

The work of the Gesellius, Lindgren, and Saarinen office combined the ideas of the international art nouveau and Jugendstil movements with a uniquely Finnish language of form. The most prominent example of the national elements in the firm's architecture is the Pohjola insurance company building in Helsinki (1899–1901). Faced with natural stone, its walls are decorated with pictures of forest animals and plant ornaments, exuding the spirit of national romanticism that abounded in the country at that time. The pro-Finnish propaganda of cultural circles had gained emphasis when strict Russification policies were introduced in the 1890s. Finland was part of the Russian Empire from 1809 until 1917, and the beginning of the twentieth century was marked by a tense political atmosphere between the two nations. The economic boom that had led to affluence in Finland in the late nineteenth century slowed down around the same time, worsening the situation.

Nevertheless, the office received abundant commissions. An extensive study on Saarinen notes that "with reference to their joint work, Gesellius, Lindgren, and Saarinen can be regarded, without any exaggeration, as the private residence architects, total-concept artists, interior and object designers of the century."[1] Along with apartment buildings for the center of Helsinki, the studio designed residences and villas for wealthy families in all parts of the country. The office also worked on several bank and office buildings, and their largest project was for the National Museum of Finland. In 1905, the trio decided to disband their joint office.[2] Armas Lindgren moved back to Helsinki and founded his own office, while continuing his academic work as artistic director of the Central School of Industrial Art. Herman Gesellius and Eliel Saarinen collaborated until 1907, when they established separate offices, while still living at Hvitträsk, the shared studio and residence of Gesellius, Lindgren, and Saarinen.

opposite
This chair was custom-designed by Gesellius, Lindgren, and Saarinen for Villa Wuorio.

Villa Wuorio

Helsinki, Finland, 1898–1901

Salomo Wuorio (1857–1938), the owner of a painting and house decoration firm, commissioned Villa Wuorio as a summer residence for his family in Laajasalo, a neighborhood in southeastern Helsinki. Originally specializing in ornamental painting, Wuorio's firm was the leading and most successful enterprise in its field in Helsinki during the late nineteenth and early twentieth century. Immediately after it was founded, the firm received contracts for painting important public buildings, which led to residential commissions in the growing city. Working both independently and together with architects and artists, the company made stained-glass windows and performed decorative painting work for numerous buildings in Helsinki, including several projects by Gesellius, Lindgren, and Saarinen. Wuorio himself was an important patron of art and culture, who donated funds for architectural and art projects. Interestingly, despite being well connected in the field, he chose to commission the design of his own summerhouse from a firm of then relatively unknown young architects. His son Gunnar later established the Gerda and Salomo Wuorio Foundation, which owned Hvitträsk from 1969 until 1981. The foundation renovated the building complex and opened it to the public.[3]

By the late nineteenth century, it had become popular among affluent residents of Helsinki to spend the summer months at summerhouses, so-called villas, built by the seashore in the outskirts of the city. The neighborhood of Laajasalo had begun to develop into an area of villas in the 1870s. Villa Wuorio is on a rocky point with a westward view of the sea dotted with islands and the maritime fortress of Suomenlinna. The name of the area, Bergvik (Rocky Bay), aptly describes the rugged terrain and setting. Part of the surroundings of the villa was left in its natural state, while the rest was developed into a formal garden. An existing cottage on the site was used as a guesthouse.

With its unfaced log walls, wooden porch columns, and decorative moldings, Villa Wuorio exudes a romantic spirit. Natural stone, which predominates in the high foundation of the house, was, together with wood, a favorite material at the turn of the century. The architectural design of the house has been described as a combination of several themes.[4] International features, including those of Swiss wood houses and art nouveau buildings, are found along elements inspired by the Viking Age and characteristics of the traditional Finnish log house. Examples for exotic additions are the wrought-iron ornaments on the

opposite
Winter view of Villa Wuorio from the sea

exterior, the window shutters, the porch columns, the notched ends of the logs, the dragonlike ornaments along the eaves, and the forged flame-shaped hinge leaves of the outer doors.

The compact form of the building is enhanced by protrusions and recessed parts, wooden and metal consoles, and log ends that jut out at each end of the facade, resulting in a playful variation of light and shade. The sea is visible in the distance, over the treetops, from the round openings at the top of the tower crowning the house. A lookout tower used for enjoying the surrounding landscape was a popular feature of summerhouses of the late nineteenth century. Taking in the beautiful view was just one of the ways members of the upper class passed their time when staying at their villas. The summer season was also spent, with due help from servants, walking in the gardens and enjoying their controlled natural setting, and sitting on verandas and in gazebos, sheltered from the sun, in the company of family members or guests. Socializing and festivities were important forms of interaction.

There are several entrances to the house from the garden, providing access to the main hall, living room, dining room, and kitchen on the ground floor. The design of the living room was inspired by the *tupa*, the main room of a traditional Finnish farmhouse, and was described in contemporary texts as "genuinely Finnish."[5] It was the central space of the house, and the other rooms of the first floor, originally the dining room and children's room, and a porch, facing south and west, were grouped around it. This type of informal lounging area reoccurs in different variations in many of the homes and summerhouses designed by Gesellius, Lindgren, and Saarinen. Apart from Finnish traditions, the work of British architect M. H. Baillie-Scott (1865–1945) was an important model for the residential architecture of the office.[6] His interiors were widely published and showed a similar spirit in their attention to craftsmanship and interior detail. Gesellius, Lindgren, and Saarinen's fireplace corners with built-in sofas and the layout of the main hall in many of their residential projects especially resemble Baillie-Scott's works. In Villa Wuorio the space is dominated by a granite open fireplace of a rough and solid appearance and a wooden ceiling with exposed beams. The wainscoting of the walls underscores the special nature of the space as does its dim lighting, with the windows facing the covered porch.

A combined sofa and cabinet piece was part of the original furniture. In the hall a *ryijy* rug known as *The Flame* by Finnish painter Akseli Gallen-Kallela was part of the interior decoration.[7] The dining room furniture is also original and reflects the national-romantic style of the time in the ornamental fretwork of the backrests of the chairs and the cupboard doors, which almost resembles embroidery. The main bedrooms were on the second floor, with servants' rooms located on the top floor. A steep staircase leads to the highest point of the house, the lookout tower.

The Wuorio family used the villa until 1964, when it was acquired by the City of Helsinki.[8] It can now be rented for celebrations.

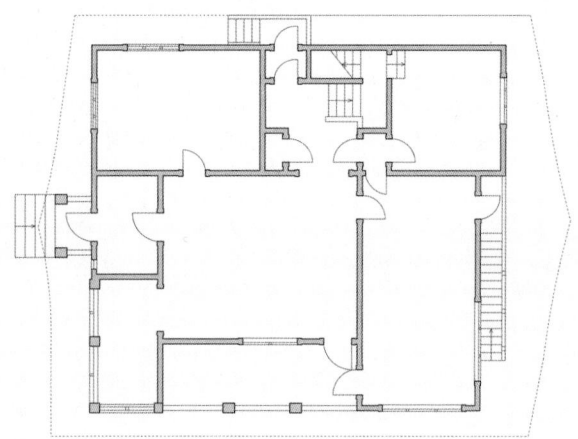

opposite
First-floor plan

top
Villa Wuorio from the southwest. The corner room was originally an open veranda.

middle left
All furniture in the dining room was custom-designed by Gesellius, Lindgren, and Saarinen.

middle right
Salomo Wuorio in the villa on his seventieth birthday in 1927

bottom
Perspective drawing, 1898

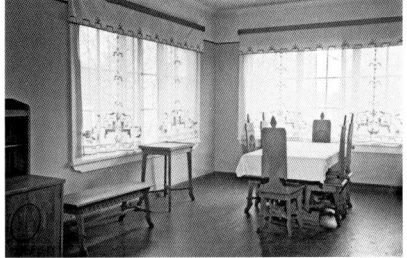

opposite
Villa Wuorio from the southeast, showing elements inspired by the Viking Age and characteristics of the traditional Finnish log house.

below
The tower with its long eaves and wooden consoles

overleaf
View of the sea from the tower (left) and from the second floor (right)

top
Armoire designed for the villa by Gesellius, Lindgren, and Saarinen

bottom
The first-floor dining room was originally a children's room.

opposite
Fireplace in the living room

Pulkanranta
Juho and Selma Saarinen's villa

Mäntyharju, Finland, 1900–1

Eliel Saarinen designed Pulkanranta as a summer residence for his parents, Juho (1846–1920) and Selma Saarinen (1845–1914). Mäntyharju, in the heart of the eastern Lake District of Finland and easily reached via railway, became a popular summer destination in the late nineteenth century. The summer homes there were typically built for civil servants of nearby towns and cities, and affluent members of the middle class who had both the means and the opportunity for leisure. Family fathers often worked in town for part of the summer, while other members of the family and servants spent the whole summer at the villa. The season spent in the countryside was usually an active social time filled with outings, guests, and parties. This was the lifestyle at Pulkanranta, where Juho and Selma moved in the spring, to return to the city after harvest in the fall. The place brought together various members of the Saarinen family, including the couple's grown children with their own families. After Juho and Selma's deaths the property was passed on to Eliel's brother Hannes and still belongs to the family. At midsummer a large number of Juho and Selma's descendants gather there to celebrate.

The design of the house coincided with the construction of the Finnish pavilion at the Paris World's Fair of 1900, and Saarinen, who spent time in Paris to supervise its construction, was often too busy to work on the drawings for Pulkanranta. When he finally completed them and the house was under construction, Saarinen's mother described it as follows: "The house looks strange; we cannot say yet that it is beautiful, but it is unusual. I don't think many people will like it."[9]

The villa is built of logs painted with traditional red ochre paint and has a steeply pitched roof and an open porch facing the adjacent lake. The landscape surrounding the house opens up toward fields on one side while gently sloping toward the lake on the other. It was designed as a parklike setting in the 1920s and 1930s. The building consists of two parts, with the living room forming a separate wing with a higher ceiling than the other rooms. Serving as the heart of the house, it is an interpretation of the *tupa*, as suggested by its unpainted log surfaces, an oven of traditional shape, and a bench along the walls. At the same time the space appears modern by facing outside in several directions, through small-paned windows on three walls that provide daylight from dawn to dusk. An open staircase leads to the bedrooms on the upper floor. A kitchen and additional bedrooms are on the first floor of the second wing. The

opposite
View of the house from the shore

hottest part of a summer's day could be spent in the shade of the porch, where the family often gathered to drink coffee and listen to piano music.

Pulkanranta blends national and international features. The materials and colors of the villa resemble those of traditional Finnish farmhouses, while the small-paned windows are influenced by the English arts and crafts movement and the door frames are inspired by Egyptian forms. The upper parts of the gables are faced with shingles, a nod to the American shingle style [10] as well as to traditional Finnish churches, which were roofed with shingles from the Middle Ages until the eighteenth century. The villa's main design elements, including multilevel spatiality, with a line of sight from the corridor of the bedroom floor to the lounging area below; the gable motifs of the exterior; and the accentuated forms of the roof, are repeated with greater diversity at Hvitträsk. Saarinen also faced the gable end of his own wing at Hvitträsk with shingles in a similar manner as at Pulkanranta. He would occasionally visit the villa and spent some time there during his last visit to Finland in 1946.

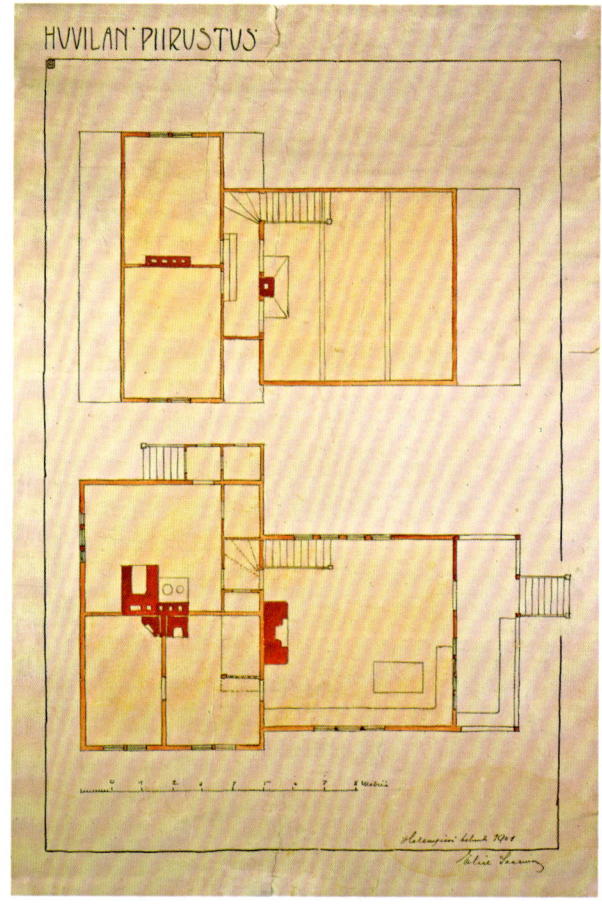

opposite
Facades (left) and first-floor
and second-floor plans

top left
Eero Saarinen near Pulkanranta
in 1922

top right
Selma Saarinen's relatives
visiting Pulkanranta in the
summer of 1903

bottom
Juho Saarinen at the villa in 1914

29

below
Porch with a ladder leading to the top floor

opposite
View of Pulkanranta from the shore

opposite
The living room focuses on a large fireplace. The stairs on the right lead to the bedrooms upstairs.

below
The chairs in the living room were designed by Armas Lindgren.

Villa W. Karsten

Helsinki, 1900

This summer residence, commissioned by pharmacist Walter Karsten (1868–1953), was built in Vuosaari in East Helsinki at the turn of the twentieth century. The construction of summer villas on seafront properties in Vuosaari had increased at the end of the nineteenth century, when steamboats began to provide regular service to the area.

Although Villa Karsten is of simple form, it reflects the modern spirit of European architecture at this time. The predominant feature of the house is its high-pitched roof with long eaves extending down to the upper edge of the first-floor windows. While the gently curving line of the eaves seen on the original plans for the building became straighter when realized, there is still a predominantly art nouveau spirit to this house with its undersized and small-paned windows and their tapering arches. The tower that is characteristic of many summerhouses by Gesellius, Lindgren, and Saarinen has here been reduced to a small round corner bay. In addition, a pair of rounded bays protrudes from the roof facing the sea. The tapering shape and ornamental ends of the chimneys are also characteristic elements of the art nouveau.

The layout of the main floor is divided into private areas for a middle-class family and the kitchen and servant's room with their own entrances. As the most important space of the house, the living room has a higher ceiling than the other spaces. As typical in villas by Gesellius, Lindgren, and Saarinen, the walls feature paneled surfaces and other wood details. Carpentry was Karsten's pastime, and he made the paneling for his villa himself. The living room's corner fireplace with fixed furnishings was another characteristic element used in the firm's domestic designs. The round bay, seating only a few people and looking out into the surrounding landscape, was called a "lantern." The upper floor originally contained two bedrooms and attic space, but has since been renovated to add another four bedrooms.

In addition to the main building there is an older cottage on the site as well as a boat shed and auxiliary building designed by Saarinen. Located on the shore of a fjord-like bay, the villa was originally surrounded by a large park created by Karsten's son Erik, who introduced, among other species, plants grown from seeds obtained in Tibet. Many of these still survive, and the rock garden planted on the slope of the bedrock still blooms in the summer.[11] Today the villa is owned by the city of Helsinki and can be rented for special occasions.

opposite
View of Villa Karsten from the sea

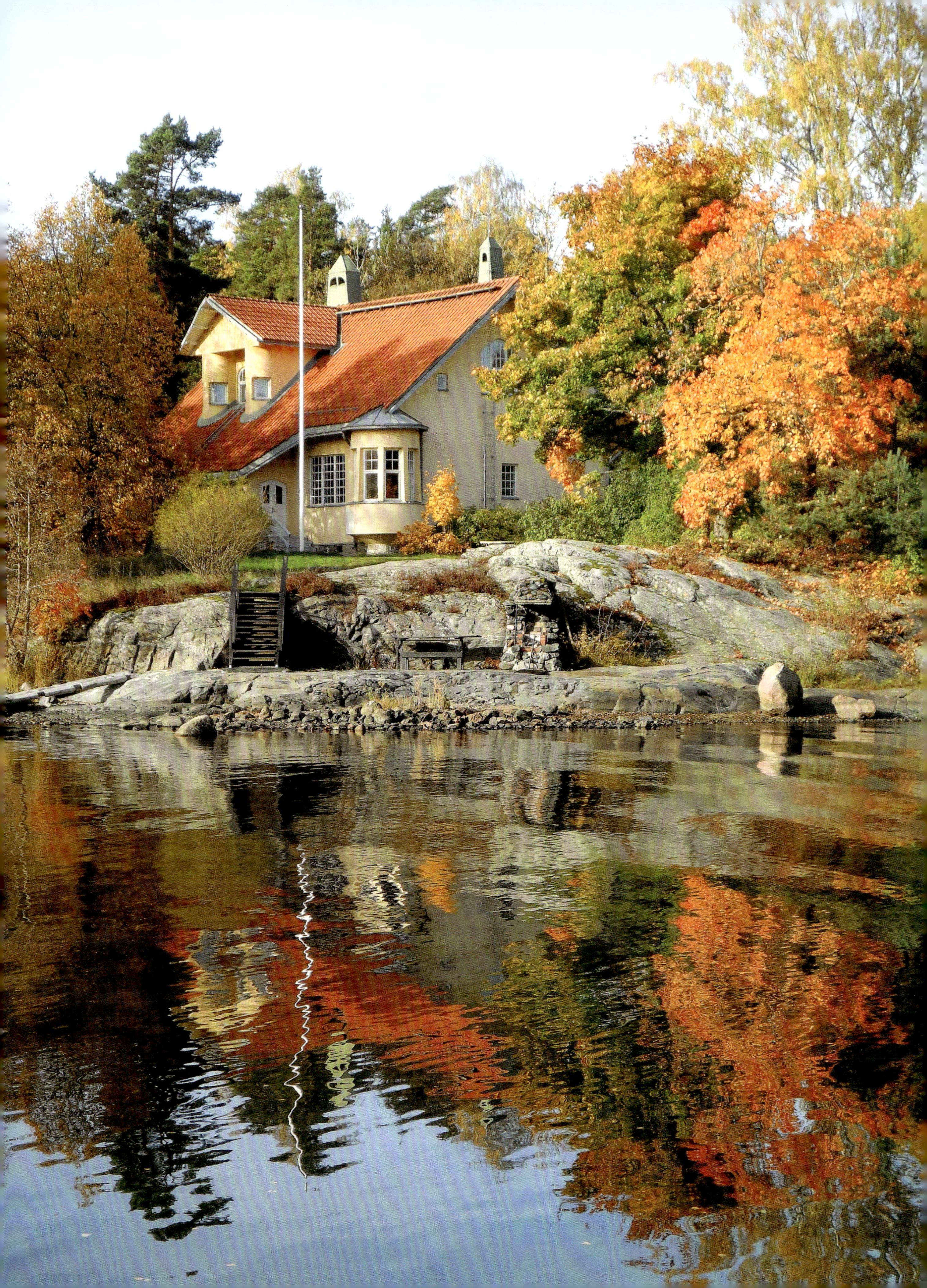

top
View of the living room, 1967

bottom
Wooden staircase in the entrance hall

top
View to the entrance

bottom
Plans, section, and facades, watercolor and ink drawing, 1900

overleaf
Garden-side porch (left) and the house seen from the sea (right)

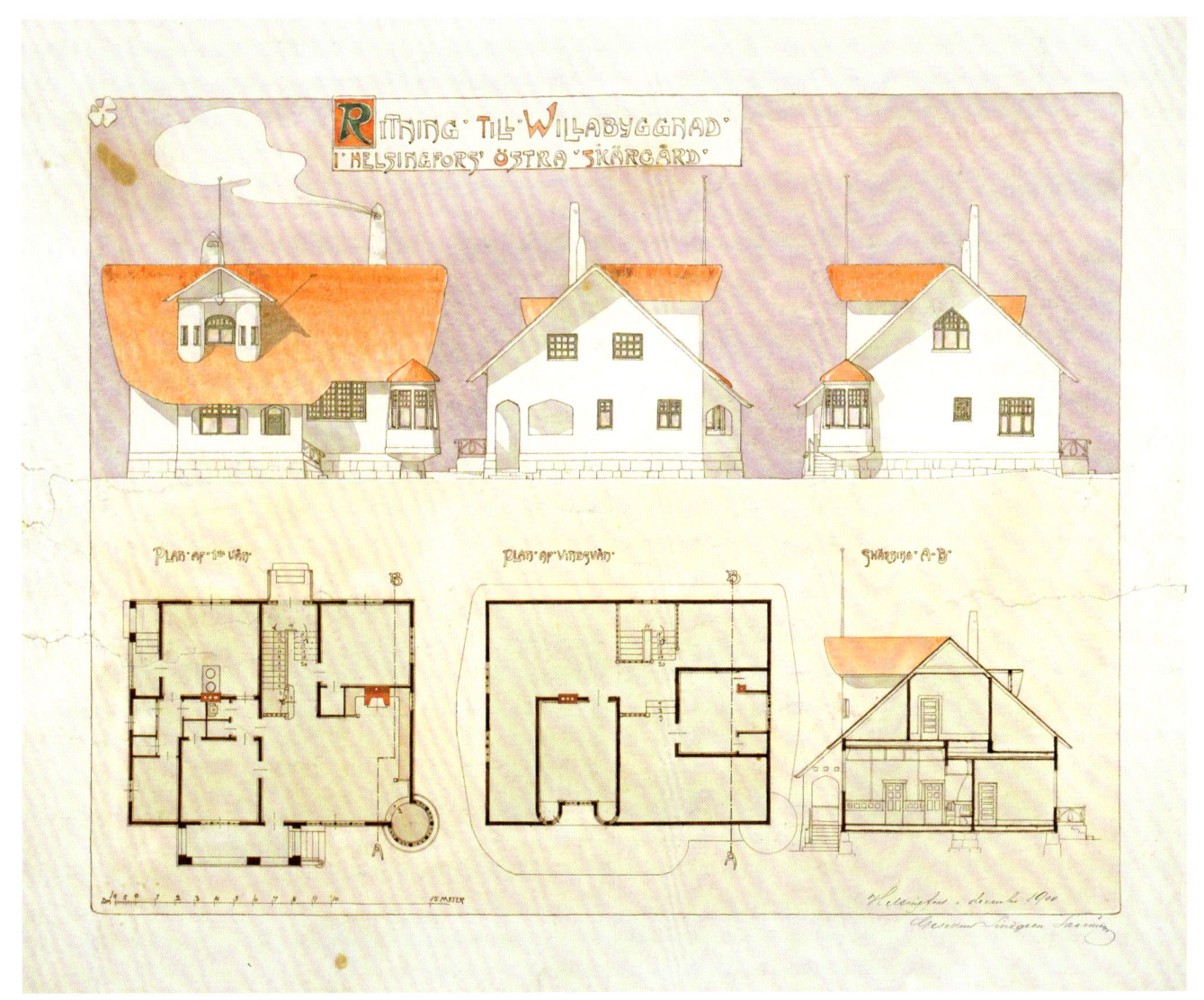

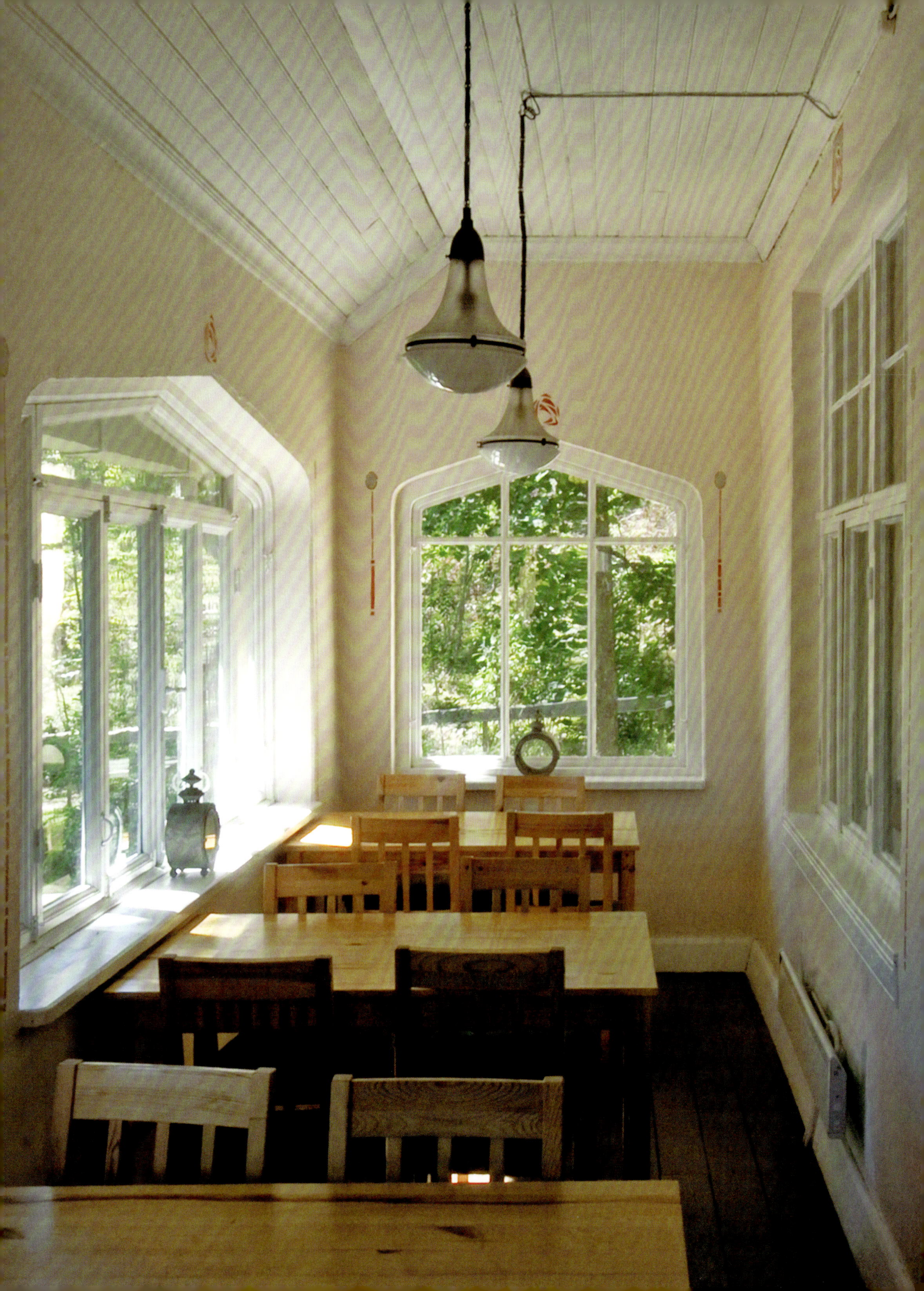

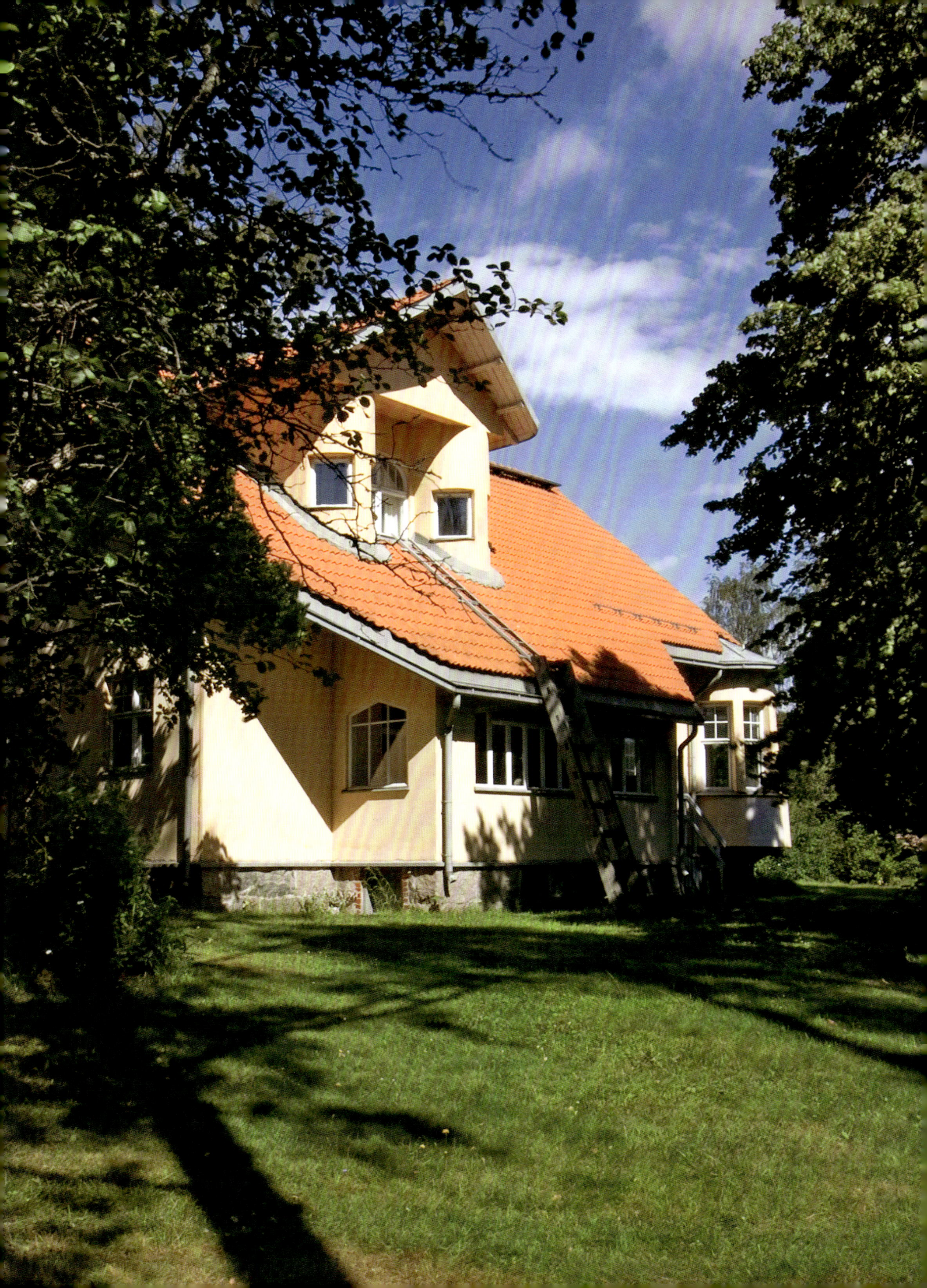

below
The lantern, looking out into the bay

opposite
Master bedroom on the second floor

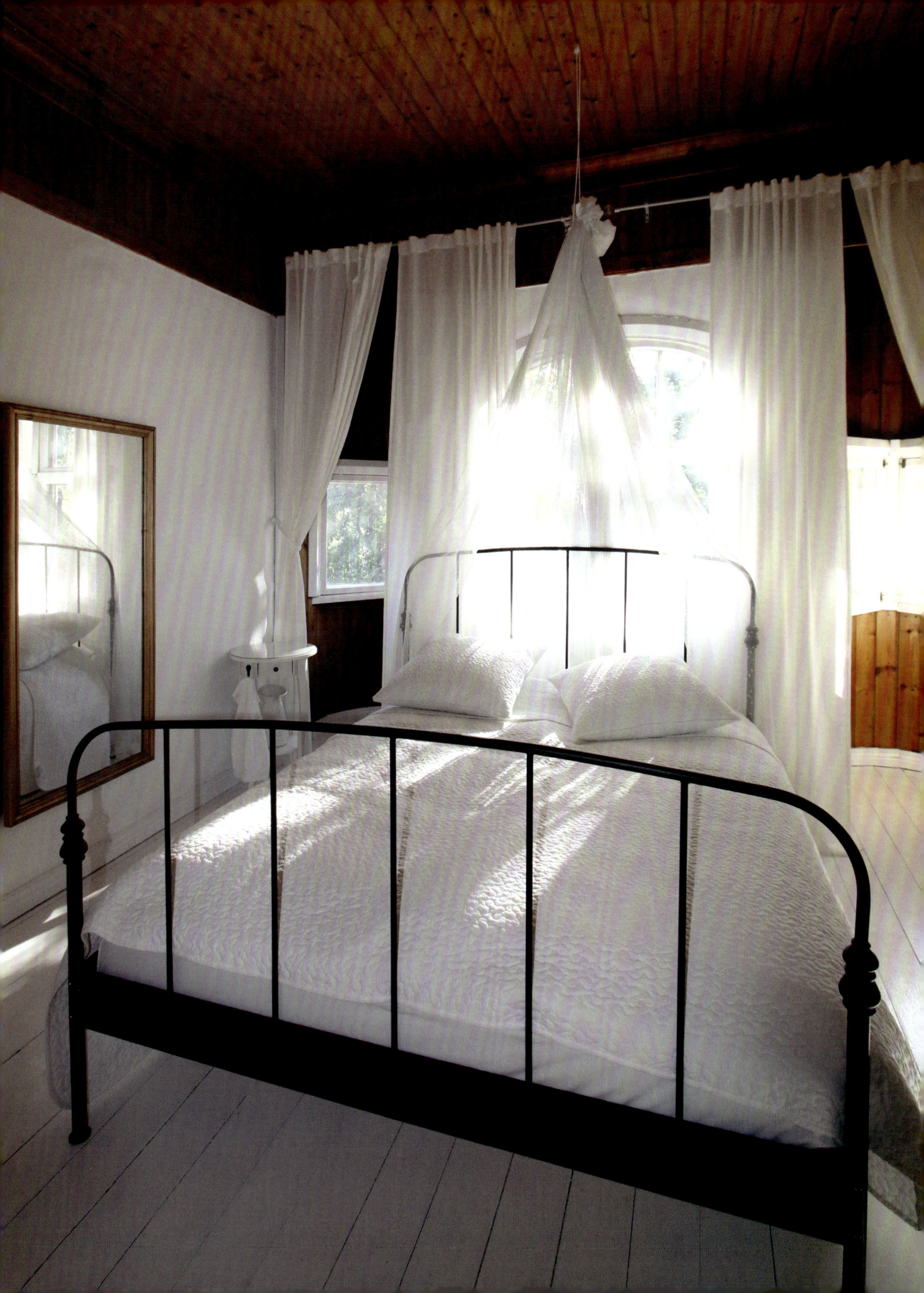

Villa Miniato

Espoo, Finland, 1901–2

Villa Miniato belongs to a series of white-plastered houses by Gesellius, Lindgren, and Saarinen that are marked by their soft, rounded forms. Along with Hvittorp, it is one of the largest summer residences designed by the office, the most impressive and best appointed of which was Suur-Merijoki (now demolished) near Vyborg (now Russia). The villa was originally commissioned by the engineer Knut Selin (1844–1914), who was property manager of the Kymmene paper mill in eastern Finland. Around the same time the office of Gesellius, Lindgren, and Saarinen also designed an extension to the company's paper mill in Voikkaa. Selin used the villa only for a few years, as did the next owner, Privy Counsellor Alfred Nyberg, director general of the State Roads and Waterways Board, who gave the villa its name. Nyberg, who was blind when he bought the house, had spent his honeymoon in Italy and had been fascinated by a description of the church of San Miniato, which reminded him of it. Subsequent owners of Villa Miniato included General August Langhoff (1856–1929), the Finnish High Commissioner in St. Petersburg, during whose period Tsar Nicholas II of Russia visited the villa. The Russian Revolution of 1917 and the subsequent declaration of Finnish independence ended the Finnish connections of many Russian officials and military men, and the next owners of the villa were businessmen.[12]

The archipelago of Espoo was a popular area for summerhouses and could be accessed by steamboat from Helsinki in the summer. Viewed from the sea, the castlelike shape of Villa Miniato stands out among a stand of delicate birch trees by the shore, with its tower and the ridge of its steep roof rising above the treetops. The house is anchored to the bedrock of the shore with foundations of natural stone, contrasting with the villa's white-plastered facades, which are punctuated by the colonnades of the originally open loggias, groups of windows, and several entrances with tapering arches and porches. A large tower, around which the whole building seems to revolve, marks the main entrance. The surroundings of the villa were mostly left in their natural state; only a terrace with a wall of natural stone was constructed next to the main entrance.

The core of the building is a two-story-high central hall, which is accessed from the vaulted lobby. The high space is given intimacy by low nooks and bays. A flat ceiling with exposed beams and partly wood-paneled walls create a warm atmosphere. With its fireplaces, nooks, built-in high-backed sofas, and small tables for socializing

opposite
Its steep red tile roof and lookout tower give the villa a castlelike appearance.

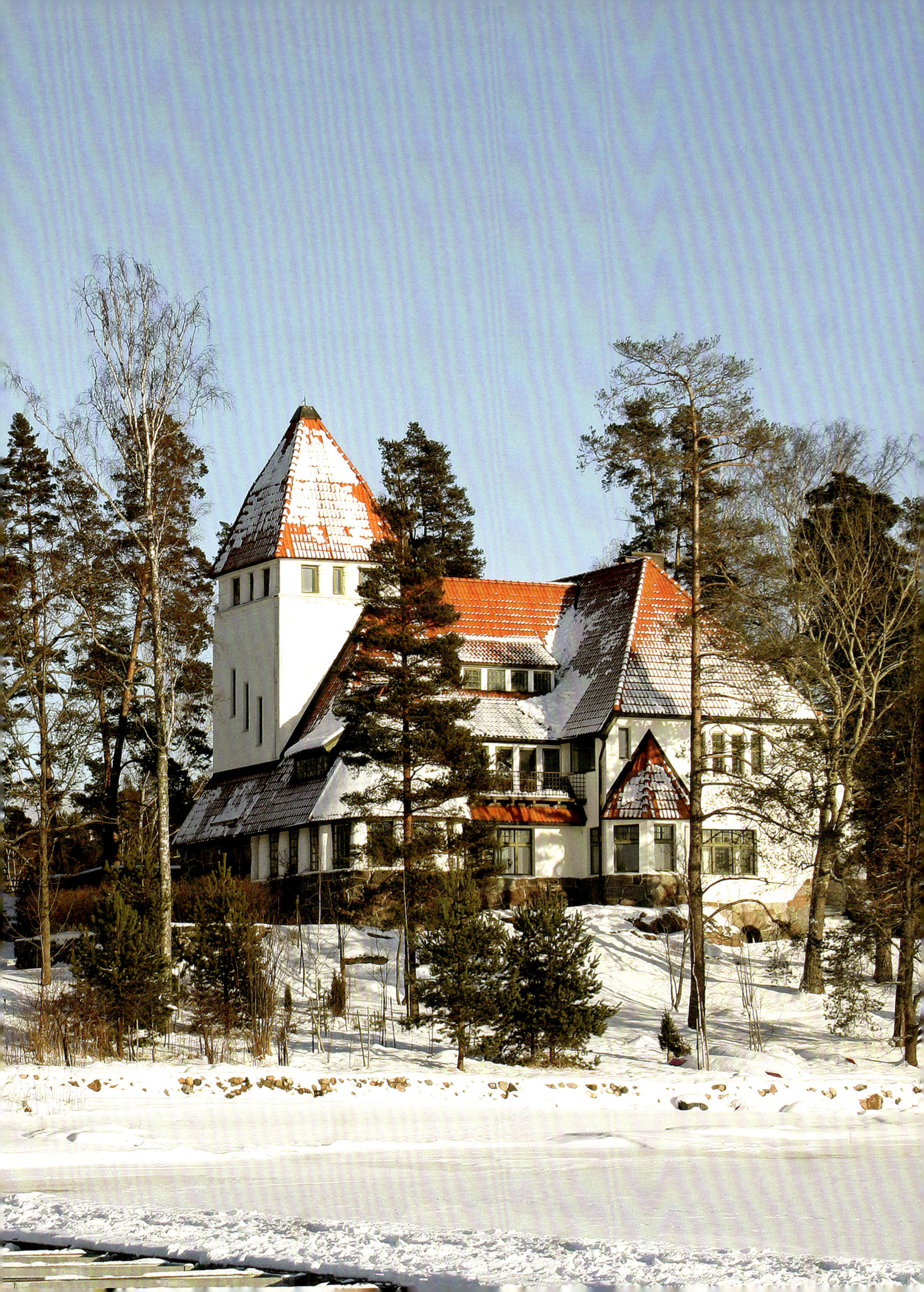

or playing cards, the space is a Finnish version of the ideals of English residential architecture at the turn of the century. The paneling of reddish stained spruce that covers the lower part of the walls provides not only a human scale for the high space but also forms a uniform background for moveable furniture and softens the acoustics of the room. The fireplace, with its unique design, featuring copper shutters and a fireguard with circular embossings, serves as a focus and eye-catching detail of the room.

The central hall leads to the dining room, library, and a terrace facing the sea. An open staircase rises to the second floor, which is divided into private bedrooms and an open gallery with wooden columns. An important detail of the staircase is a lanternlike light at the top of the handrail, with the electrical wiring hidden inside the architectural form, which Gesellius, Lindgren, and Saarinen also used in the stairways of apartment buildings designed by the firm. Although the hall is surrounded by rooms on almost all sides, it receives plenty of daylight, particularly from the high staircase window and the upstairs gallery.

Villa Miniato is one of the works by the architects that received international recognition and was soon published in European architectural journals, such as *Dekorative Kunst* and *Deutsche Bauzeitung* in Germany. The villa is still privately owned.

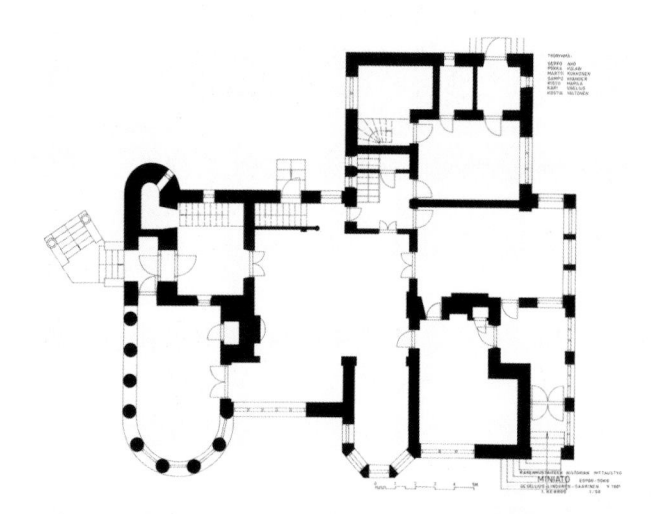

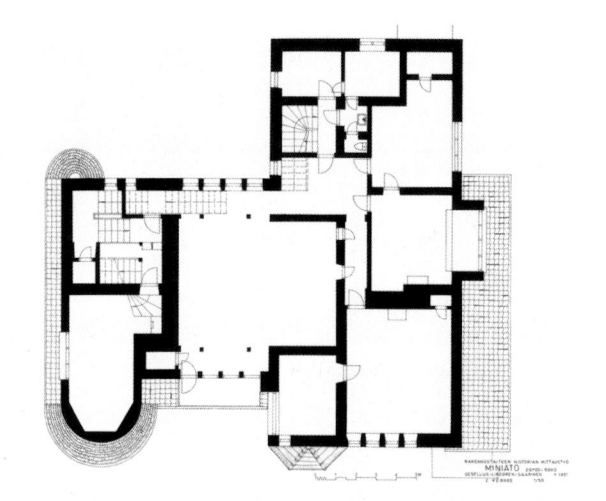

opposite
First-floor (left) and second-floor plans

top
Watercolor of Villa Miniato by Saarinen, 1901

bottom
The fireplace in the living room in its original position near the window

45

top
A detail of the main door shows a woman giving birth to the house.

bottom
The custom-designed lamp at the staircase. The door visible in the background leads to the courtyard.

opposite
View from the hall to the main staircase and entrance. The *ryijy* rug on the wall, The Flame, was designed by Akseli Gallen-Kallela for the Finnish pavilion at the Paris World's Fair of 1900.

overleaf
View of the *tupa* from the second floor

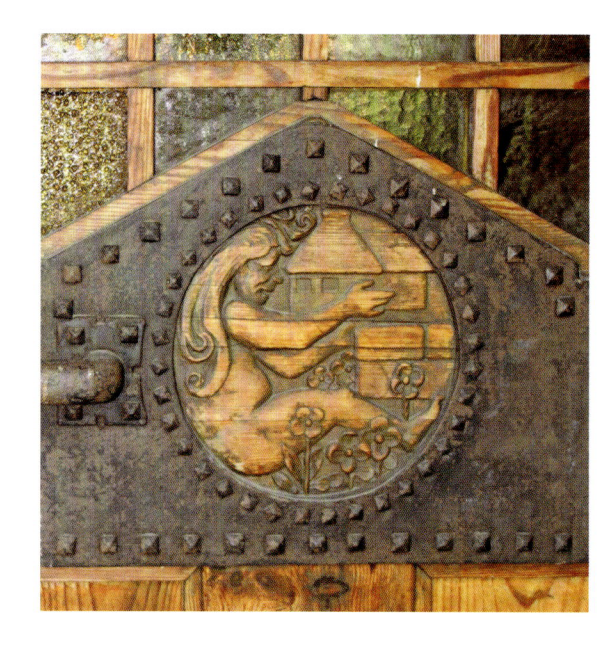

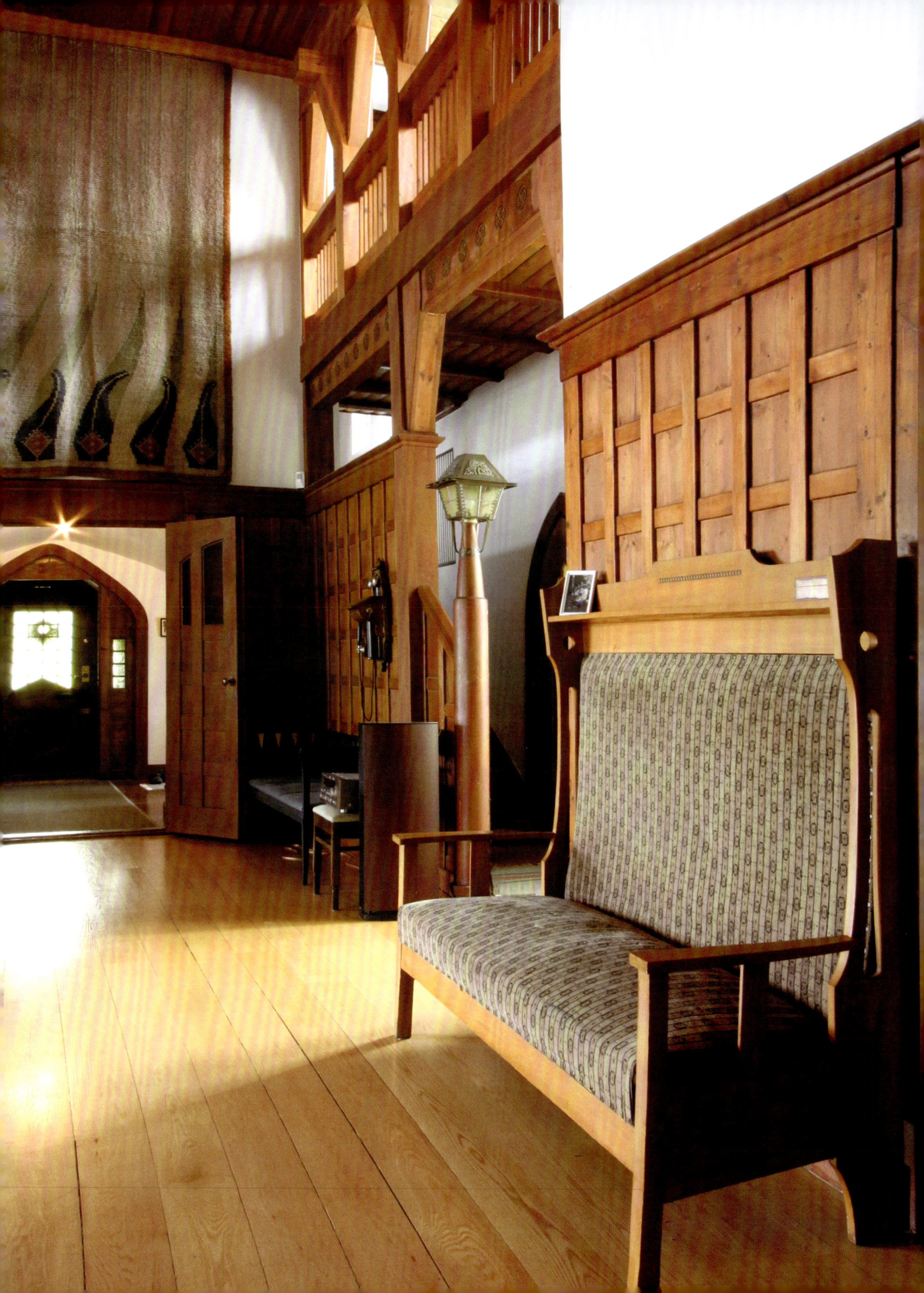

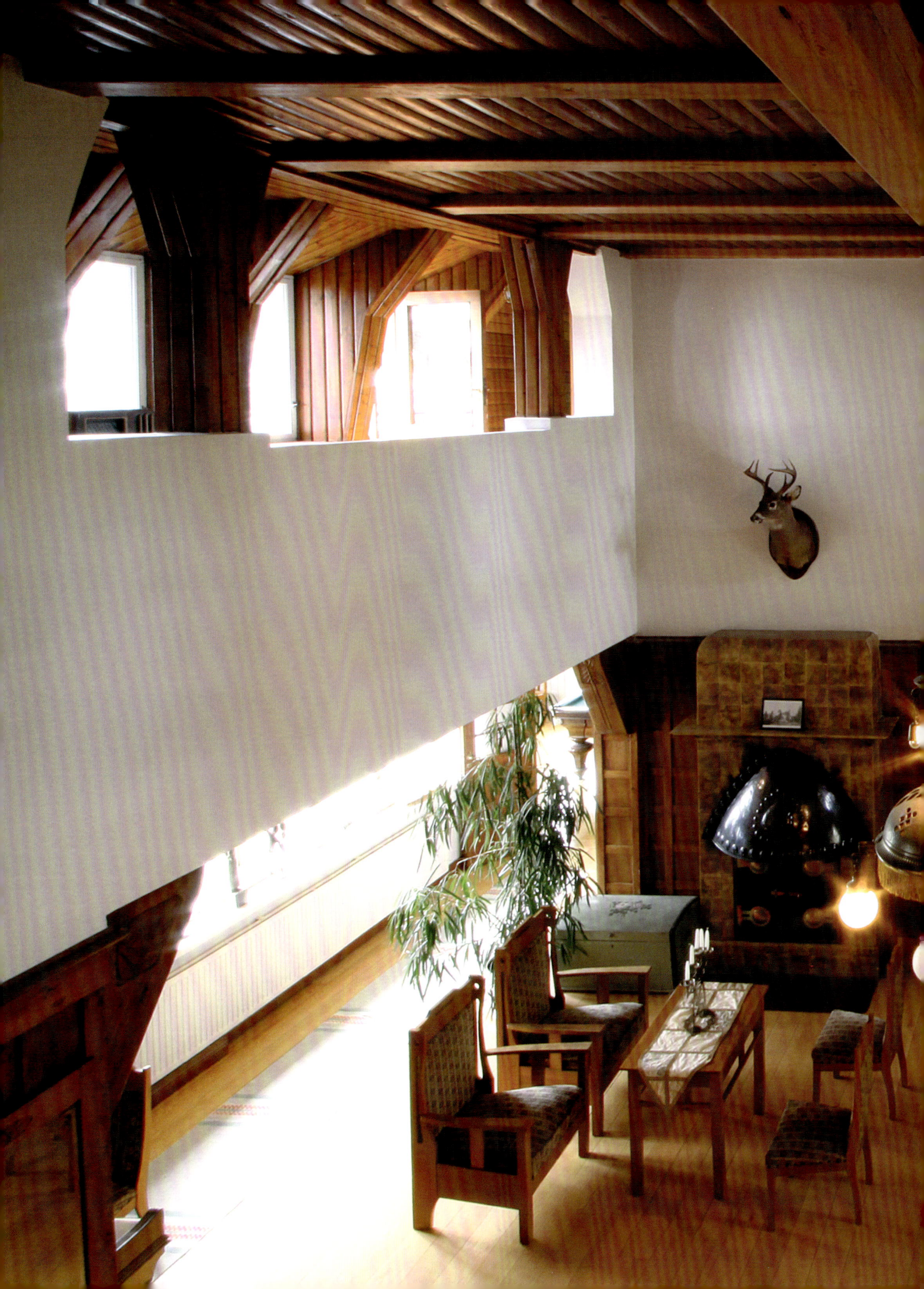

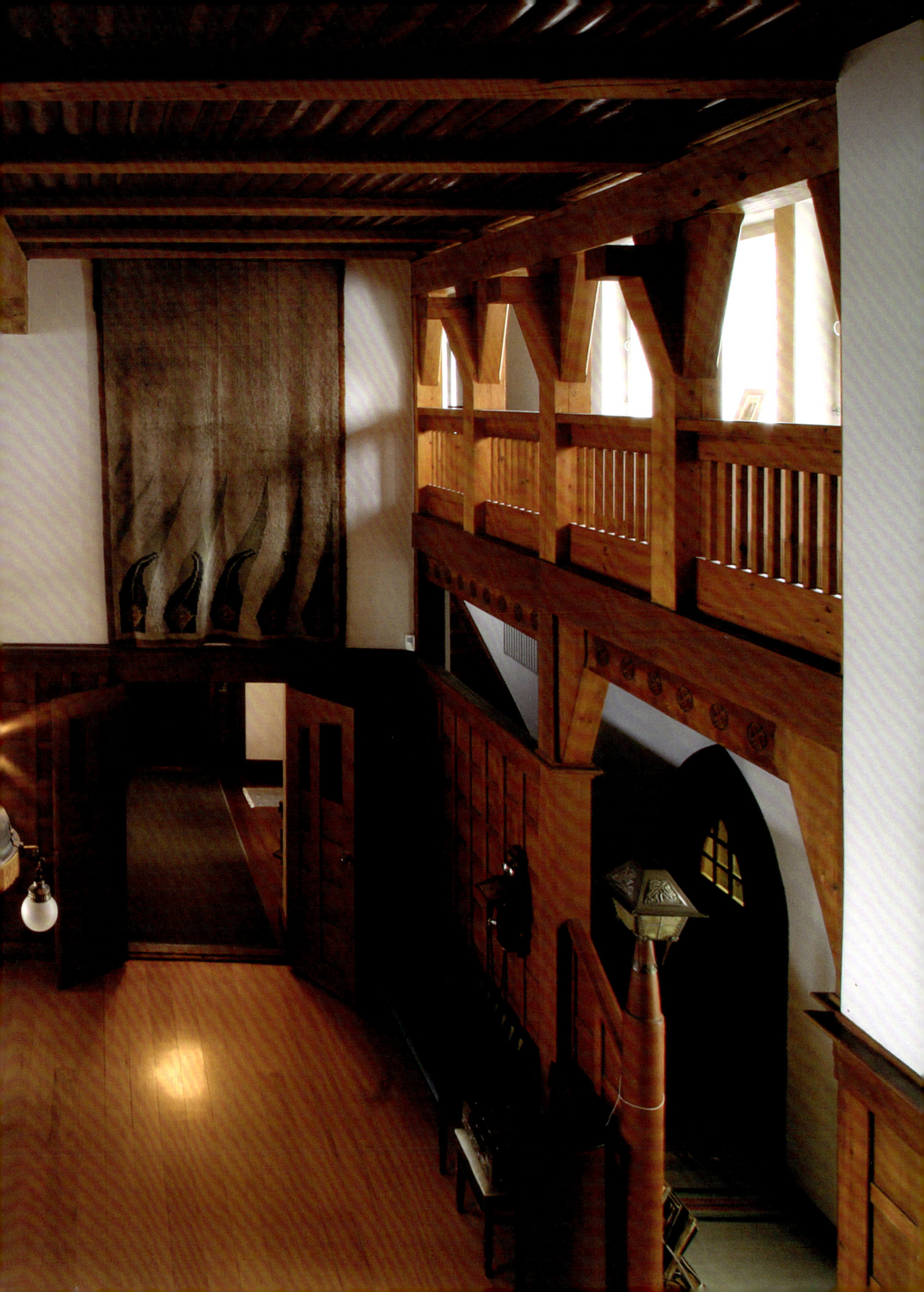

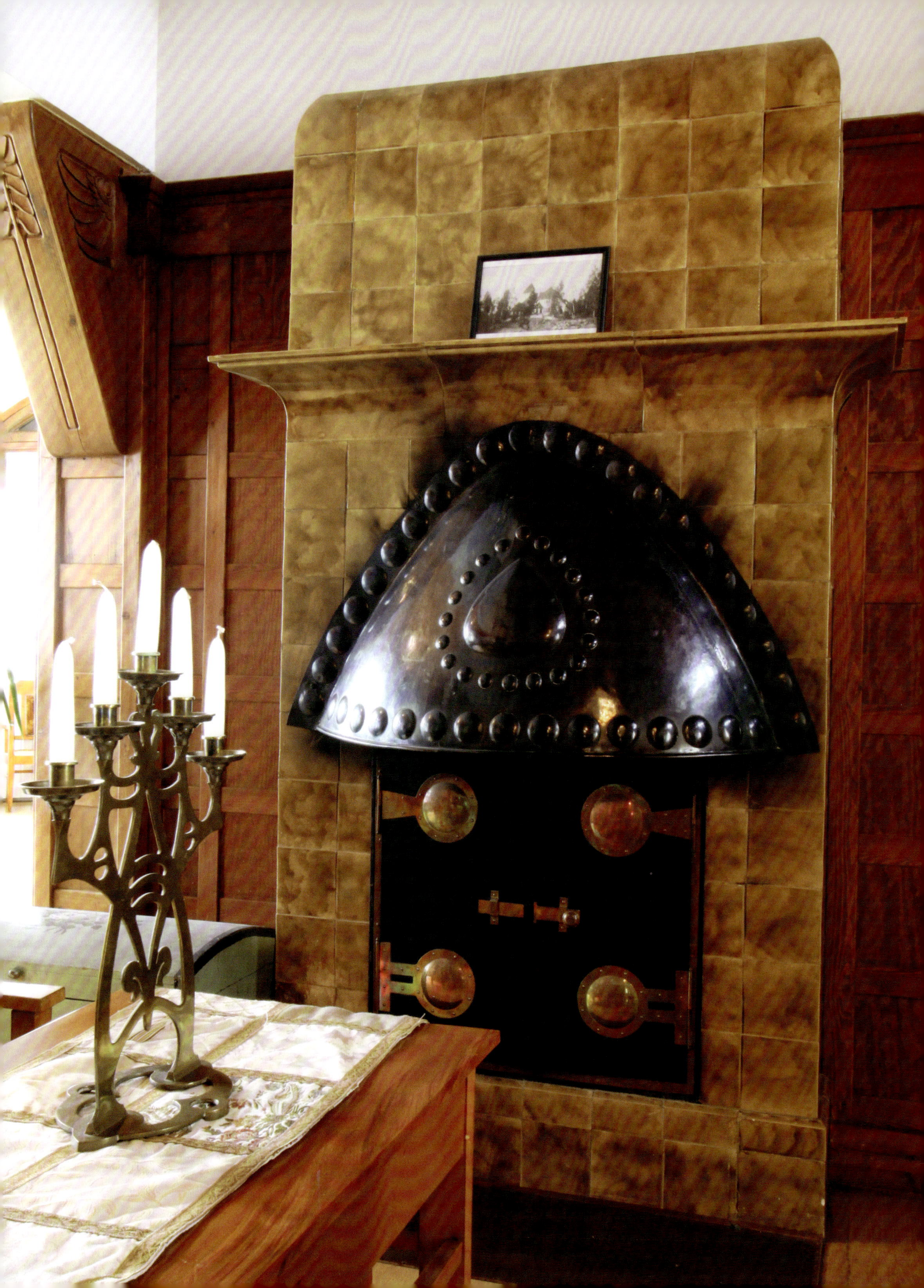

opposite
Tile stove with original metal embossings

below
The sitting corner opens to the seaside through a bay window.

top
Tile stove in the dining room

bottom
Study, with Hannes chairs and table by Saarinen, 1908

opposite
Dining room

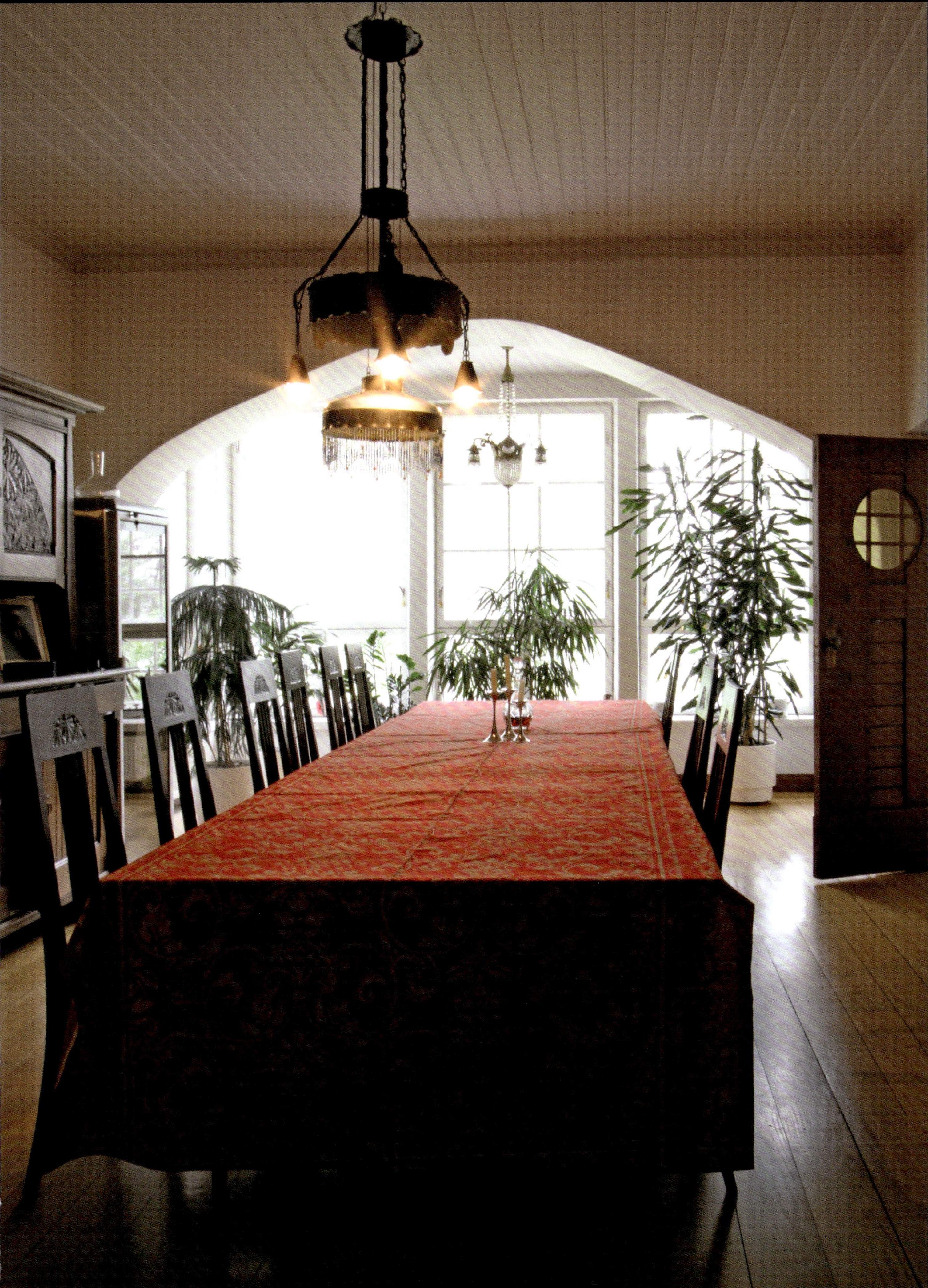

below
The first-floor billiard room was originally an open porch.

opposite
The tower looks out to the sea.

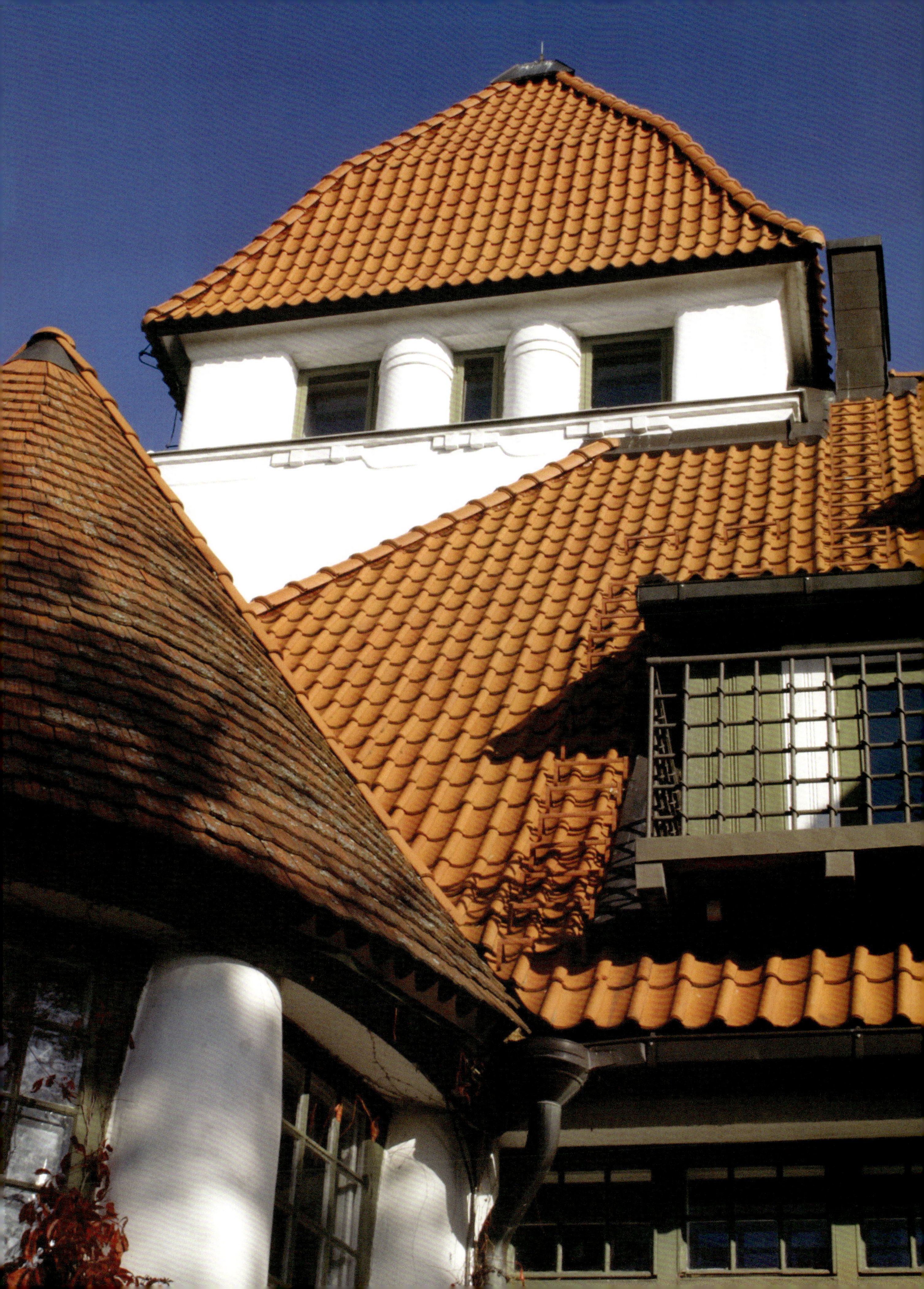

Hvittorp

Kirkkonummi, Finland, 1901–2

Lake Vitträsk near Helsinki belonged to the outlying areas of the city that became popular locations for summer residences at the turn of the twentieth century. The lake is bounded by steep outcrops of bedrock, lending a rugged atmosphere to the landscape. Ancient rock paintings discovered by the composer Jean Sibelius are evidence that people have frequented the shores of the lake since prehistoric times. The birth of the villa community was helped by the arrival of the railway, which was built from Helsinki to Turku in southwest Finland between 1896 and 1903. The nearest station on the line was only a few miles from the lake. There was also fairly easy access to the area by steamboat from Helsinki along the seashore.

It was here that Robert E. Westerlund (1859–1922), the owner of a music store in Helsinki, commissioned his summer villa. Before moving to the city in 1896 and becoming a dealer in sheet music and instruments, Westerlund worked as a pharmacist in Oulu, in North Finland. Aside from his interest in music, he also had a passion for botany. Both pastimes found a home at Hvittorp.[13]

Through Westerlund's connections in the music industry, the villa community of Vitträsk was visited by leading figures in Finland, such as composer Jean Sibelius and conductor Robert Kajanus. By commissioning Gesellius, Lindgren, and Saarinen to design his summer residence, he also brought the architects to the shores of Lake Vitträsk, where they would come to live and work.

Making skillful use of differences of elevation, the designers placed Hvittorp on a steep slope leading to the lake. The house has two main aspects: facing the lake as a castle of natural stone, and the forest as a wooden villa with a peaked roof. The main entrance to the ground floor was originally on the lake side of the slope. A visitor would approach the villa gradually, first experiencing the landscape and views, before seeing the dramatic volume of the house with its towers, gables, and balconies. Hvitträsk was approached in a similar way; the first view greeting the visitor was that of the gable end of the Saarinen wing and the log tower of the Lindgren wing.

The surroundings of the villa, whose exterior design included terraces with walls of natural stone and plantings, were originally dominated by a formal garden with arrangements of sanded walks and flowerbeds, all designed by gardener Svante Olsson and later by his son and garden architect Paul, both of whom were masters of Finnish garden design. The setting by the southern lakeshore included an artificial island. Westerlund

opposite

Hvittorp in the middle of winter

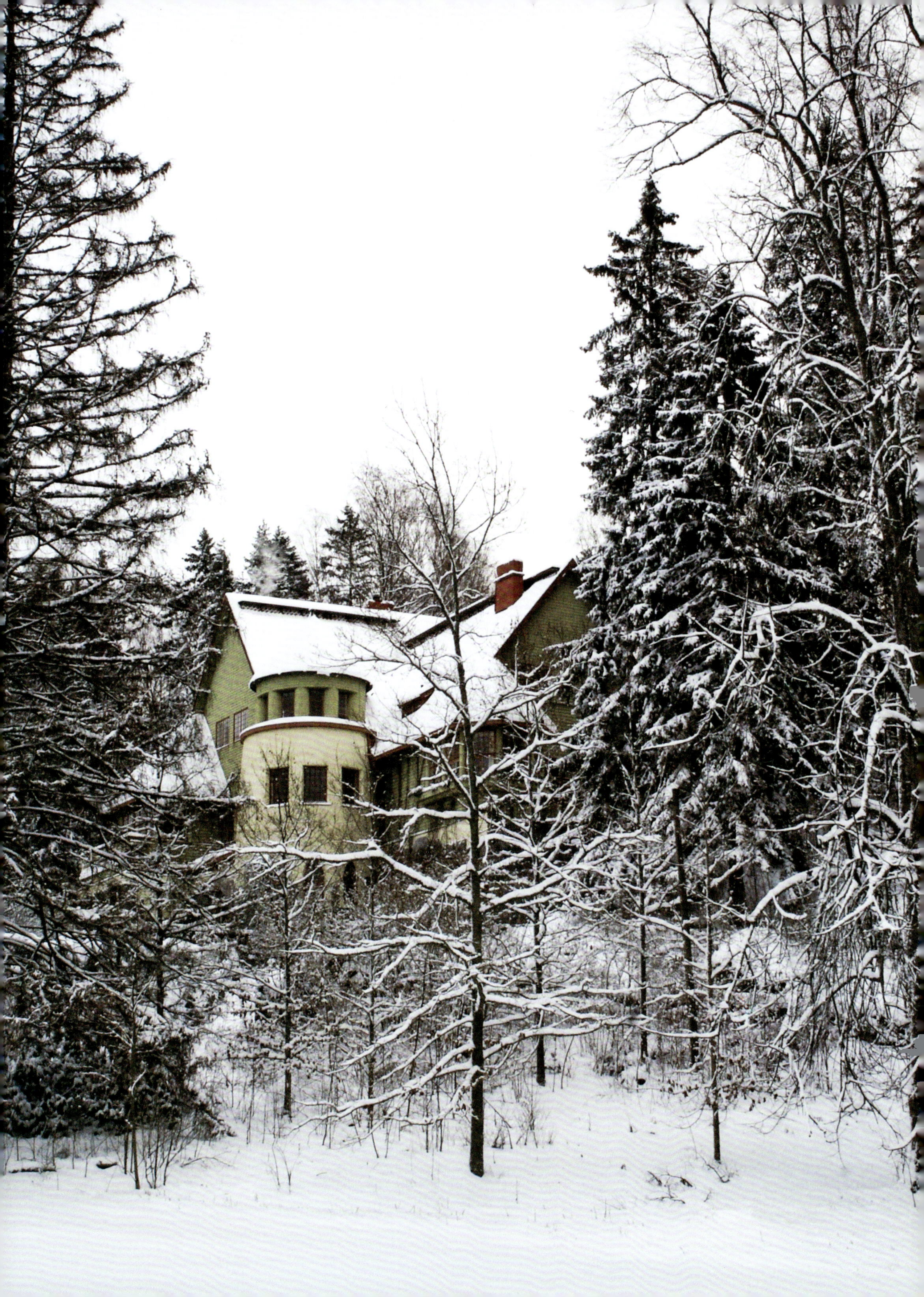

was personally interested in the garden and its care and commissioned Saarinen to design a gardener's house and a sauna building on the site.[14] Like at Hvitträsk, the setting was a mixture of woodland wilderness and tended parklike grounds. The romantic yearnings characterizing the turn of the century and a partly explicit tendency to employ the natural setting as a symbolic expression of Finnish identity are evident here.

The design of large villas was usually a collaborative process at the office of Gesellius, Lindgren, and Saarinen, and there was probably a division of tasks, as drawings by Lindgren and Saarinen suggest. While a sketchbook used by Lindgren contains drafts of the volume of Hvittorp and its tower, as well as drawings for the final version of the facade,[15] archival material from Saarinen, in turn, includes sketches for the interior.

The exterior of Hvittorp is complex, with bays and balconies on several levels, and a terrace opening in various directions with views of the surroundings and the lake. The steep slope of the site made it possible to have entrances to both the ground floor and the second, or main, floor. Vertical access within the house was along the main staircase, used by family and guests, and a narrow staircase for the servants. A similar functional and social hierarchy was employed in other villas, for instance at Hvitträsk.

The vaulted space of the ground floor, which contained the dining room, reflects a medieval mood. The original wall and vault paintings by artist Väinö Blomstedt (1871–1947), who also owned a villa in the area, extended the room in an illusionary way, depicting views of natural surroundings. One of the scenes was of a monk fishing by foaming rapids; another was a hunting motif showing a European elk in a stand of birches along a lakeshore. The paintings were replaced with frescoes by Gunnar Clément in the 1940s.[16] The original ornamental painting work was carried out by Wuorio's firm.

The core space of the main floor, the music room, is inspired by the *tupa*, similar as at Hvitträsk and other villas by the firm, with a large fireplace by one wall and a wooden colonnade separating the staircase on the other side, both elements typical for the firm. The wooden interior surfaces were suited to performing and listening to music. The room extends all the way through the house, receiving daylight from two directions through stained-glass windows, and is dominated by the sculptural row of wood columns and the sturdy log beams of the ceiling. The importance of the space is underlined by its height of one-and-a-half stories. A slightly higher floor level sets off a bay facing the yard, where a small group could gather to socialize, from the rest of the large space. The music hall with its public function was separated from the adjoining rooms, possibly for reasons of sound insulation.[17] Important details of the space included the fireplace frieze's meandering line of stylized twisting garlands, wrought-iron decoration, and embossed work. As in other rooms at Hvittorp, the space also contained a corner with a built-in sofa.

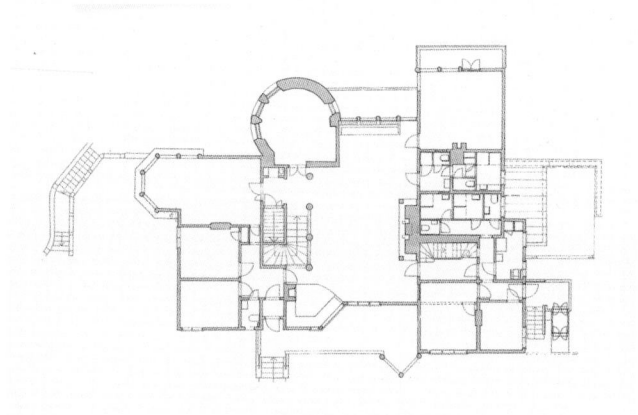

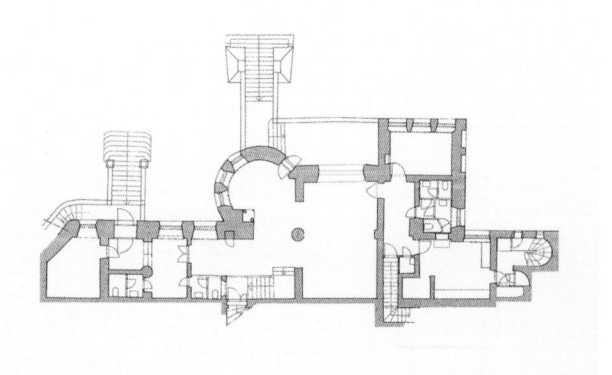

Also on the main floor were a combined library and smoking room in the tower, several salons, a piano room, a ladies' room, the master bedroom, and four additional bedrooms. The top floor was used to store and display Westerlund's significant collections of East Asian porcelain and shells and held several guest rooms. The individual bedrooms were decorated in various ways and partly fitted with Westerlund's antique furniture. Although Hvittorp did not become a total work of art furnished by Gesellius, Lindgren, and Saarinen, artists who collaborated with them in several other projects contributed in various ways. The versatile artist, artisan, and designer Eric O. W. Ehrström (1881–1934) designed metal elements and light fittings, of which the chandelier in the music room has survived. Ehrström also made the copper embossings of the main door, featuring spiraling motifs of water plants and rose designs.[18] Loja Saarinen created the ceramic mask motifs for the fireplaces.[19]

Westerlund had to give up the villa in 1914. The economic problems resulting from World War I took a toll on Finland, and building work had become expensive. During the following years, the villa changed owners every few years because of social unrest and unstable conditions. Westerlund's son Gustaf owned the villa for some time as did Westerlund's father-in-law, bank director and municipal politician Alfred Norrmén. During Norrmén's ownership (until 1940) the villa was fitted with electric lighting and water supply. Under the next owner, many of the features of the original interior design were removed. During World War II and afterwards, the house suffered, due first to the constantly changing tenants and then to being kept empty, because the border military zone leased from Finland by the Soviet Union after the war was in the immediate vicinity of Lake Vitträsk.[20] In 1963, Hvittorp was purchased by the Lutheran congregations of the city of Espoo and is now used for special events and meetings.[21]

opposite
Second-floor (left) and first-floor measuring drawings

left
The villa seen from the lake side in 1906

right
Watercolor of Hvittorp from the lake side by Saarinen, 1902

top left
Dining room with original wall paintings by Väinö Blomstedt

top right
Watercolor of the dining room by Saarinen, 1902

bottom left
Music room

bottom right
Watercolor of the music room by Saarinen, 1902

opposite
The chandelier in the music room was designed by Eric O. W. Ehrström.

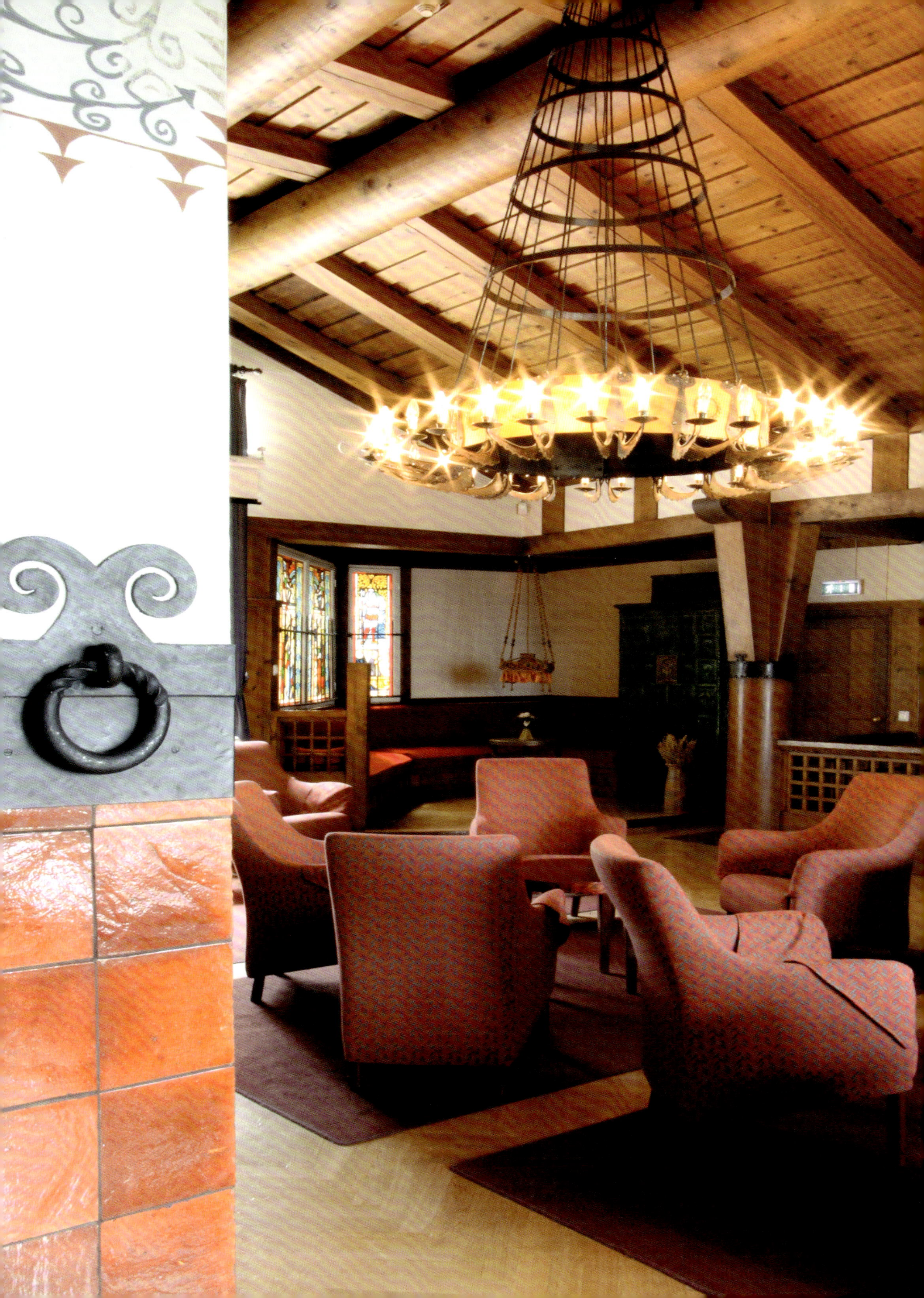

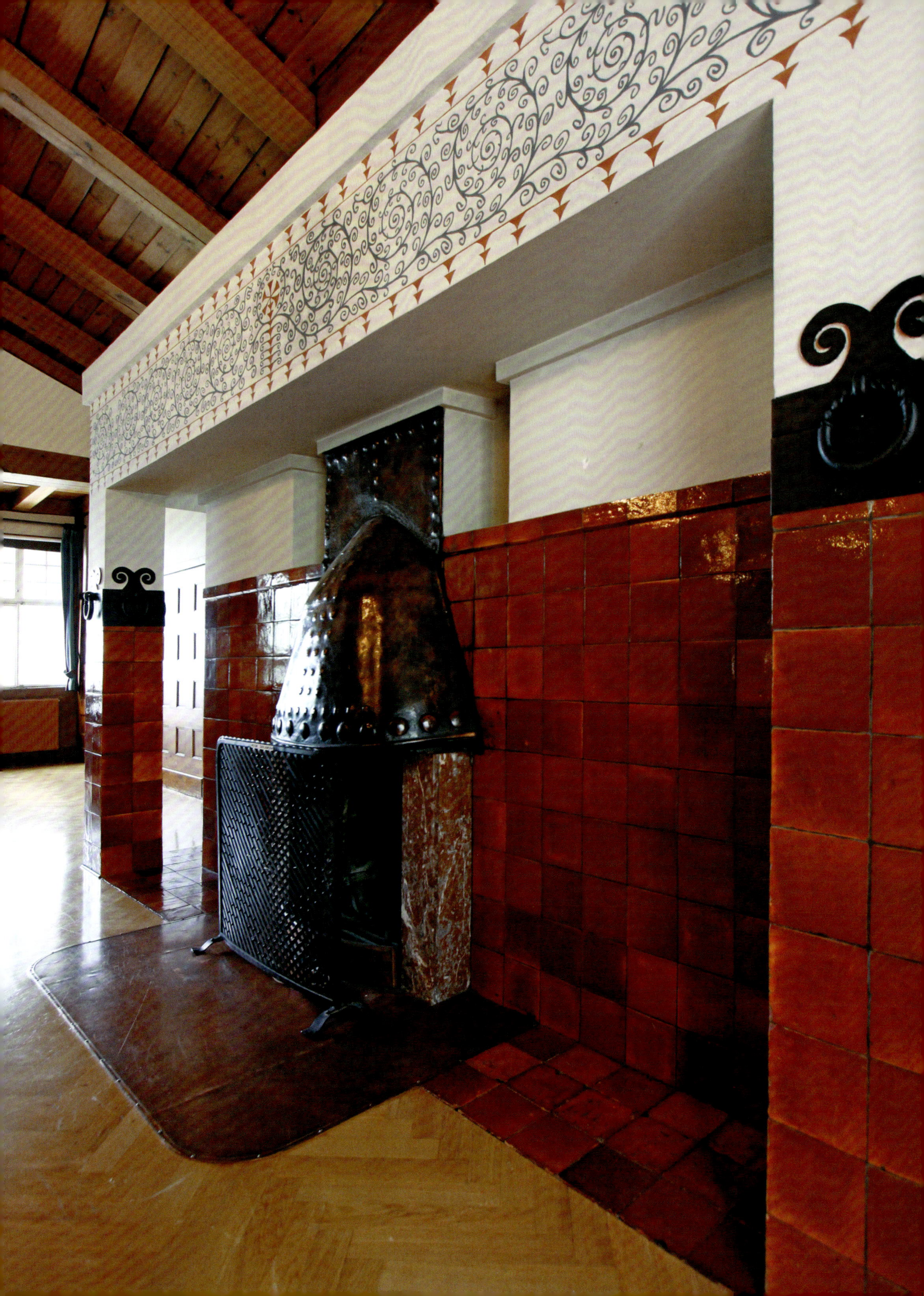

opposite
Fireplace in the music room

below
Wooden columns mark the staircase.

below
The entrance door features copperwork by Ehrström, who collaborated with Gesellius, Lindgren, and Saarinen on several projects.

opposite
The main facade from the north

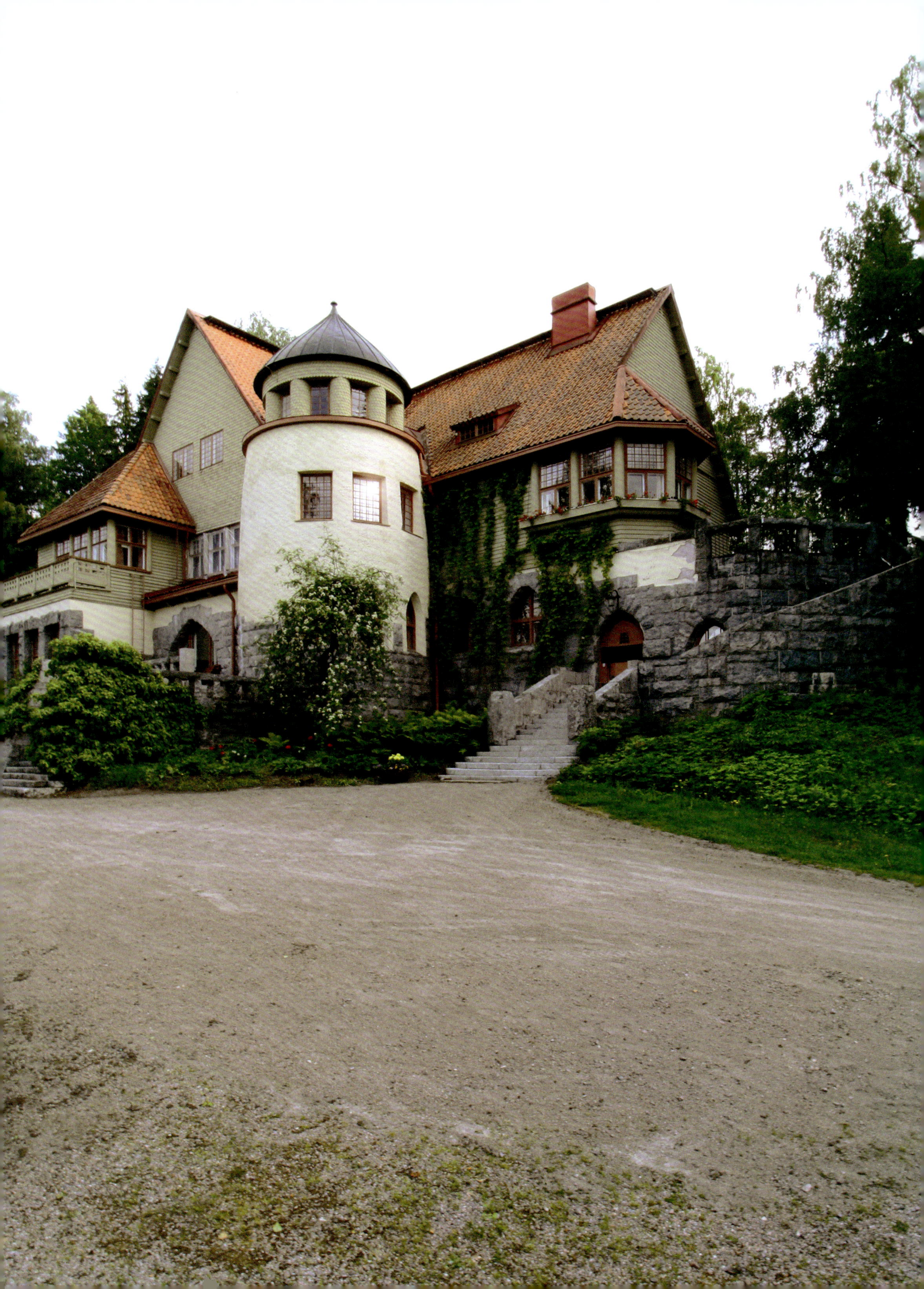

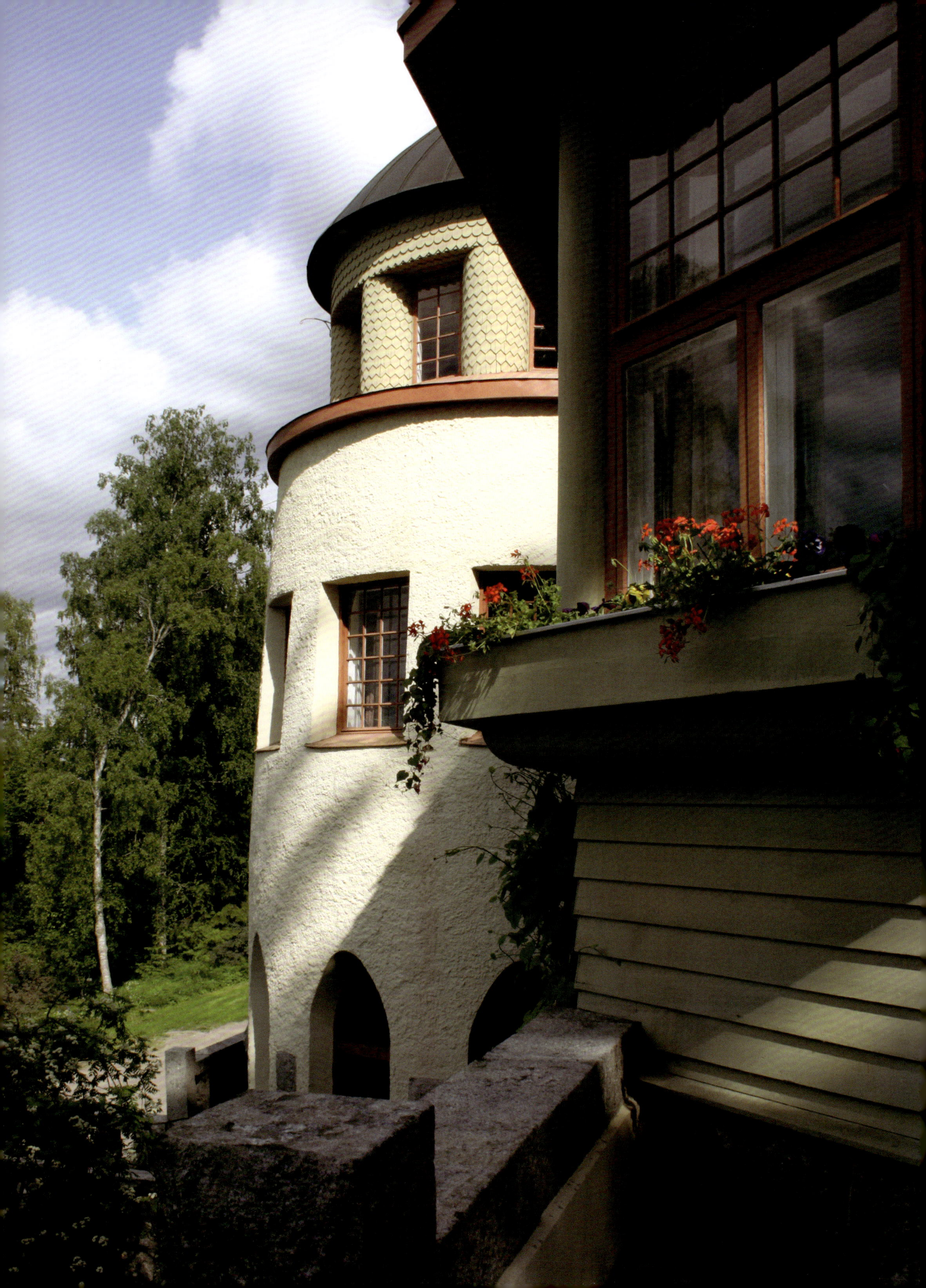

opposite
The round tower dominates the villa.

top
View to the lake from the salon

bottom
Second-floor salon

below
A cabin and sauna house is near the lake.

opposite
View from the east

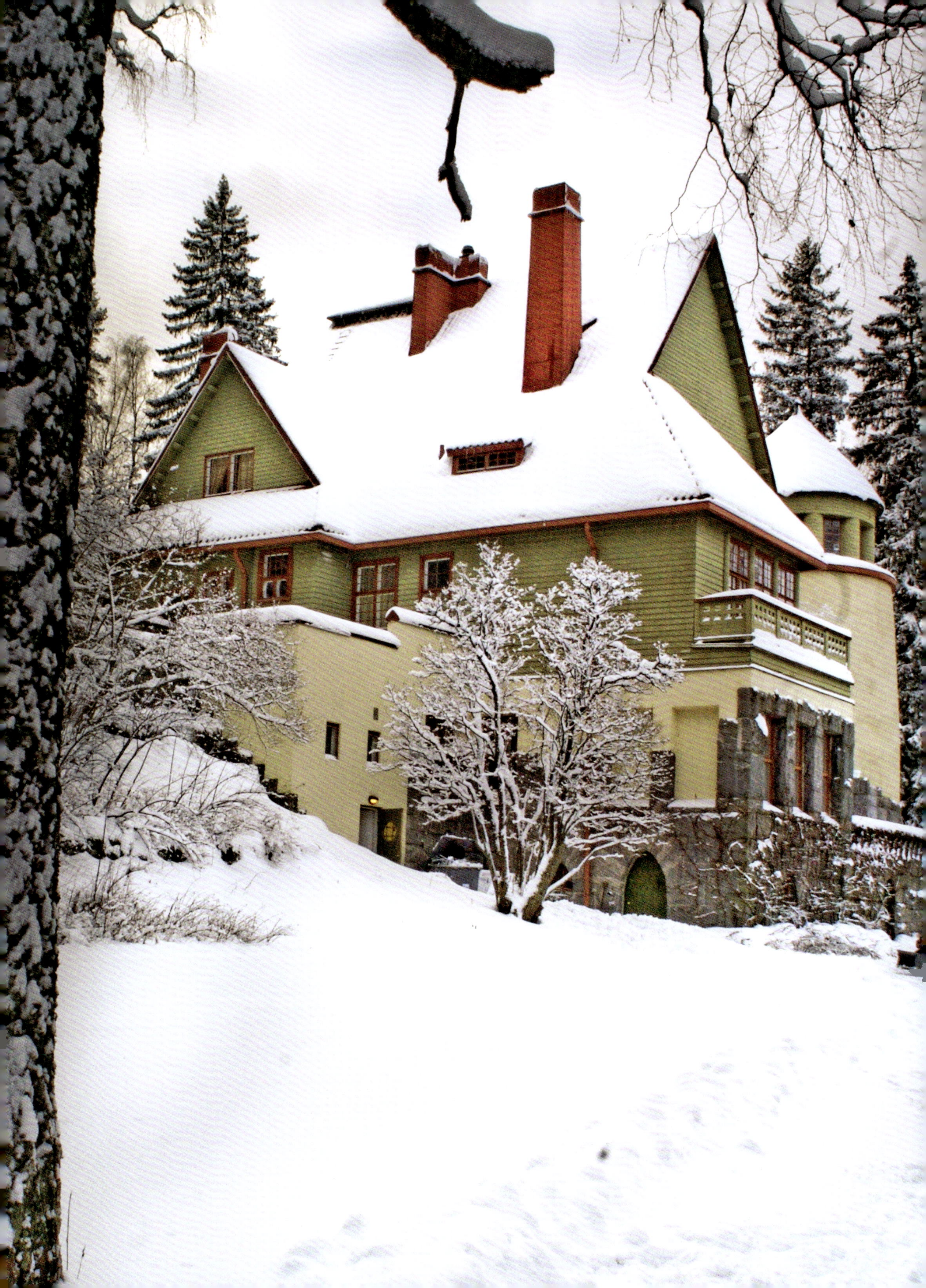

Hvitträsk

Kirkkonummi, 1902

Like many other Finnish artists at the turn of the century, the architect trio Herman Gesellius, Armas Lindgren, and Eliel Saarinen built their joint residence and studio complex in natural surroundings far from the bustle of the city. The building served as the architects' calling card, crystallizing their main architectural goals, but Hvitträsk was also a home in the true sense of the term, especially for the Saarinens—and this despite the upheaval in Saarinen's personal life soon after the house was completed. Eliel and Mathilda Saarinen divorced in 1903. Both remarried in March 1904, Mathilda to Herman Gesellius, and Eliel to Herman's sister Louise (Loja), with whom he had two children, Eva Lisa (called Pipsan, born in 1905) and Eero, born in 1910. As Eliel observed: "So Hvitträsk was all a home could mean to us; there Pipsan and Eero grew up and there Loja and I were united in that spirit which, I like to think, is the fruit of love." [22]

In the early 1900s, the residence, located in a wooded area near Lake Vitträsk, was reached by train and horse-drawn carriage. The last section of the way led uphill through rugged forested terrain to the building complex. Its sheltered yard was bordered by the yard building's stone tower and a wall enclosing the terrace. The first view was of the main building, which rises up from a steep downward slope and is built of stone and wood. The elements and materials that were popular at the time blend in a uniquely harmonious way in the exterior. The house is connected to its surroundings through pergolas, terraces, and stone walls, while gables and towers add variety to the upper level. The main house contained the studio of the architectural office and the apartments of the Saarinen and Lindgren families. In the original building the complex architecture of the Saarinen wing was complemented by an archaic log castle used by the Lindgrens, which was dominated by a tower and was destroyed in a fire in 1922. (This wing was rebuilt according to a design by Eero Saarinen in 1929–36). On the other side of the yard is a log building that was originally the home of Herman Gesellius. The complex as a whole, which evolved gradually in response to the needs of the family and the architectural firm, is characterized by free form, asymmetry, and elements that relate to each other in a rhythmic manner.

The landscaping at Hvitträsk included a rose garden and a tennis court, as well as a beach with a changing room at the lakeshore for those who wanted to refresh themselves on a hot summer's

opposite

View of Hvitträsk from the lakeside

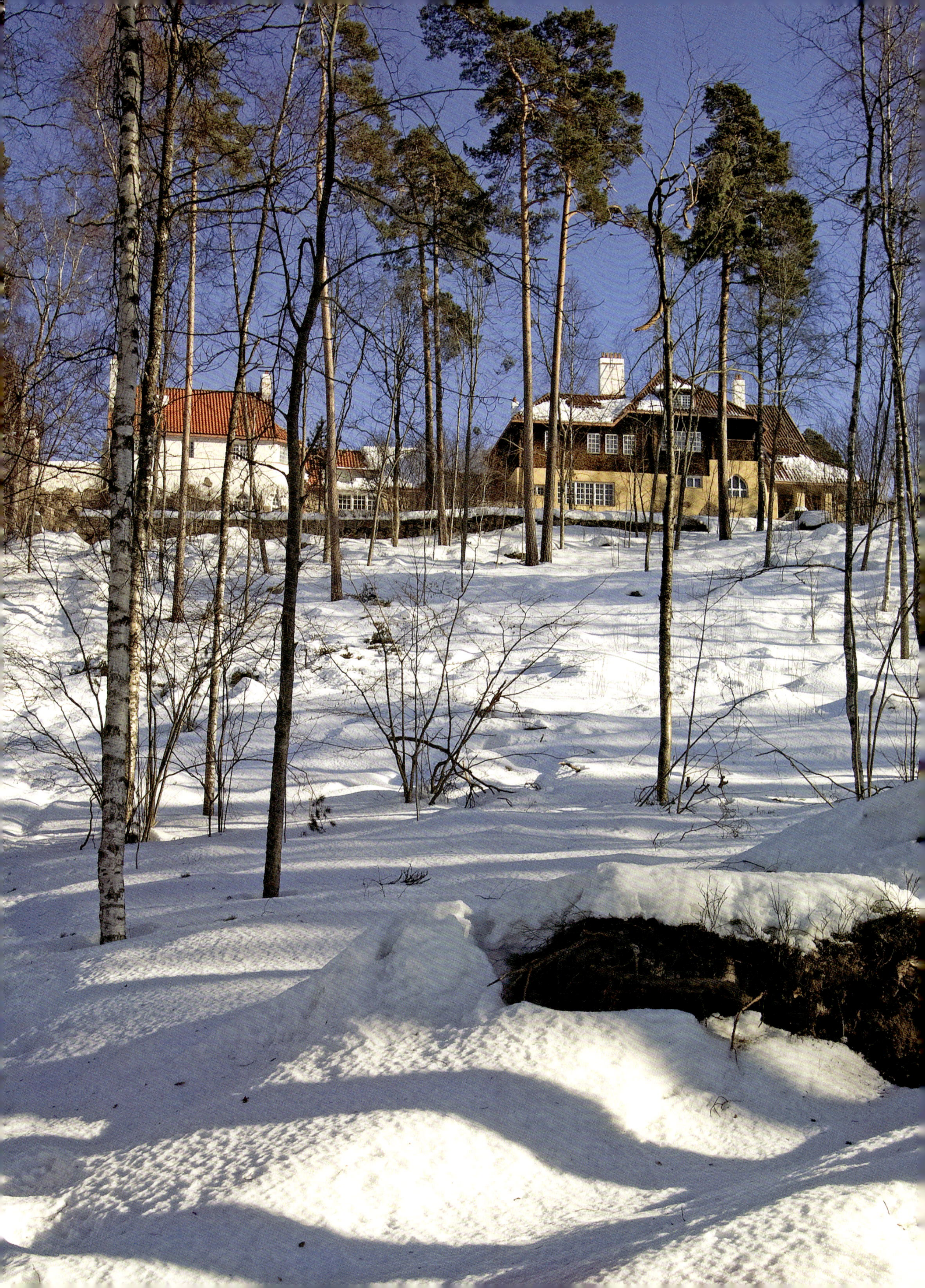

day. Loja Saarinen in particular was interested in plants and their care and tended the flowerbeds in the formal garden. Hvitträsk offers a powerful experience of place. The house has several entrances, and the yard and the balcony, from which the surrounding landscape can be admired, are accessed from various rooms. In similar fashion, Saarinen House engages in a dialogue with its setting, although it represents a more urban design and does not open outward as much as Hvitträsk does.

The building complex was both a home and a place of work. The two were often not distinguished from each other, and especially for Saarinen work was integrated in his family's life. Along with the members of the household, employees of the office lived part of the time at Hvitträsk. Of the firm's associates the artist couple Eric O. W. and Olga Ehrström lived there for years. Both architect Frans Nyberg (1882–1962), who assisted Saarinen for many years, and architect and town planner Otto-Iivari Meurman (1890–1994), described the spirit at Hvitträsk as informal, with enjoyable moments of leisure punctuating the busy days. In the summer, the team would interrupt their work to go swimming in the lake, and after a long work day, Loja would serve sandwiches and Hungarian wine.[23] Nyberg recalled how Eero, or Poju, as he was called, would make octahedrons and dodecahedrons out of paper in the studio. Meurman notes how "the architectural assistants were regarded as members of the family, with their own rooms and sitting with the family at the dining table, and being invited to join guests in the large main room." Describing Saarinen's way of guiding his assistants' work, Meurman writes that "the relationship between the master and the assistants was free, warm-spirited and marked by trust. The world-famous architect could ask a young and inexperienced budding colleague for his opinion."[24] Various cultural figures also visited Hvitträsk, from the Finnish painter Akseli Gallen-Kallela to composer Gustav Mahler and writer Maxim Gorky.

The studio space, which had fireplaces with built-in sofa nooks at both ends and was later modified and further developed by Saarinen in his studio at Saarinen House at Cranbrook, was dominated by large drawing tables. In the winter, billiards was played in the library area of the studio. In addition to a large window facing north, the studio also offered a view of the courtyard.

In Saarinen's residential architecture Hvitträsk can be seen as a point of departure—the architect would repeat and transform many of its features and architectural ideals in his later houses. The central hall, resembling a *tupa*, included a large fireplace and a cozy nook by the window with a sofa by the wall. The dining table in this space was used for dinners with friends. Custom-made furniture and textiles, rugs, and curtains created by Loja Saarinen complement the designed entity. The Saarinens' wing at Hvitträsk is marked by spatial multidimensionality, with lines of view from one level to another. A staircase leads from the central hall to bedrooms and guest rooms several levels above. The pronounced ambience of the shared spaces is characterized by sturdy log walls, dark-colored surfaces, and a vaulted roof of medieval inspiration. The bedrooms are of a lighter color and more intimate in scale.

After the gradual disbanding of the architectural office and the death of Herman Gesellius in 1916, the villa remained in the ownership of the Saarinens. Eliel Saarinen visited Hvitträsk each summer until World War II; in the winter tenants took care of the house. As they grew older, the Saarinens decided to give up the house, and it was sold as a private residence in 1949. At the turn of the 1970s, Hvitträsk was turned into a museum, which was acquired by the Finnish state in 1981. The building in the yard was converted into a restaurant in the 1970s.

top left
Loja Saarinen at the Saarinen wing entrance in the 1910s. In the background, the wooden Lindgren wing and its tower, which were destroyed by fire in 1922, are visible.

top right
Pipsan and Eero at the entrance to the Lindgren wing, ca. 1917

middle
View of the studio around 1911, with (left to right) Frans Nyberg, Pipsan Saarinen, and Eliel Saarinen.

bottom
Original site plan with first-floor plan of the Saarinen and Lindgren wings and the studio

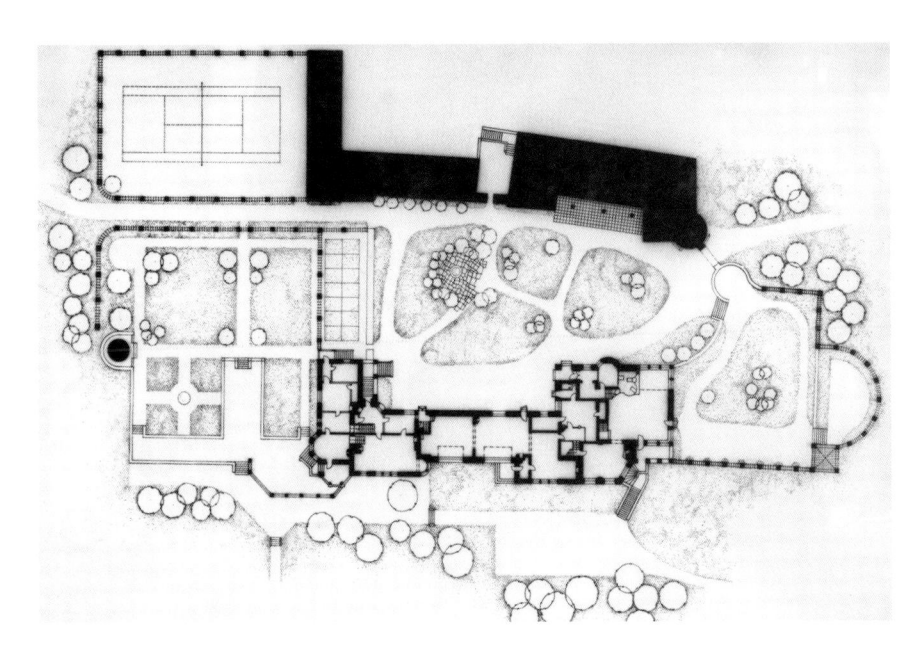

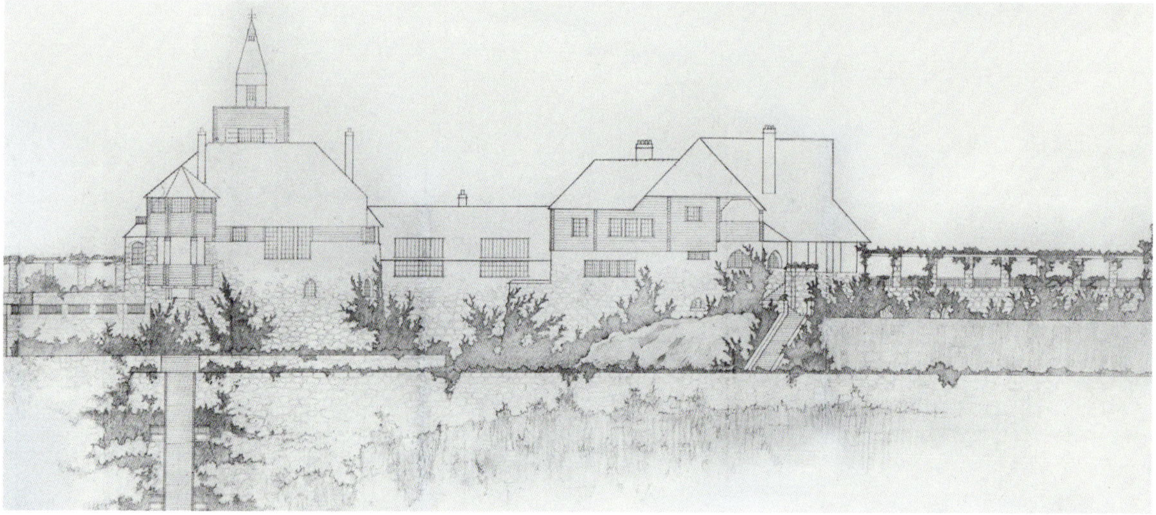

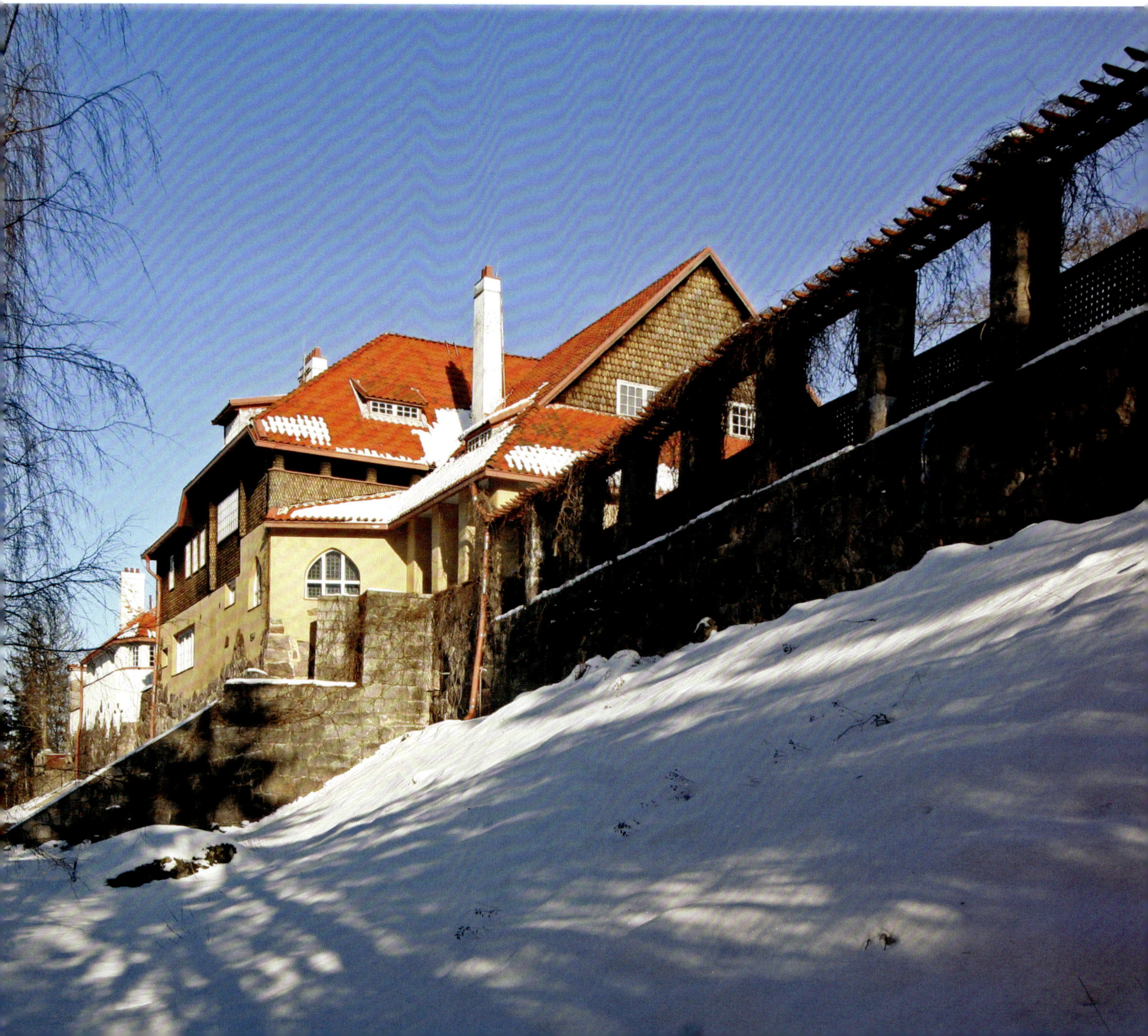

opposite, top
Lakeside facade, pencil drawing by Saarinen, circa 1907

opposite, bottom
Winter view of the lakeside facade and porch

top
Loja, Eliel, and Juho Saarinen sitting next to the fireplace, ca. 1915, with Eero reading at the table

bottom
The rug in the living room, *The Flame*, was designed by artist Akseli Gallen-Kallela.

top
Painting by Saarinen of the view from the living room to the dining room

bottom
View from the large fireplace in the living room to the dining room

opposite
This ground-floor room in the Lindgren wing is also known as "the poker pit."

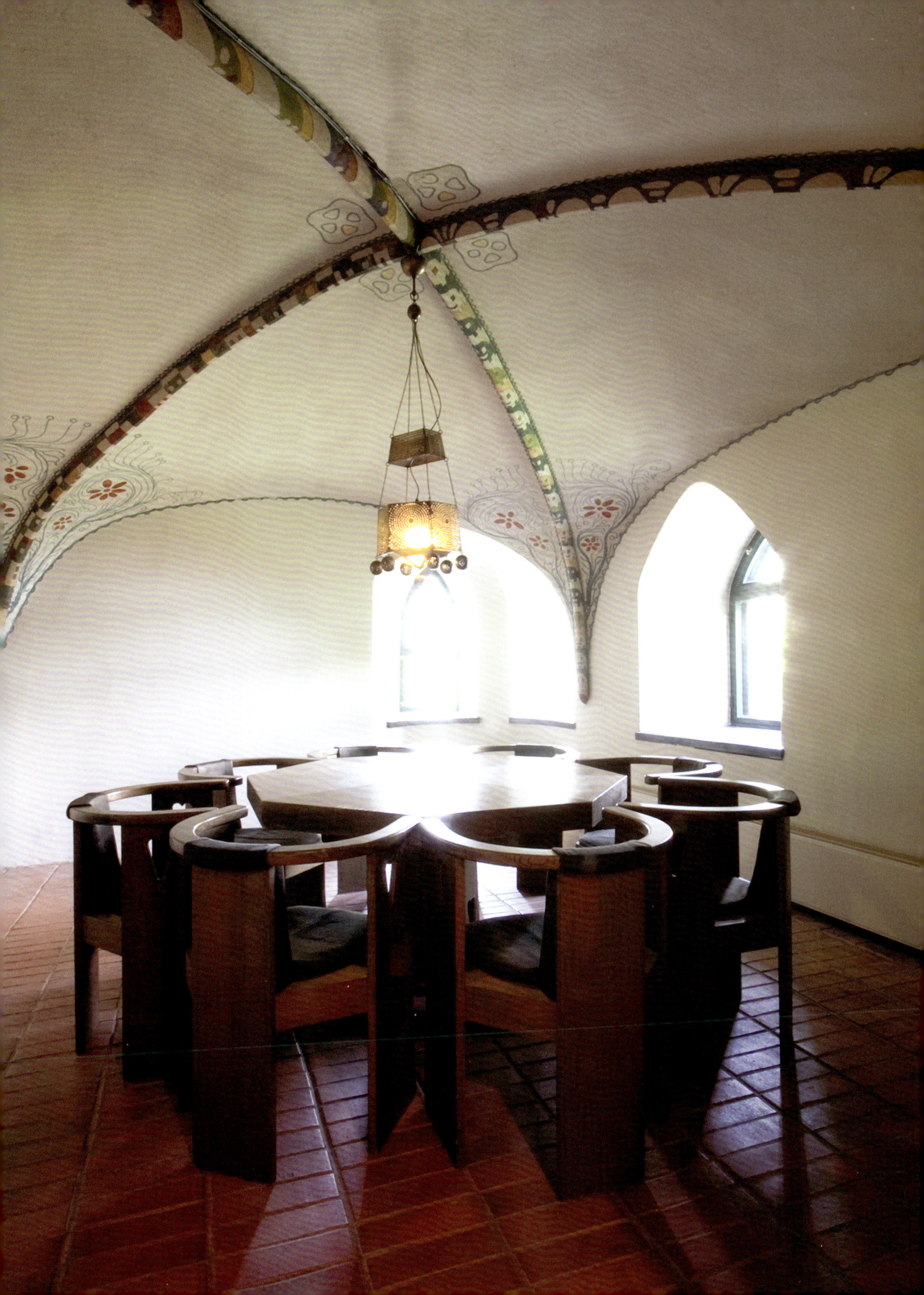

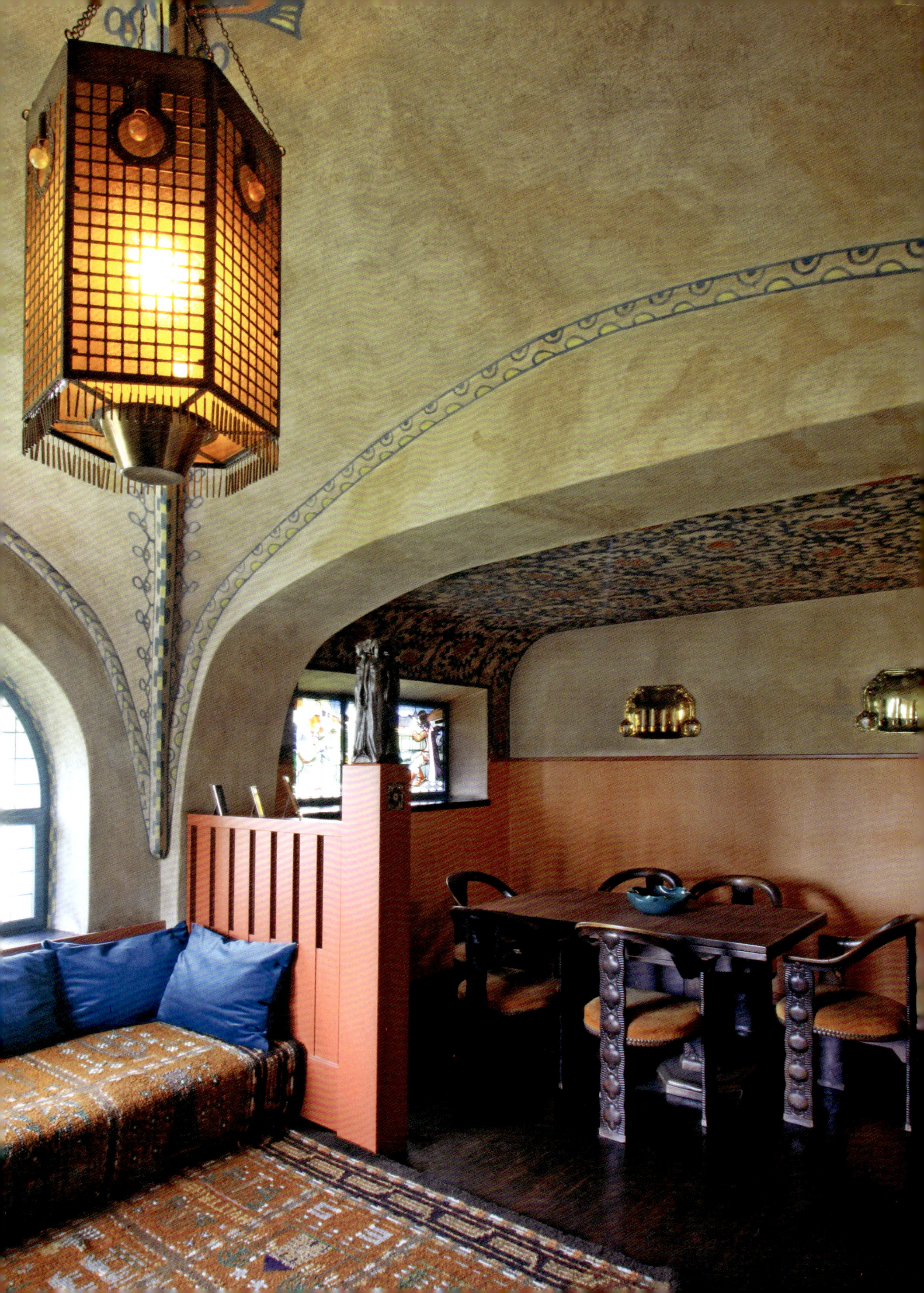

opposite
View to the dining room. The lamp and the sculpture on the sofa railing were designed by Loja Saarinen.

bottom
The rug in the fireplace corner of the dining room, known as *The Story of Hvitträsk*, was designed by Eliel Saarinen.

top
Dining room table. In the background is Olga Ehrström's stained-glass work *The Rivals* (1904–5), symbolizing "the switching" of the spouses. It shows Eliel Saarinen and Herman Gesellius serenading Mathilda Saarinen, who, after her marriage with Saarinen, married Gesellius.

top left
Bedroom chair known as "Loja chair," 1903

top right
Detail of the "Loja chair"

bottom
View from the bedroom to the flower room. The chairs and table in the latter were designed by Saarinen, 1910.

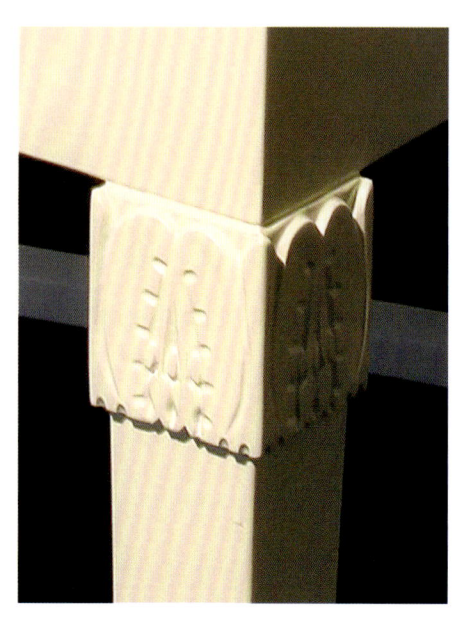

80

top
Eliel Saarinen painted this picture of Eero, Loja, and Pipsan (from left to right) in Hvitträsk in the 1910s.

bottom
Fireplace corner in the library

top
Desk and chair in the library corner of the atelier, designed by Saarinen, 1907

bottom
Saarinen's studio with Gesellius's atelier in the background

opposite
The plaster relief *The Angel of Resurrection* by Hungarian sculptor Géza Maróti (1875–1941) in the studio

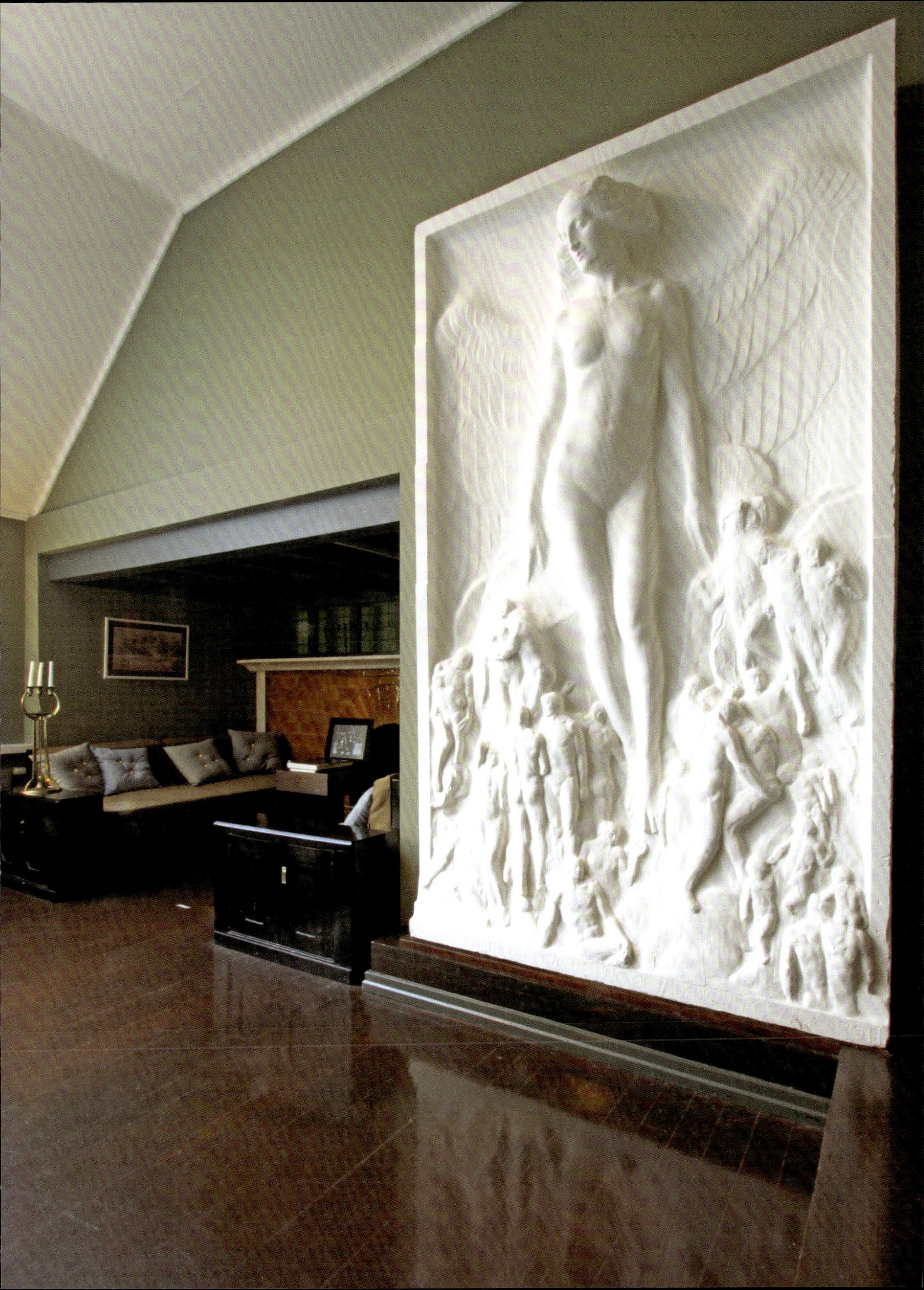

below
The children's play room, interior from 1908–9. In its place was originally the architectural assistants' bedroom with a stair leading to the atelier.

top
Pipsan's room, known as "the rose chamber," with an oil pastel portrait of Pipsan by Géza Maróti on the back wall

bottom
Second-floor bedroom in the Saarinen wing, with a portrait of Loja by Eliel on the wall

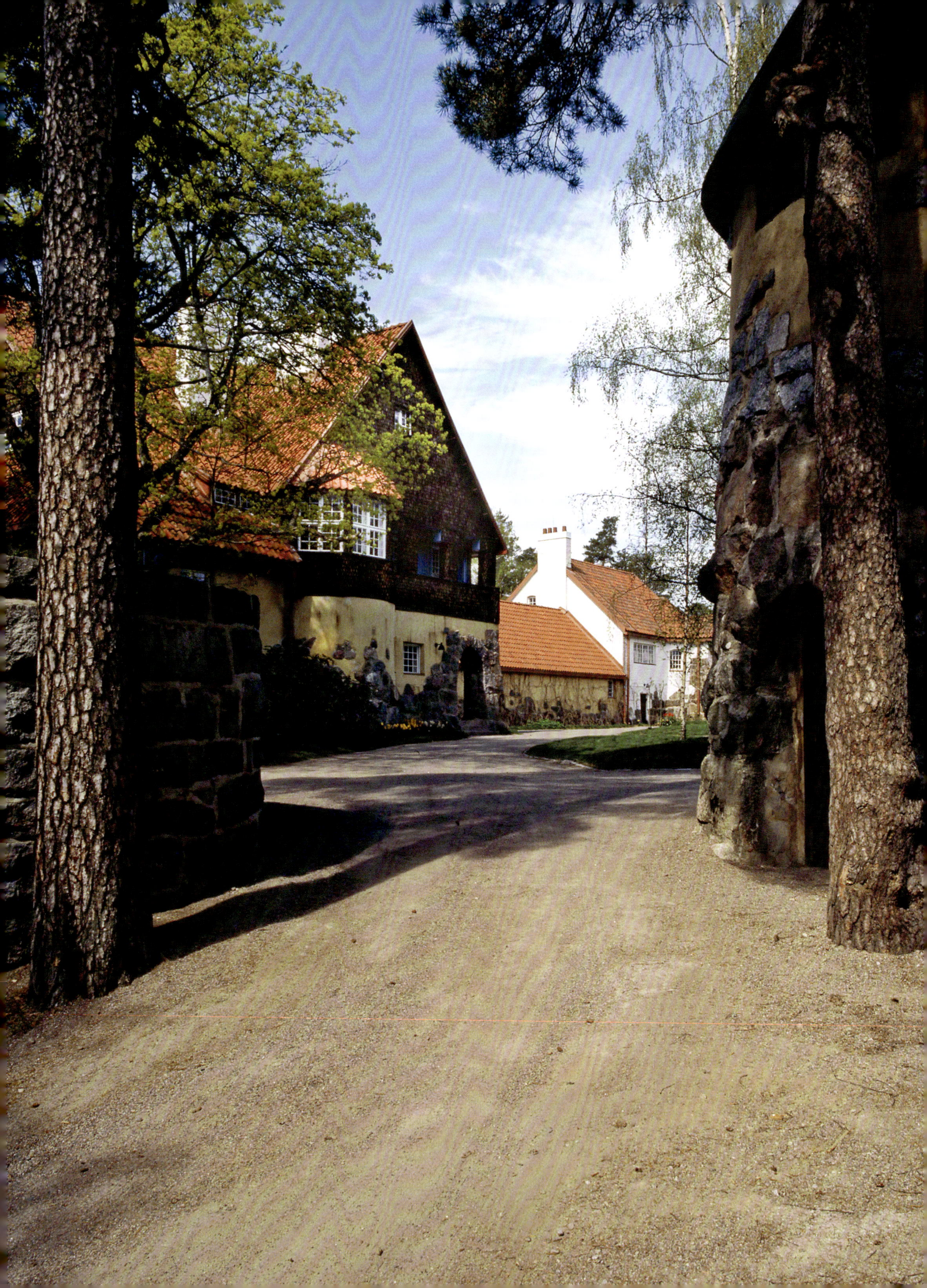

opposite
The original view of approach. The north wing, seen in the background, was rebuilt according to a design by Eero Saarinen in 1929–39.

left
Main entrance to the Saarinens' home

right
Entrance to the kitchen

overleaf
Winter view from the courtyard

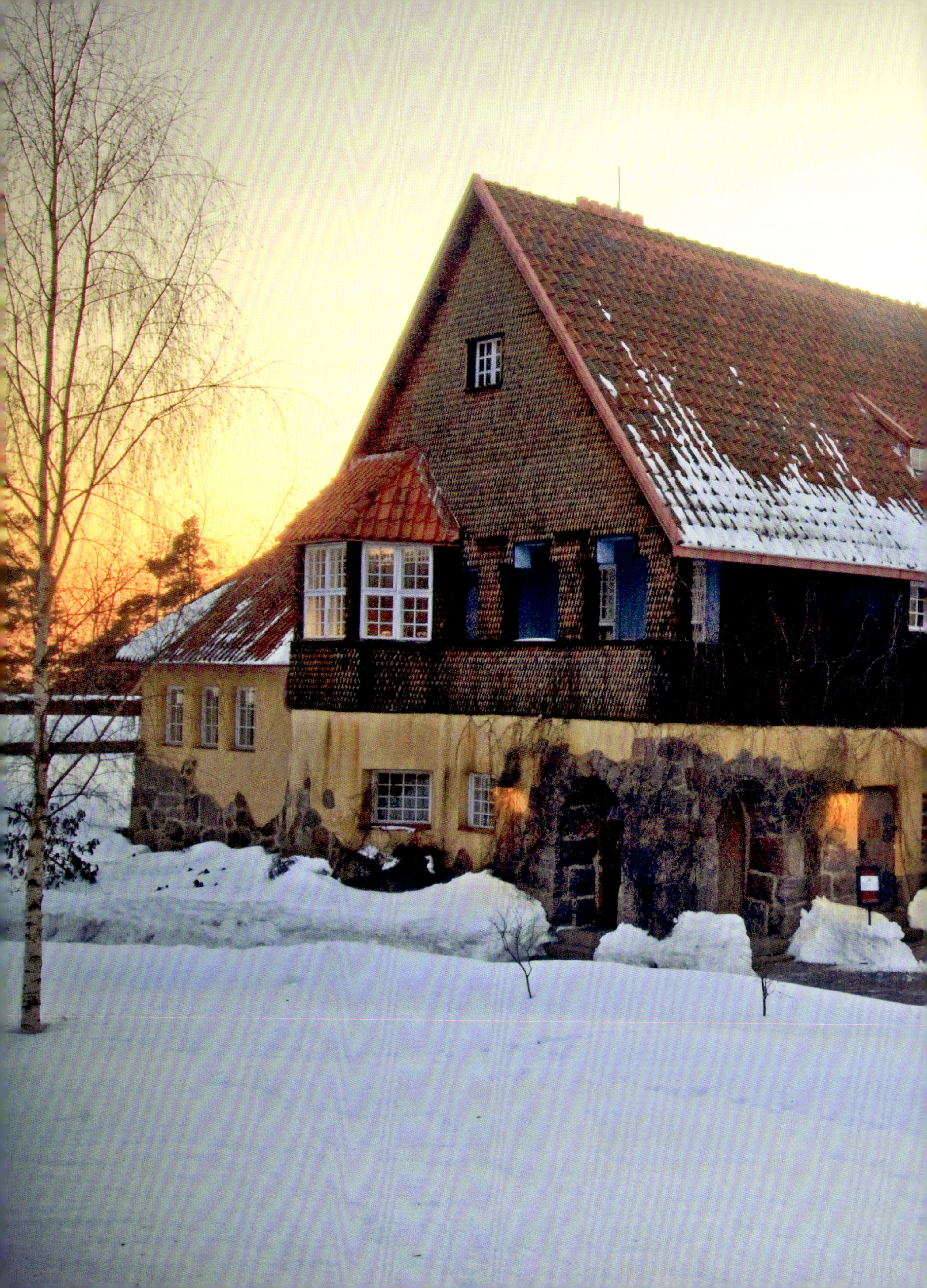

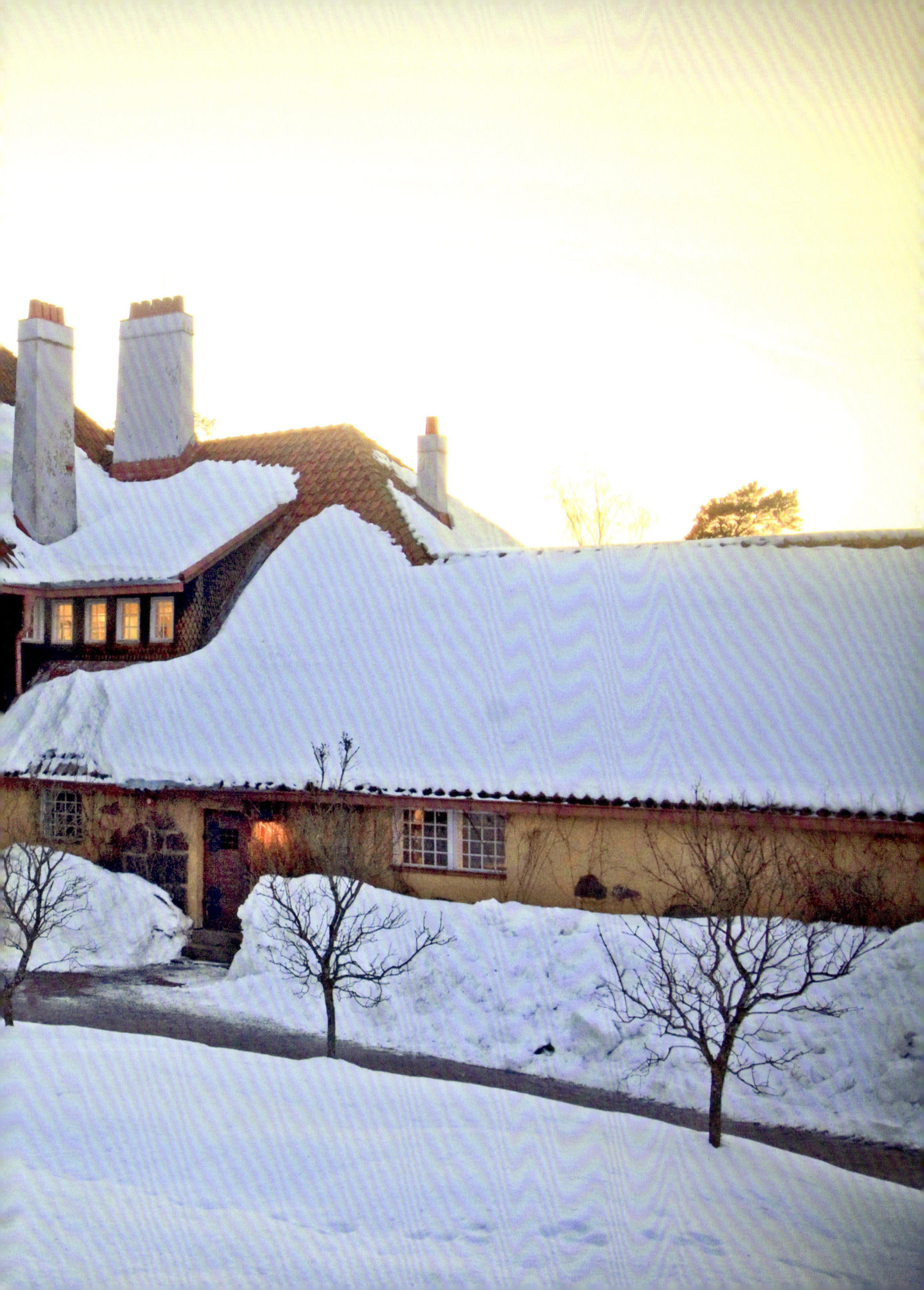

Summerhouse for A. and E. Lindberg

Vihti, Finland, 1903–5

The summerhouse that Amanda Lindberg, the owner of a farm in Vihti, and her daughter Emmy hired the firm to build for them was probably designed mostly by Saarinen. After the death of Emmy's father, mother and daughter managed the farm by themselves, and its old main building was in a state of poor repair. The contemporary building with modern comforts that Saarinen created served as a residence for Emmy for a while. She later became an important figure in the region and was a pioneer of so-called agritourism in Finland,[25] when, in 1918, she acquired a rest home and boarding house where many notable Finnish figures came to spend their time.

The site of the villa was a slope opening onto farmland. From the house the family's old farmhouse could be seen in the distance, beyond a garden and fields. Saarinen gave the mansard-roofed villa, which was partly faced with shingles, a unique appearance through a few carefully considered accents. The eaves are bordered by fretwork moldings, and the chimneys feature round ornaments, which also appear in the window frames. Other special features of the rural villa are its balconies, one above the entrance porch and the other facing the garden, which are almost as large as the rooms on the second floor to which they are connected. At the front facade, the colonnade supporting the semi-circular balcony creates a monumental impression. Today the house is painted in dark colors and is known locally as the Black Villa. The original color scheme, however, was predominantly light.

The main entrance, leading to the dining room, is on the central axis of the house, which ends in an open porch on the other side. Adjoining the dining room is a comfortable living room with many pieces of early-twentieth-century furniture. Built-in furnishings included a lounging corner with a sofa; a small bay held a table, chairs, and plant stands. Both main rooms have colored tiled stoves. In 1908, a few years after the house was built, Saarinen custom-designed furniture for the living and dining rooms. While the living room furniture was made immediately, the dining table and its chairs were not produced until the 1990s. Today the house is privately owned.

opposite
View of the approach to the villa

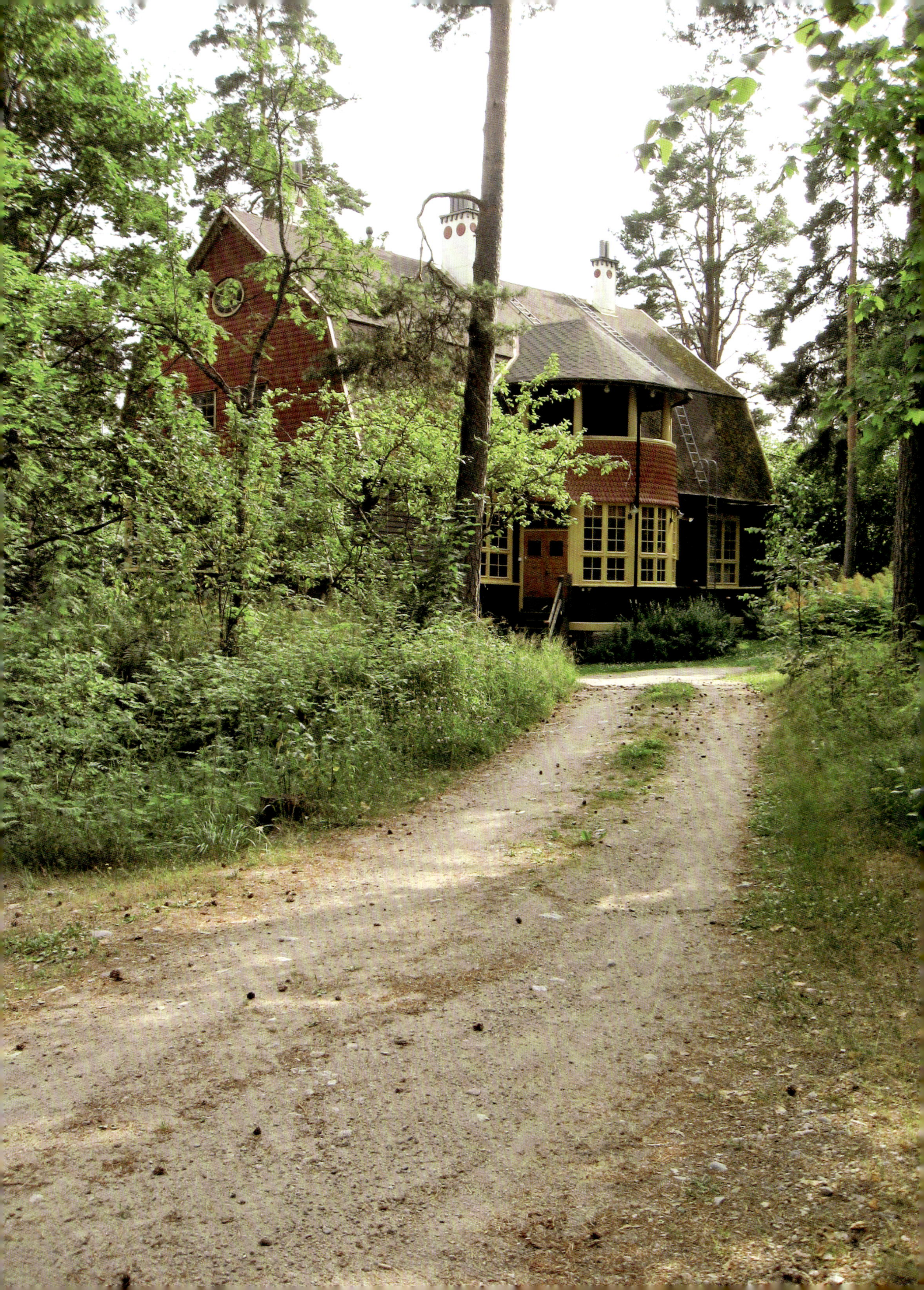

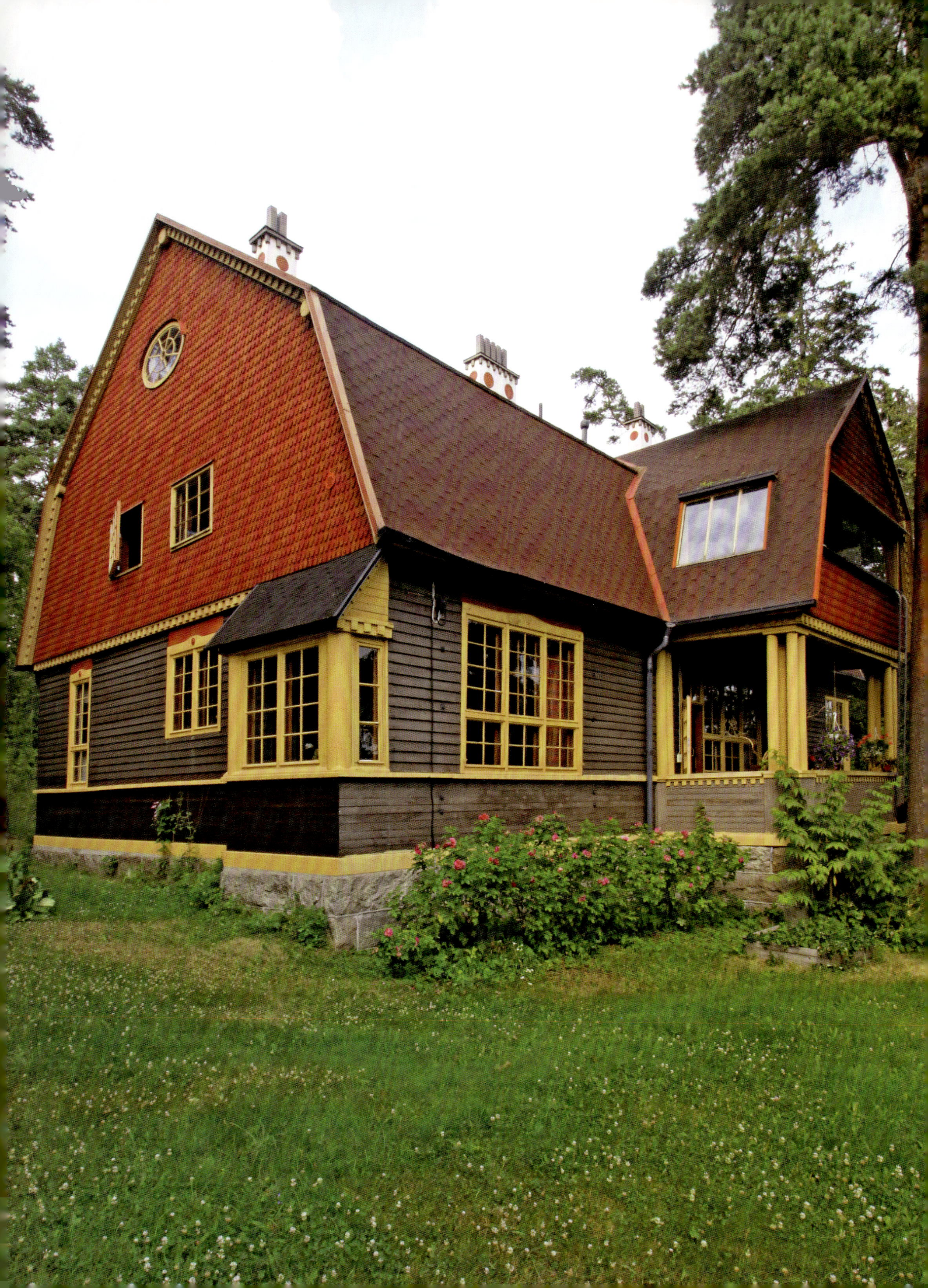

opposite
View of the house from the garden

top left
Emmy Lindberg

top right
First-floor plan, watercolor and ink drawing, 1903

bottom
Watercolor and ink drawing of the southwest facade, 1913

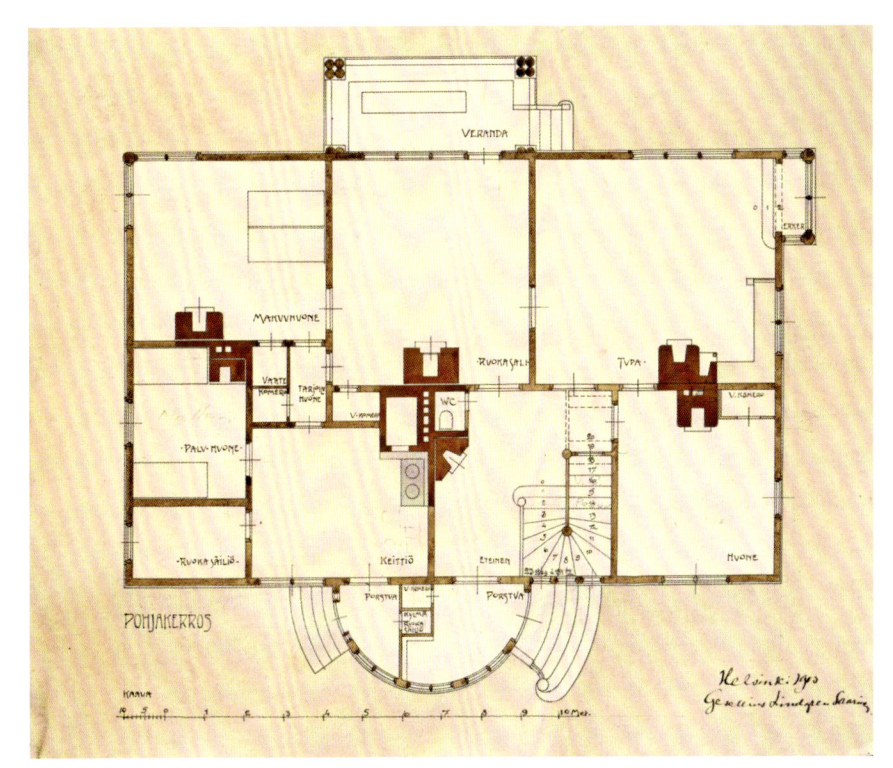

93

94

opposite, top
Living room coffee table and chair, watercolor and ink drawing by Saarinen, 1908

opposite, bottom
Living room armoire and sofa, watercolor and ink drawing by Saarinen, 1908

top
Detail of the living room chair

bottom
First-floor living room

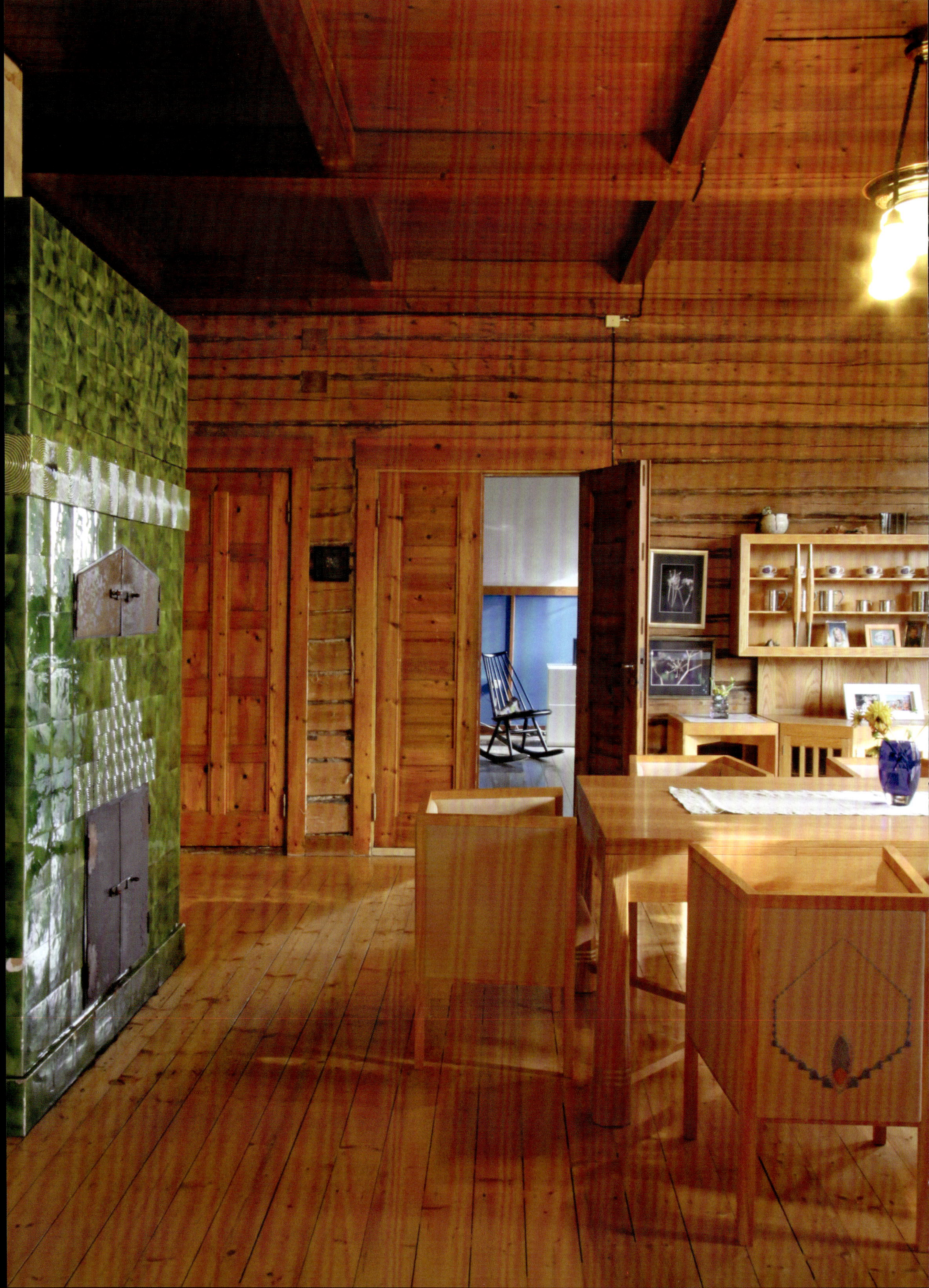

opposite
The green tile stove and the chairs in the dining room were custom-made for the house.

below
On the dining room wall is a *ryijy* rug (known as *The Rose*), designed by Saarinen in 1904.

below
An open porch faces the garden.

opposite
The main entrance has a shingle-clad entrance tower with a colonnaded porch on the second floor.

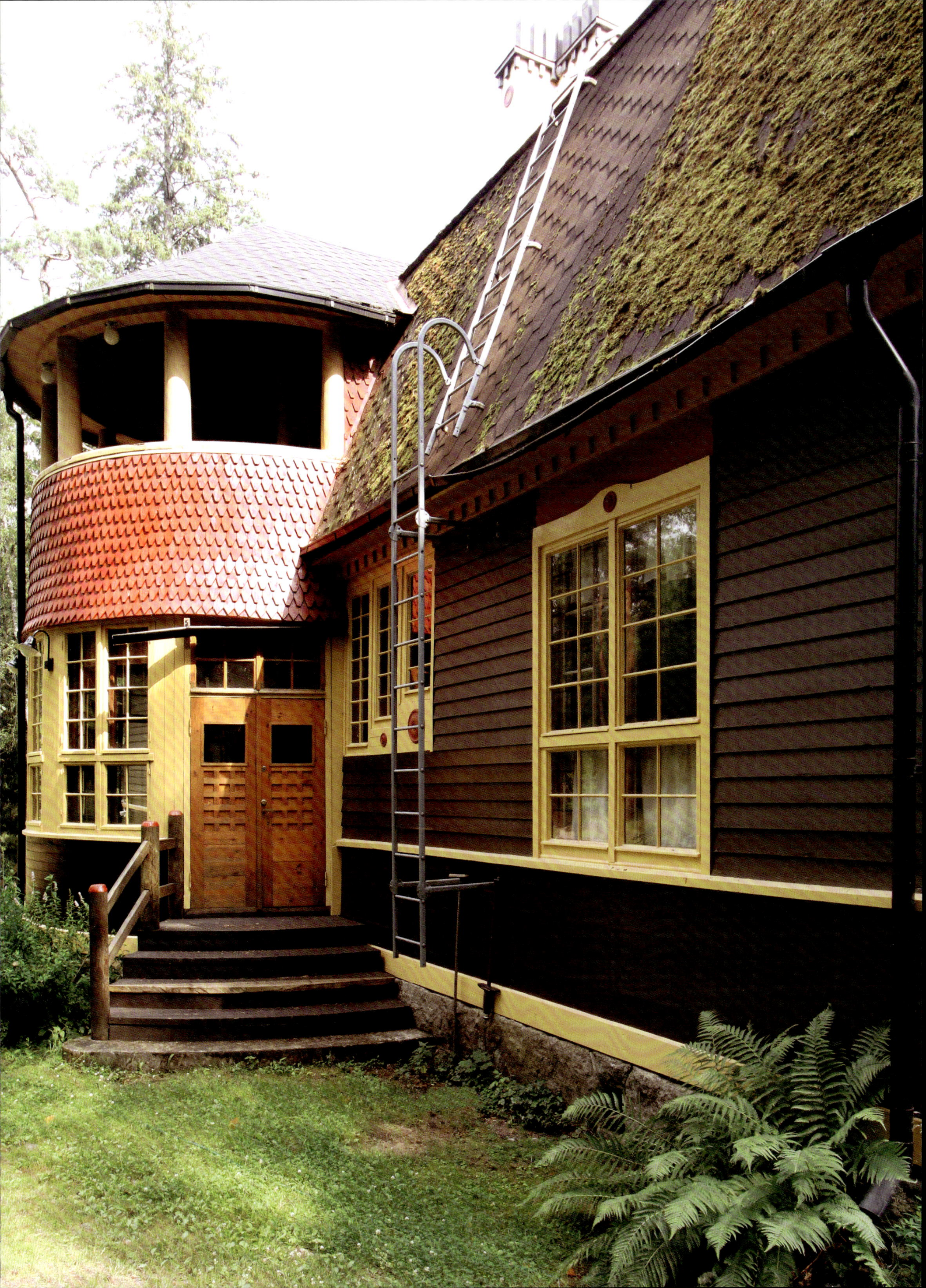

Eliel Saarinen in Finland

1907–23

After establishing his own office, Saarinen's most widely noted works were monumental public buildings and large town planning projects. He participated in numerous architectural competitions for projects of different types and sizes, but the majority of his designs and plans remained unrealized, such as his winning competition entry for the Finnish Parliament (1908), a competition entry for the Peace Palace in The Hague (1906), and his design for Kalevala House (1921) as part of the town plan for Helsinki's Munkkiniemi-Haaga district. Although the economy recovered, political instability continued in the 1910s, and before long World War I broke out in Europe. Finland's declaration of independence in 1917 and the ensuing civil war further slowed the building industry. The new Finnish banknotes, which were introduced in 1922, were designed by Saarinen.

Among the architect's realized works of the period are the city halls of Lahti (1911–12) and Joensuu (1910–14), built of red brick with tall towers, which became important elements of the local townscapes. He also designed, together with Herman Gesellius, two railway stations, the Helsinki Railway Station, for which he won the competition in 1904 and which was constructed throughout most of the 1910s, and the railway station of Viipuri (Vyborg) (1904–13). Both stations had spacious vaulted halls holding ticket offices and waiting halls. The Helsinki Railway Station has become a landmark of the city with its red granite facade and tall clock tower. The station in Vyborg was almost completely demolished in 1941.

Saarinen's interest in town planning led him to submit competition entries for the plans of Canberra in Australia and Greater Tallinn in Estonia in the early 1910s, but the town plans that occupied him for several years during that period were the Munkkiniemi-Haaga plan and the related general plan for Greater Helsinki. Saarinen's fascination with this area of work continued after his emigration to the United States in 1923, where soon after arriving he worked on the large-scale Chicago Lake Front plan.

The concept of creating a total work of art, for which Gesellius, Lindgren, and Saarinen's residential architecture had become known, developed on a different level of scale in Saarinen's urban visions.[1] Nevertheless, the architect continued to take on private commissions and designed a number of houses during this period.

opposite
Saarinen designed the "Hannes chair" for his brother Hannes Saarinen in 1908. It is made of mahogany with ebenholz details.

Villa G. J. Winter

Taruniemi, Sortavala, Russia, 1908–11

This summerhouse on cape Taruniemi at the shore of Lake Ladoga was commissioned by Dr. Gustaf Johannes Winter (1868–1924), the senior physician of nearby Sortavala's town hospital. By the 1910s, the features that had characterized the national-romantic style popular around the turn of the century—complex forms and asymmetry—had given way to more austere, classicist designs. Villa Winter has an almost symmetrical layout, whose simple shape, together with the imposing columns framing the porch, is reminiscent of the formal ideals of classicism. The exterior materials of the building make a bold statement. The upper floor and balconies are covered with shingles, continuing the tradition of Hvitträsk and Pulkanranta, while the plastered walls of the first floor are left exposed, and the foundation, the porch, and its columns are covered with large stones set in mortar. This rustic pattern of natural stones creates a surprising contrast with the refined decorations based on a leaf motif surrounding the entrance. Stylized geometric or ornamental details became typical of Saarinen's work in the 1910s.

The villa stands on a small mound near the shore, with a masonry staircase leading up to it from the lake. Castlelike in appearance, the building dominates its setting, which included a terrace by the shore, plantings, a gazebo, as well as natural areas that were left untouched. Winter was a gardening enthusiast and took great care in selecting varied and partly rare plants from Europe, Asia, and North America for the site. Architect and botanist Bengt Schalin (1889–1982) was responsible for the terraced arrangement of the banks of earth surrounding the villa, while Winter himself designed the rest of the garden.[2]

The main entrance to the building faces the garden and leads to the primary space of the house, a large hall containing a living room and dining area with built-in sofas. Surrounded by windows on three sides, the space is filled with light throughout the day. The bay containing the dining area provides a view of the rugged lake scenery. The hall's wooden paneling and ceiling with wood beams are reminiscent of the architect's earlier domestic work at the turn of the twentieth century. A half-open wooden staircase leads up to the second floor, where the family's bedrooms were located.

After World War II, the Sortavala region was ceded to the Soviet Union. During the Soviet era, Villa Winter served as a sanatorium, a site for sports camps, and a recreation facility. It is now part of a resort area. Despite its wide range of uses through several decades, the house has preserved many of its original features. Parts of the park and its botanic garden have also survived.

opposite
Natural stones and wood-clad walls give the building its solid appearance.

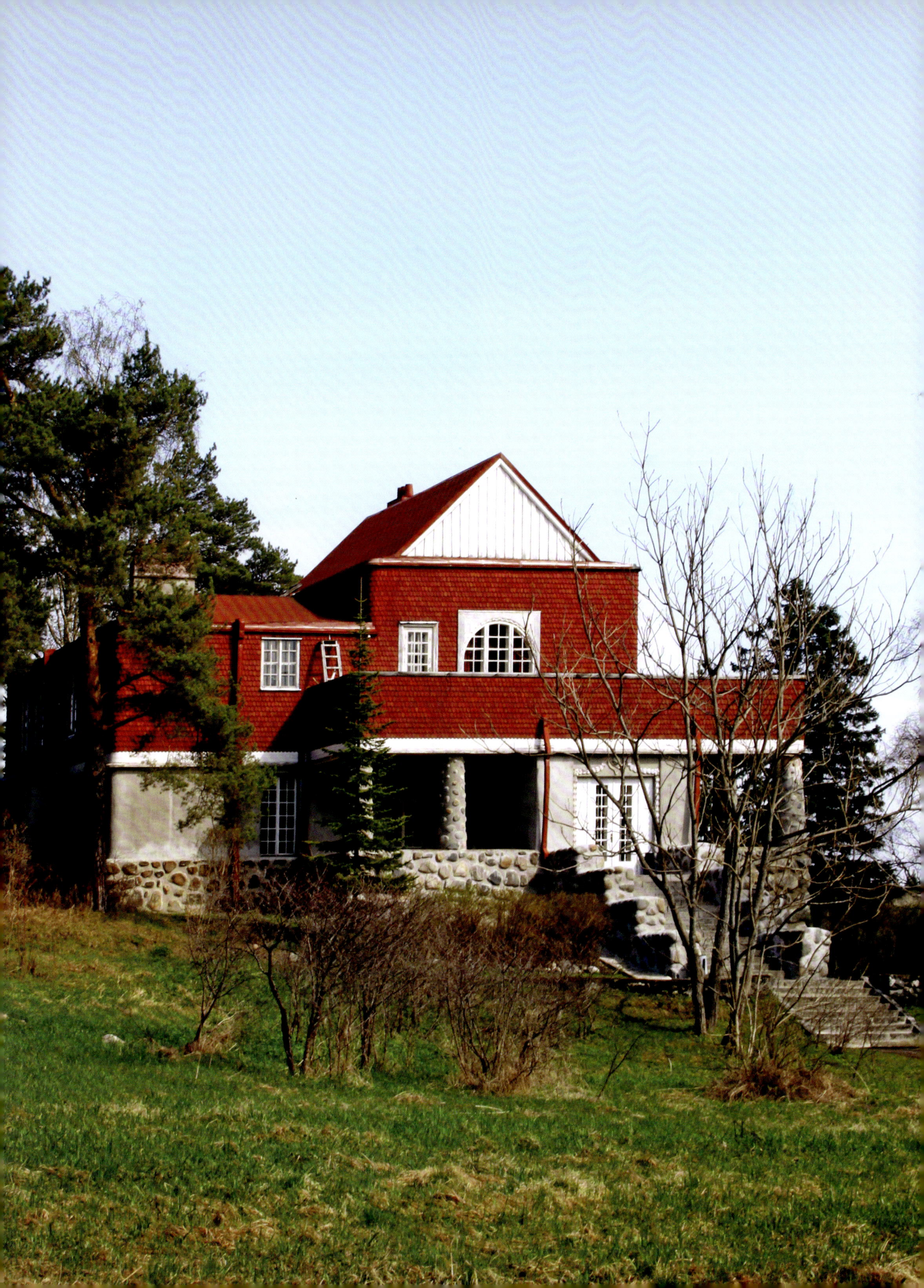

top
Pencil perspective drawing by Saarinen, 1909

middle
Doctor Winter in his garden in the 1910s

bottom left
This aerial view of the villa and its surroundings shows that the composition of the garden played an important role.

bottom right
First-floor plan

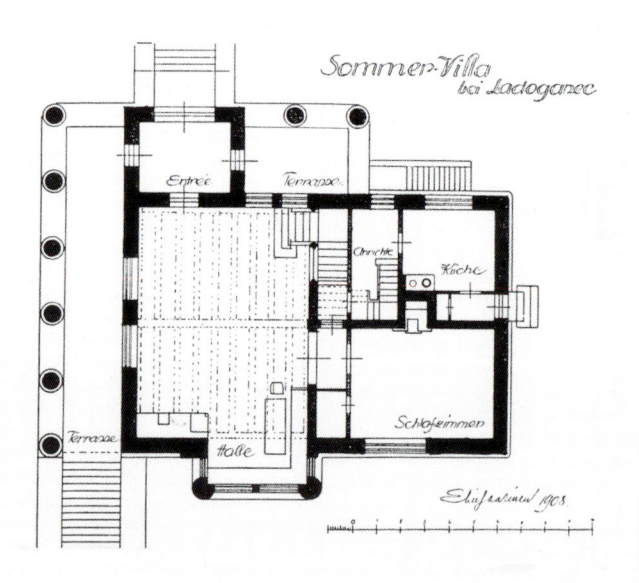

top
Main entrance

bottom
Wide stairs lead down toward the lake.

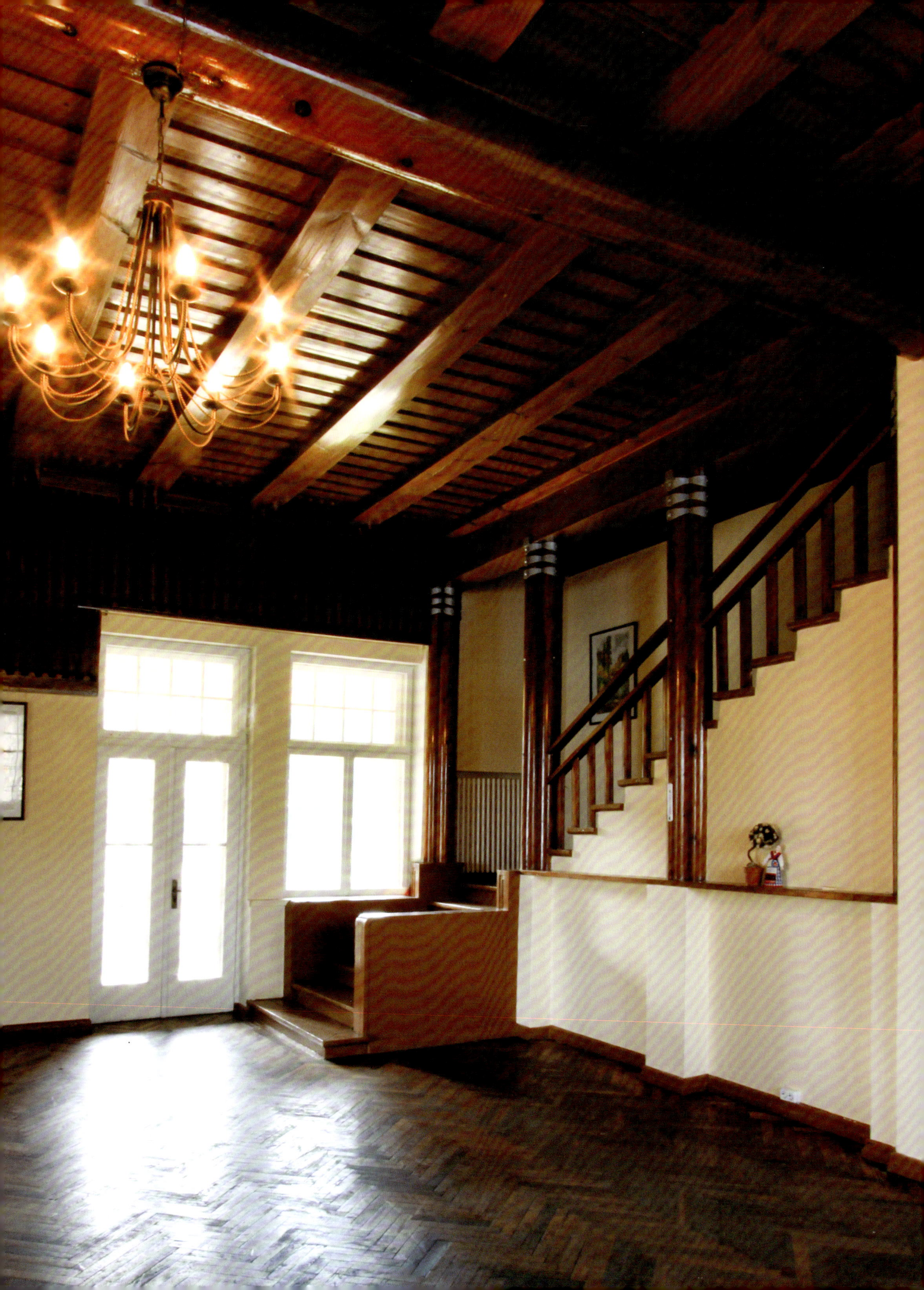

opposite
A wooden staircase leads to the bedrooms from the hall.

top
Detail of wooden stair posts with metal bands

bottom
First-floor hall

Villa Granagård

Kauniainen, Finland, 1909–10

In the early twentieth century, the villa community of Kauniainen, west of Helsinki, became popular with citizens of Helsinki, who moved there to live in more natural surroundings. Among them were Loja Saarinen's and Herman Gesellius's sister Antonia (Toni, 1871–1939) and her husband Bertil Paqvalen (1861–1943), a lemonade manufacturer and bookkeeper, who bought a plot in Kauniainen to build their family home. The house was located along a slope leading to the shore of Lake Gallträsk and connected to the landscape through terraces and pergolas. Part of the site was reserved for a large garden planted with vegetables, berries, and fruit, in order to keep the family as self-sufficient as possible. Toni in particular was interested in a natural and organic lifestyle, and the benefits of a vegetarian diet.[3]

Villa Granagård has a friendly appearance, with its mansard roof—a popular roof type in the 1910s, because it permitted bedrooms to be built in the attic story—and board-and-batten cladding painted yellow and white. The most important rooms of the main floor were the drawing room, which covered the width of the building, receiving daylight from two directions, and the dining room, with a large bay window facing the garden. Other rooms on this floor included a ladies' room, the hall, the kitchen with its serving corridor, and a servant's room. Loja Saarinen designed some of the built-in furnishings, in particular the fireplace in the living room and the sofa nook. The family began to take in paying summer guests in 1911, and part of the top floor was renovated for use as a separate apartment during the summer. In the early 1920s, the second floor was rented out on a year-round basis, and for many years the apartment was occupied by tenants, including cultural figures such as the painter Sigrid Schauman (1877–1979) and the poet Elmer Diktonius (1896–1961), who lived at Villa Granagård for several years. The building was refurbished into apartments for two families in 1966 and is still inhabited by descendants of the original owners.[4]

opposite

Southwest facade

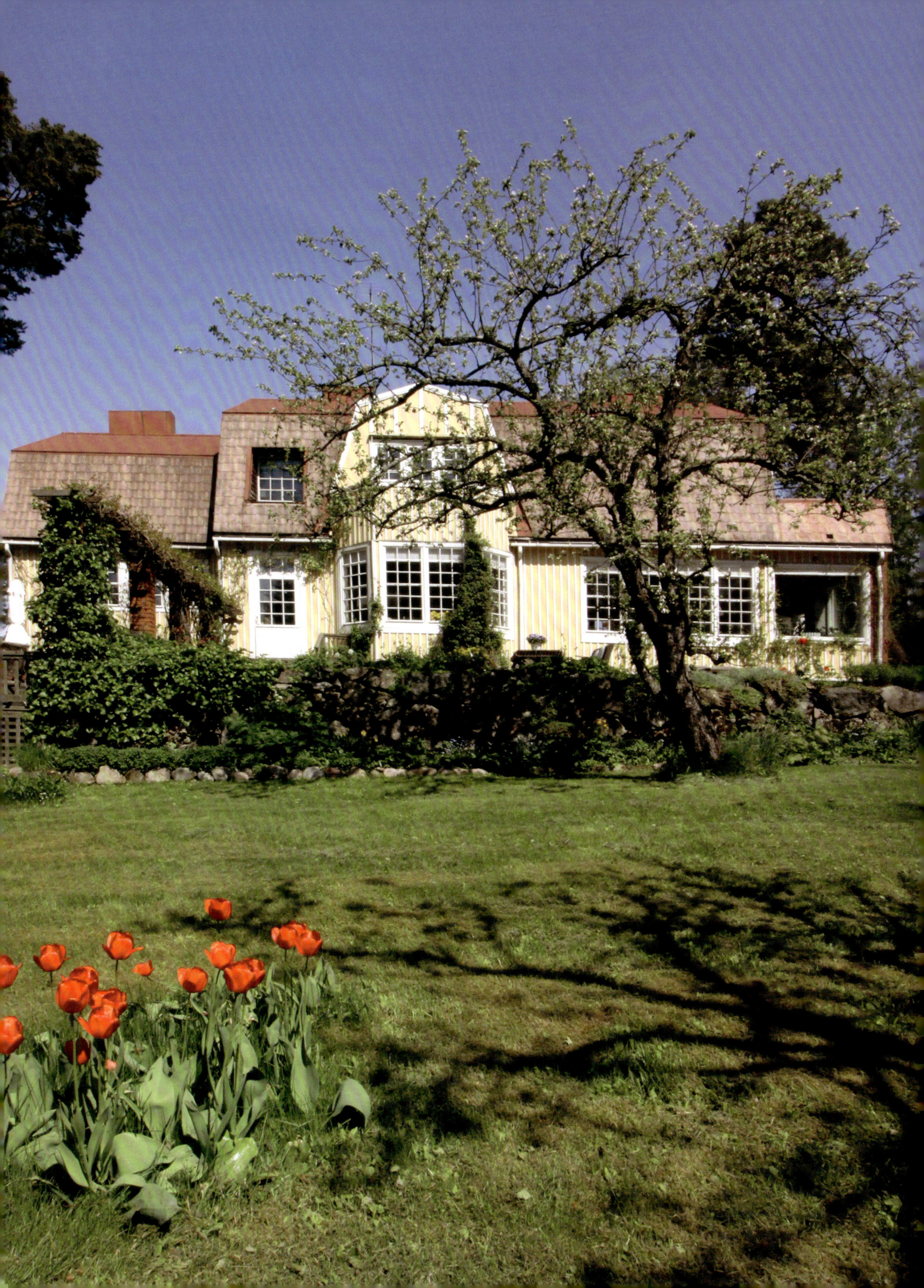

top
First-floor plan, reconstruction drawing by Tytti Valto, 1982

middle
View of the living room in 1967

bottom
The original roof was clad with wooden shingles similar to the ones used at Hvitträsk.

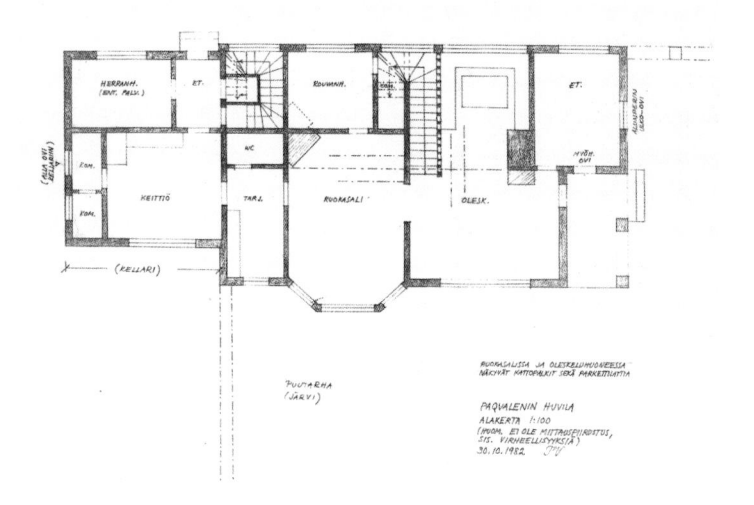

top
Watercolor perspective by Saarinen, 1909

bottom
Northeast facade with the entrance courtyard

below
The cocktail glasses on the middle shelf were designed by Saarinen.

opposite
The original pantry is now used as an entrance space, seen here with the kitchen in the background.

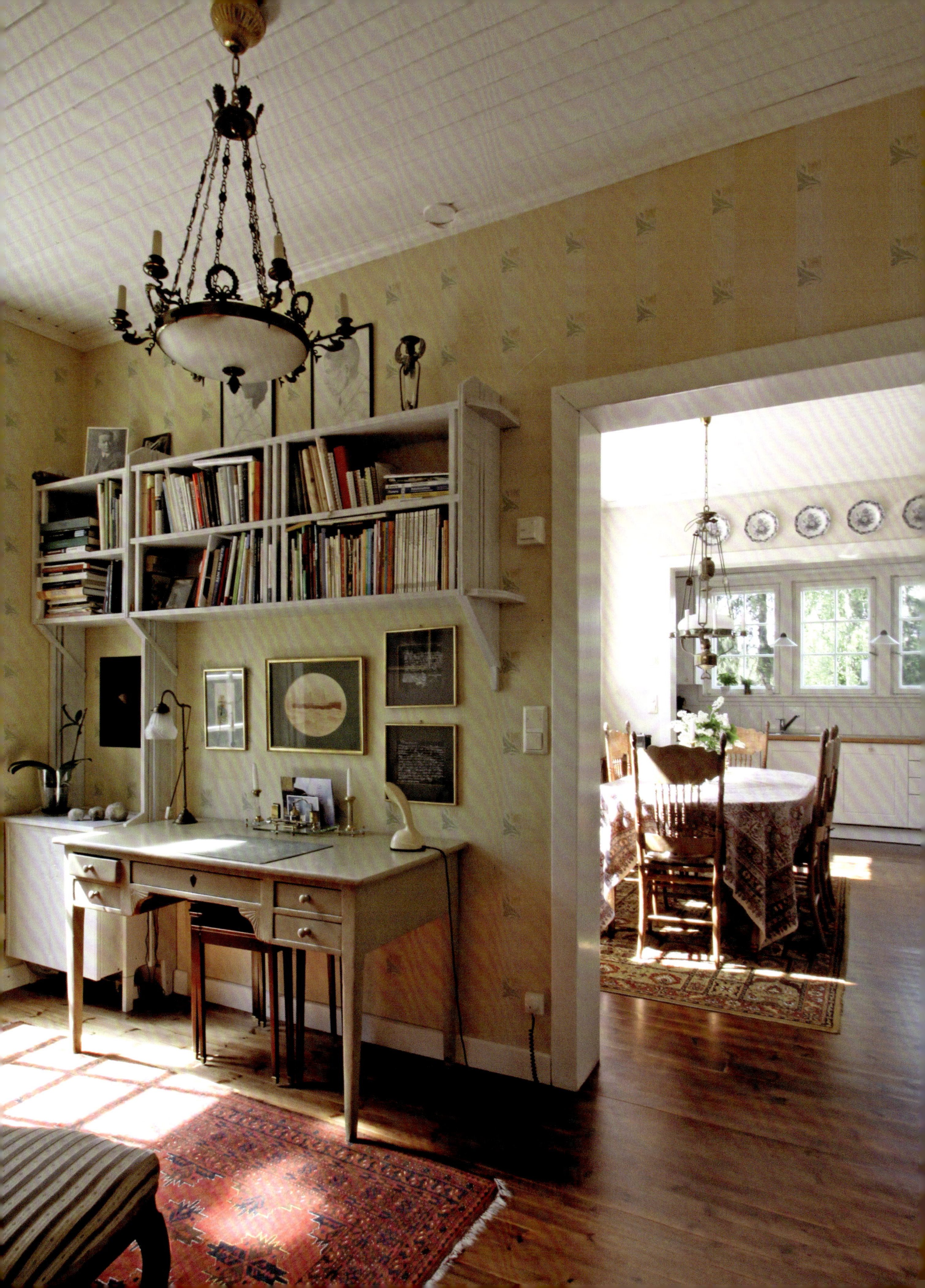

below
A view to the garden from the original dining room bay window

left
Entrance hall with replica of Saarinen's chair

right
Second-floor bedroom. The portrait on the wall is of Heinrich Gesellius, Antonia Paqvalen and Loja Saarinen's grandfather.

top
Loja Saarinen designed special tiles with faces for the stove.

bottom
Courtyard door

opposite
First-floor living room with green tile stove and Hannes chair

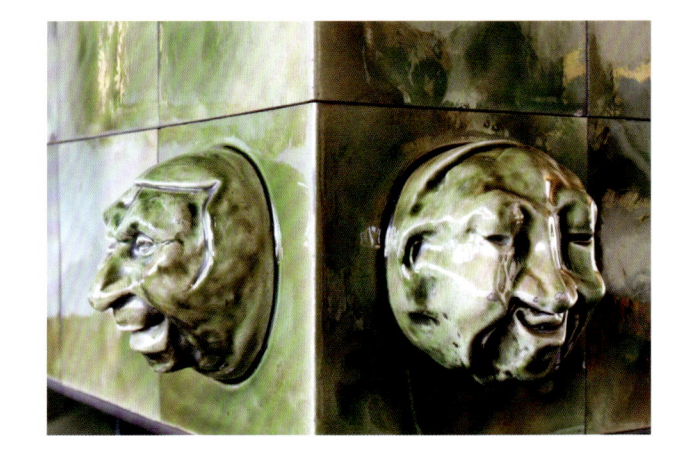

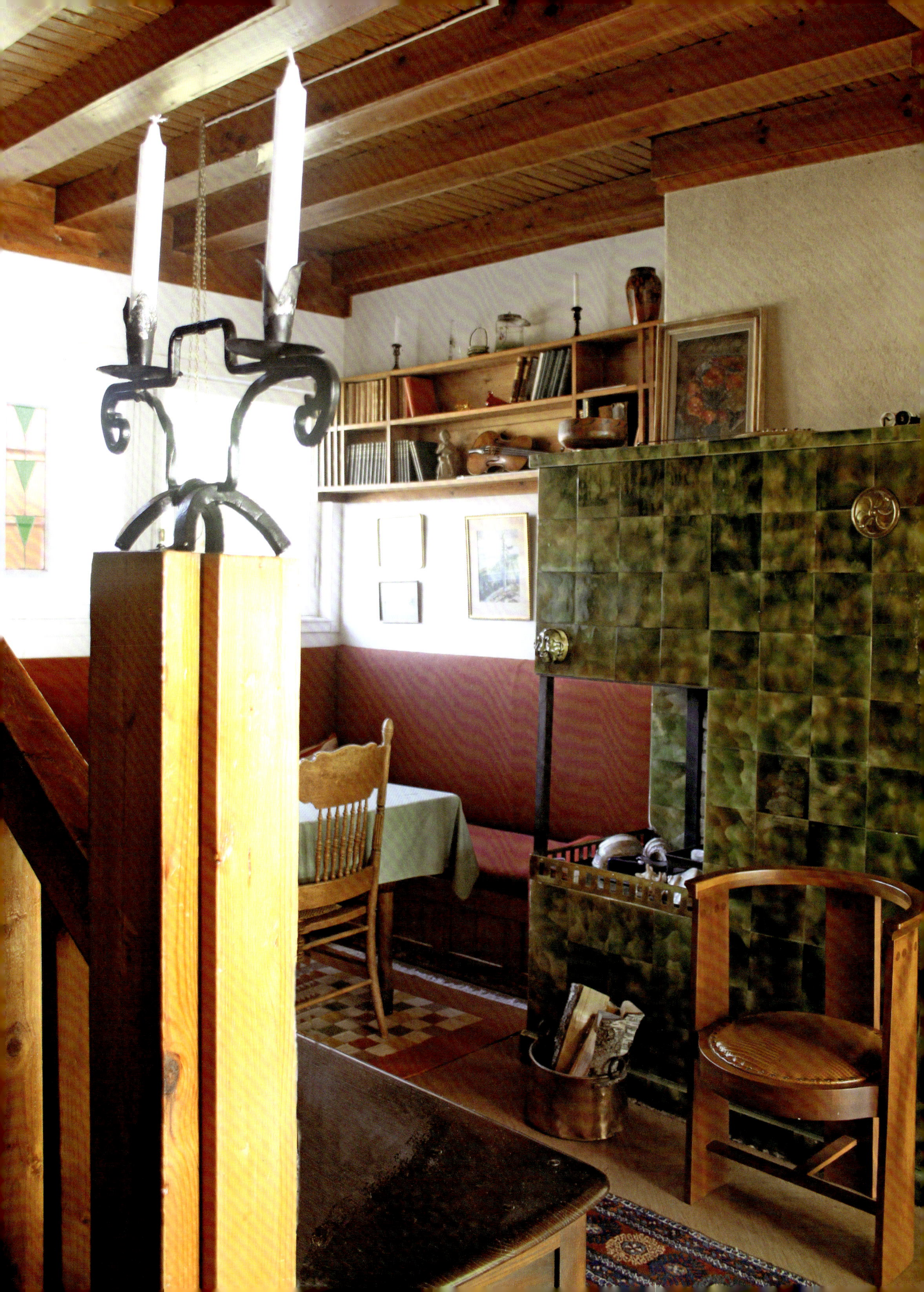

V. Sjöström Studio

Helsinki, 1909–10

The Kulosaari (Brändö) community in Helsinki was founded in 1907. The island, which was accessed by ferry before a bridge was built in 1919, was meant to provide a verdant and spacious living environment that stood in contrast to city life and would support a healthy lifestyle with opportunities for sports and recreation. Several artists and architects moved to Kulosaari Island soon after the community was established; Armas Lindgren was among the community's founding members. One of the artists moving to the island was Saarinen's friend painter Frans Vilho (Wilhelm) Sjöström (1873–1944), who bought a plot at the southeast end of Kulosaari on a ridge that was still in an untouched state. Saarinen designed a large villa and studio complex for the site, only part of which was built. Nonetheless, the villa consumed most of Sjöström's income from his paintings, and he would spend less than ten years there before he moved to Central Finland in 1918.[5]

Sjöström's work often depicted bright daytime scenes. The villa's terrace, facing south and west, and garden offered excellent opportunities for studying light and color. The house itself, covered by a mansard roof, has an asymmetrical volume with a square tower at the main entrance. A sphinx statue guards the porch entrance at the building's other end. The walls of the studio were whitewashed to aid the artist in his use of a pure palette. The two-story house as realized had a spacious living room, dining room, and kitchen on the first floor, with bedrooms on the upper floor. Sjöström's high-ceilinged atelier was also on the first floor. He executed decorative paintings in some of the villa's rooms, remains of which still exist. The atelier was renovated in the 1920s and divided into smaller rooms. Today the house is privately owned.

opposite

A view from the gate to the main entrance

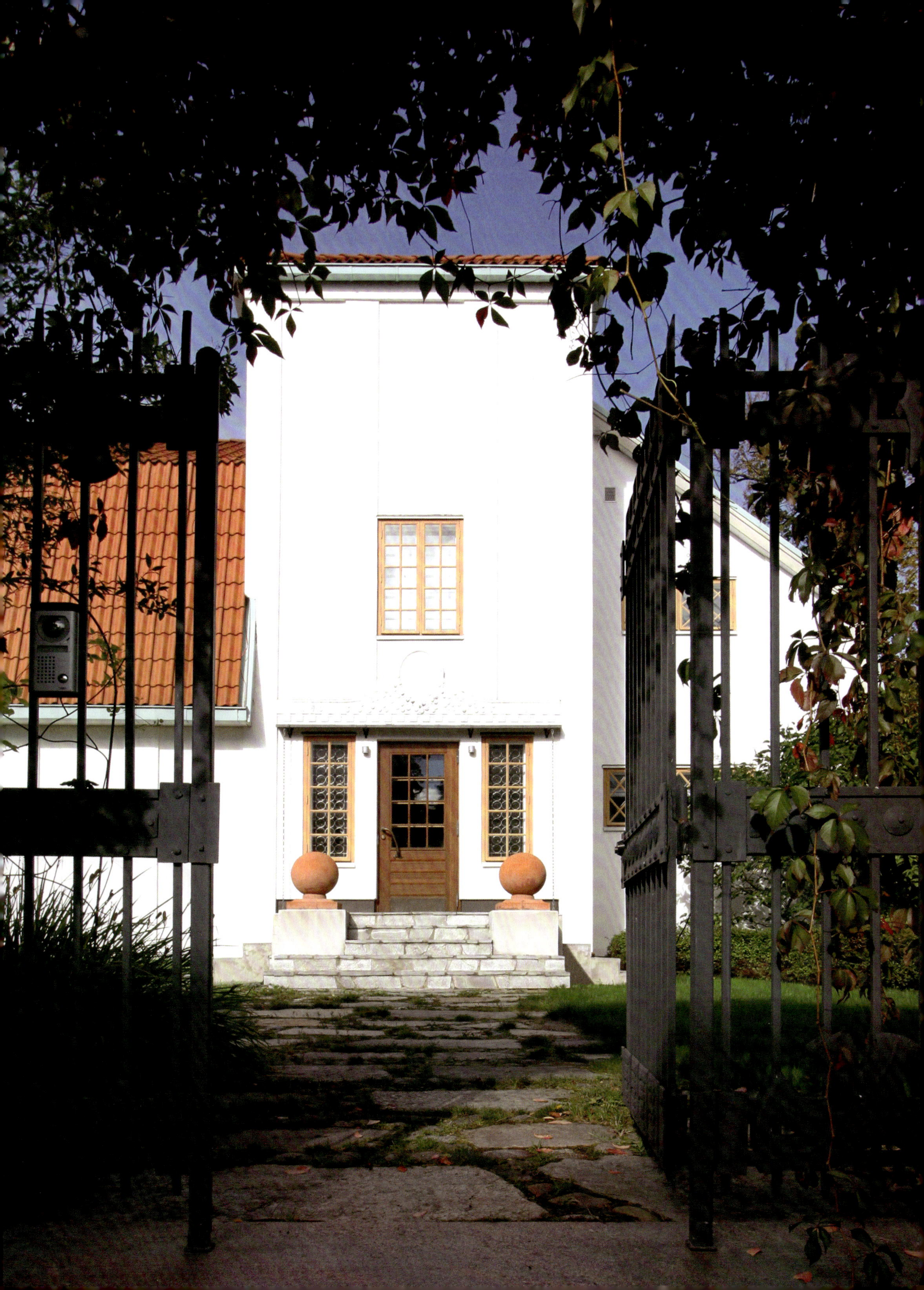

top
Vilho Sjöström in Paris, circa 1907

middle
Perspective drawing of the atelier by Saarinen in 1909. The house is a mirror image compared to the final design.

bottom
First-floor plan, 1929. The original atelier was later turned into a dining room.

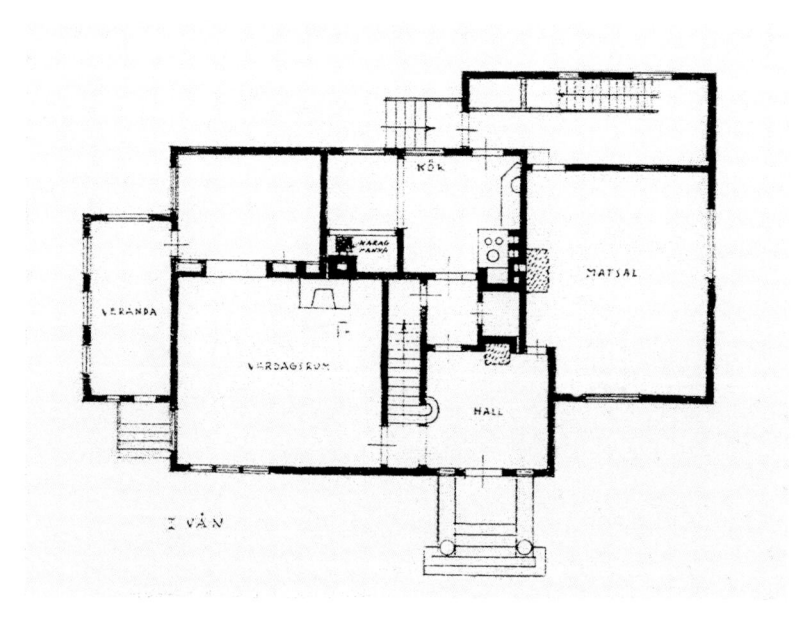

top
View of the house from the garden

bottom
The large windows mark Sjöström's atelier.

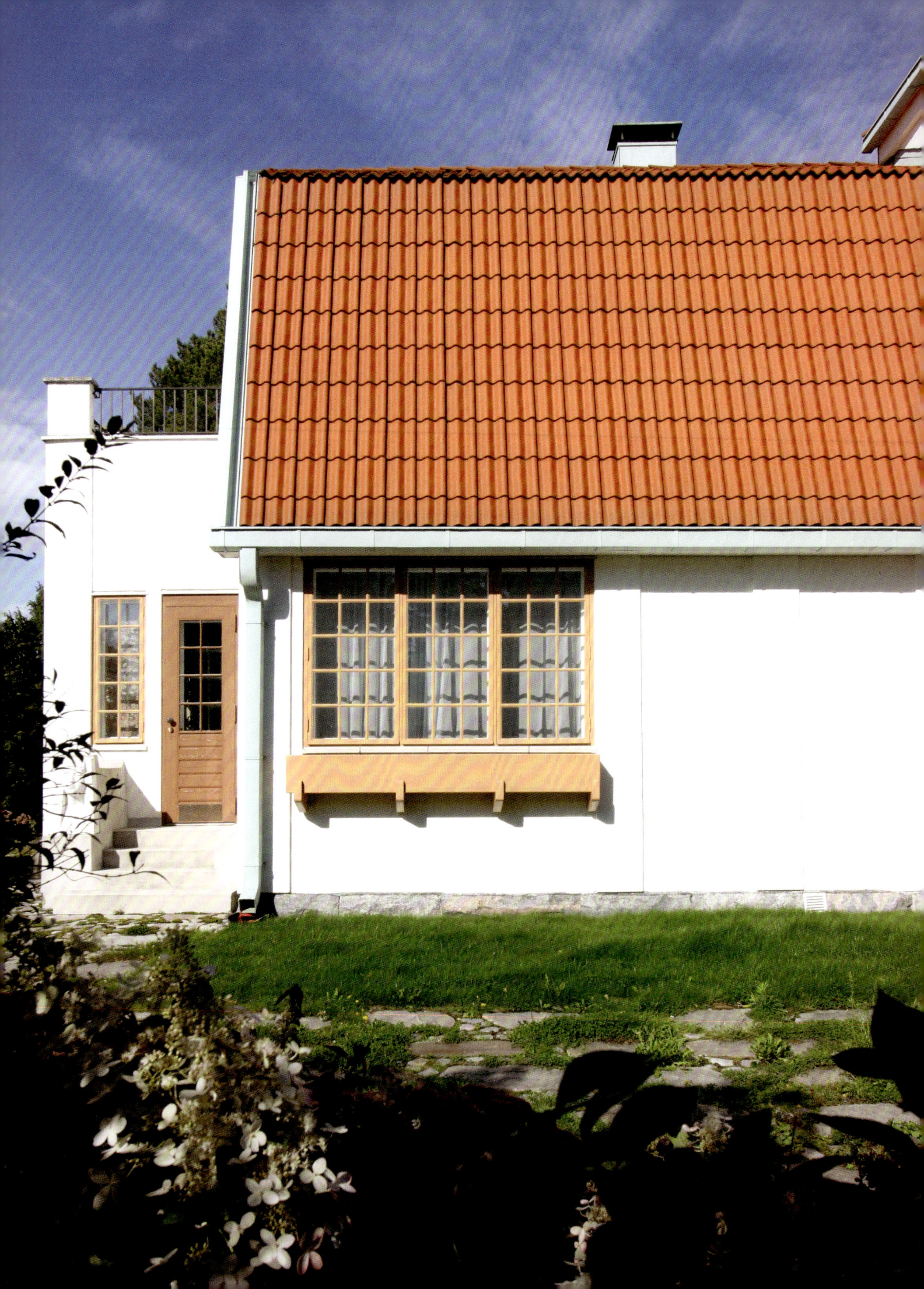

opposite
View from the garden

below
The sculpture by the garden entrance was designed by Sjöström.

below
Entrance hall

opposite
View from the living room toward the entrance hall

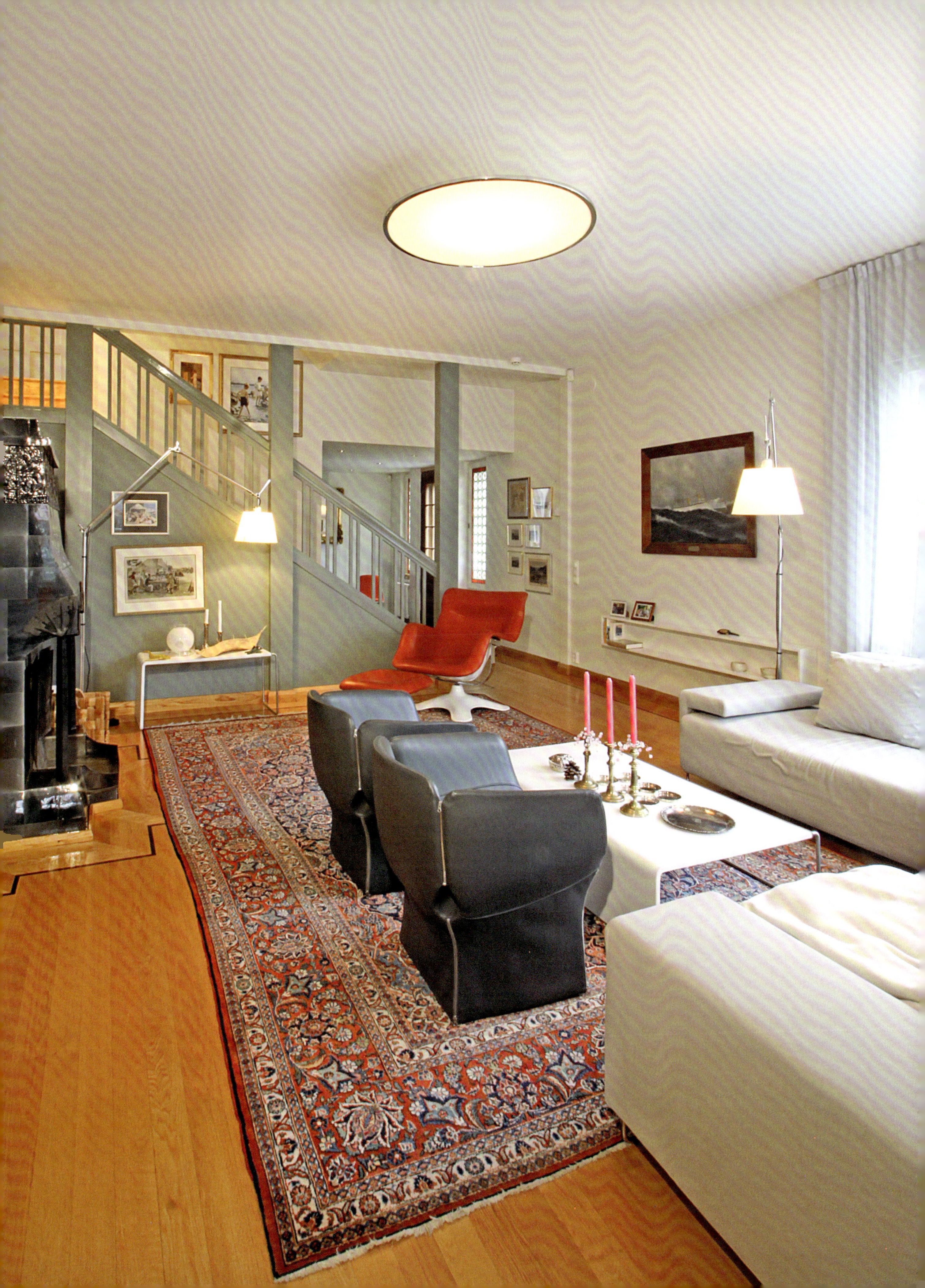

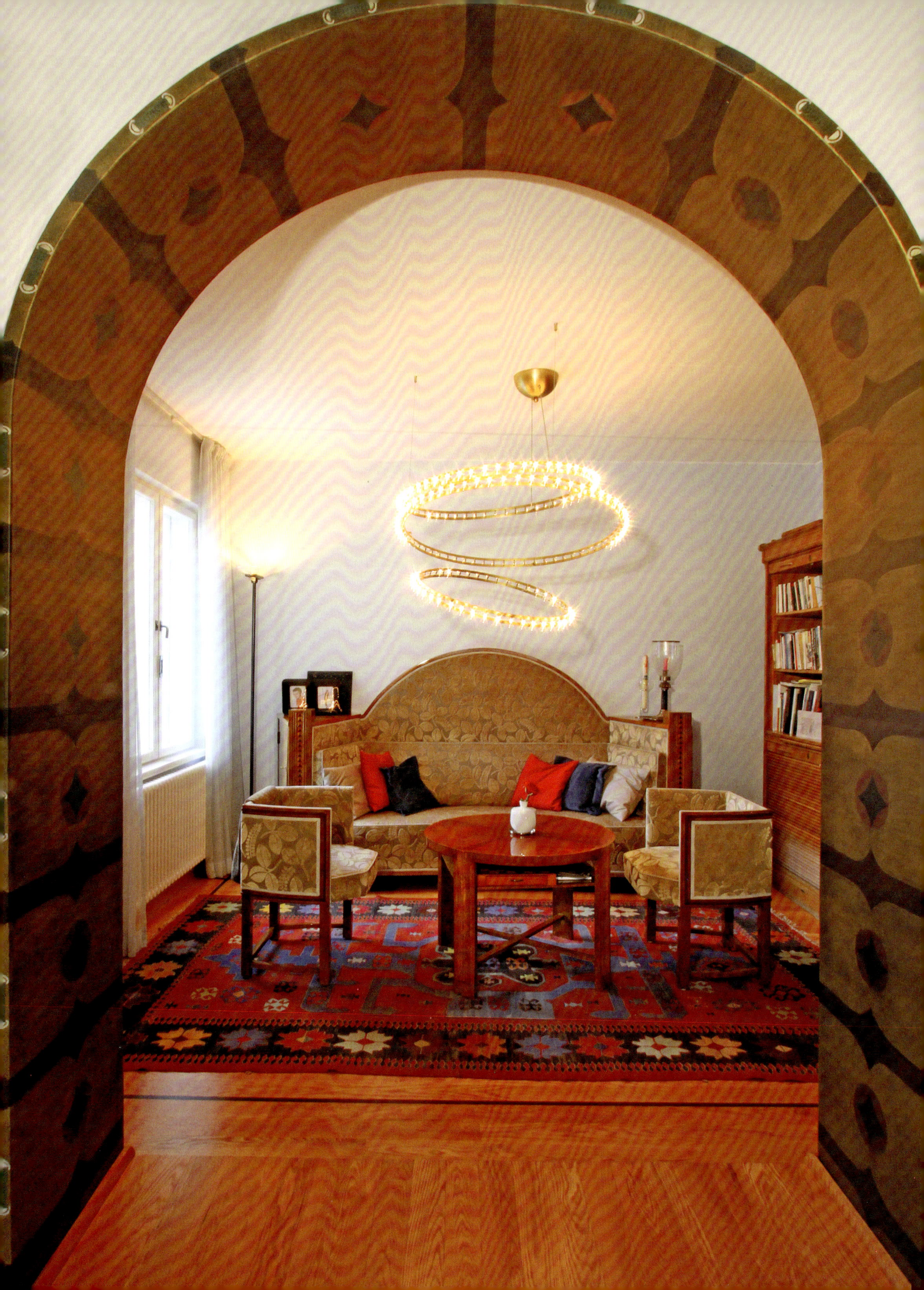

opposite
Library with furniture made of silver birch, designed by Saarinen around 1908. The set was in production in the 1910s.

below
Living room with original tiled stove

Villa Keirkner

Helsinki, 1916–18

This palatial urban house in Helsinki's Kaivopuisto neighborhood was commissioned by August Nilsson Keirkner (1856–1918), a Swedish-born engineer who moved to Finland in the 1880s and established a successful ironworks factory and an export sawmill at Inha in Central Finland. After the Keirkners moved to Helsinki in 1907, they bought an apartment building designed by Gesellius, Lindgren, and Saarinen in Luotsikatu Street.

The family's lifestyle was elegant, marked by numerous parties and society events. Together with his wife Lydia, Keirkner was an avid collector of mainly Finnish art, including works by Akseli Gallen-Kallela, Pekka Halonen, Albert Edelfelt, Helene Schjerfbeck, Ville Vallgren, and Hugo Simberg, as well as a few foreign masters, such as Marc Chagall. The family owned one of the largest private art collections of the time—later bequeathed to the Finnish National Gallery's Ateneum Art Museum—and the villa the Keirkners commissioned was to house their collection in addition to serving as their home in retirement.

Keirkner himself died before he could move into his new residence, but his wife Lydia (1861–1945) lived there until 1937, when the villa, known as the Marble Palace because of its white Finnish marble facade, was bought by General Rudolf Walden, a leading figure of the Finnish paper industry. During this time, Marshal C. G. Mannerheim, who became Finland's sixth president in 1944 and who lived in the same neighborhood, was a frequent guest at the Marble Palace. After World War II, the building was rented by the Supreme Military Court to hold a trial concerning the caching of weapons after the war. Acquired by the Finnish state in 1949, the villa was the location of the Labor Court and the Helsinki Court of Appeal for several decades. Today it is no longer used by the Finnish state, and its future has not yet been decided.

In addition to the art collection the house holds, there are also several fixed works of art by painter Olga Gummerus-Ehrström (1876–1938), and sculptors Emil Wikström (1864–1942) and Gunnar Finne (1886–1952); the latter created the lynx figures of the villa's gateposts. A frieze with animal motifs introduces a slight element of humor to the solid classicism of the exterior. The original design for the facades was more elaborate and included, among other features, a relief above the main entrance, ornaments above the fenestration, and sculptures decorating the tower, all of which remained unrealized. A tower accentuating the main entrance was a motif often used by Gesellius,

opposite
View from southwest

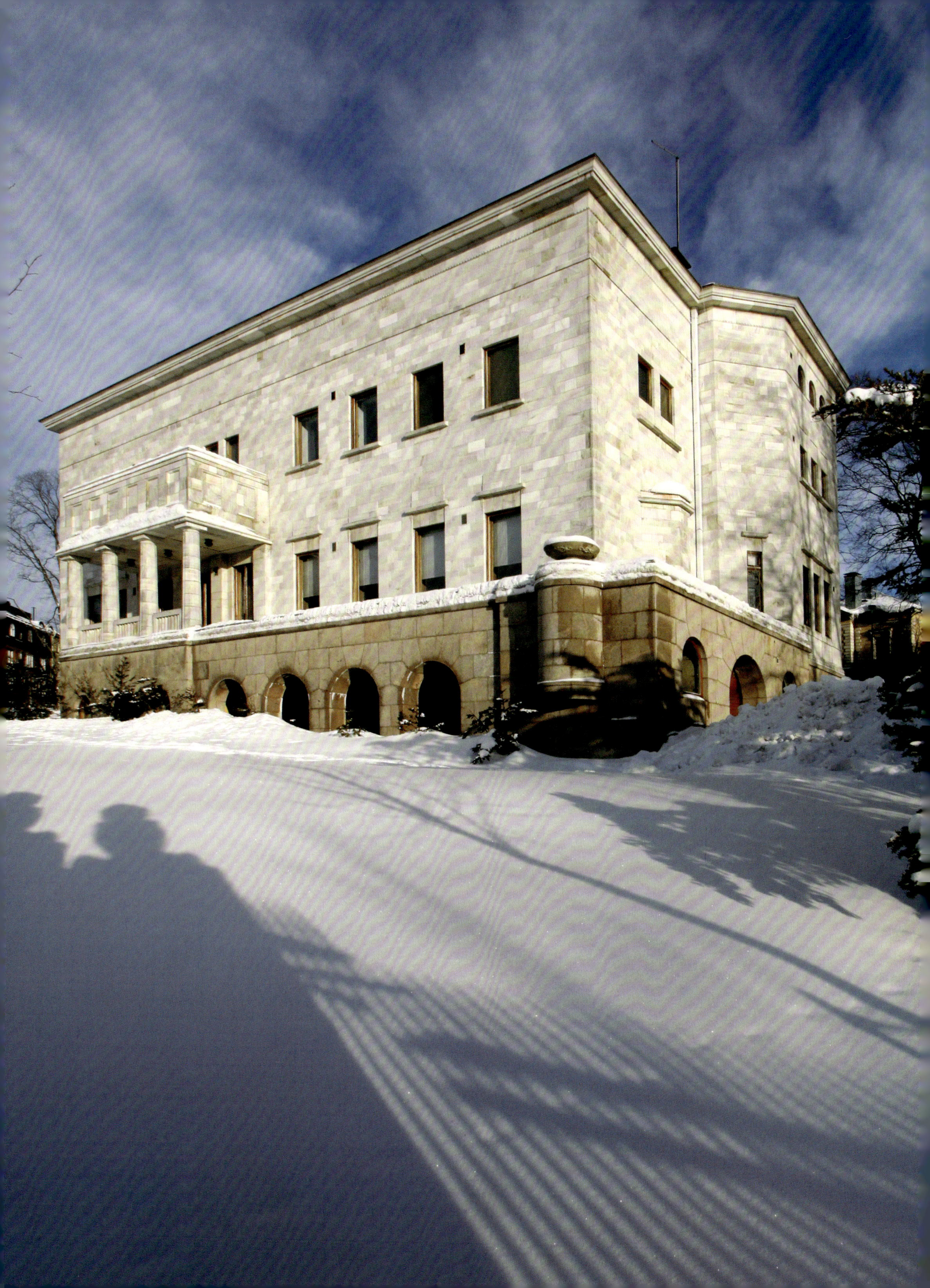

Lindgren, and Saarinen in their villa designs of the art nouveau period. At Villa Keirkner it is an important vertical element balancing the volume of the buildings, and Saarinen gave it a markedly monumental shape.

The villa's spaces for entertaining and receiving guests and the lookout tower are placed on top of each other on one side of the house. The kitchen, master bedroom, and servants' quarters are on three levels on the other side of the building. The affluent Keirkners fitted their house with modern features of the highest standard, including the first lift to be installed in a private residence in Finland. The couple did not have children, and a significant part of the house was designed especially for their art collection. The luxurious and spacious first-floor hall, an upper hall on the second floor, and the studio were used to exhibit the largest paintings and sculptures.

The stunning dark-hued entrance with wood paneling, the adjacent hall, and the Turkish room on a landing of the main staircase form the core part of the house. The hall is covered in oak paneling except for a wall at the end of the space, which originally had a fireplace and is faced with green tiles surrounded by a series of wood reliefs sculpted by Finne and depicting scenes of Keirkner's life. The hunting and fishing motifs of the chandeliers are also by Finne. The bronze frieze over the fireplace in the library was designed by Wikström, and the stained-glass paintings in the entrance hall are by Gummerus-Ehrström.

The Turkish room is screened from the lower hall by wooden columns. Dimly lit, with a dark coffered ceiling and decorative wooden blinds in arched windows, the room was furnished with a divan and ottomans with stuffed cushions, kelim carpets, and small tables; the walls were lined with gold-colored wallpaper with relief printing. A fascination for exotic styles had influenced the interior design of upper-class homes since the late nineteenth century. The lighter and less somber mood of the other rooms in the same building underscores the diversity of the interior design. As far as is known, Saarinen did not design custom furniture for Villa Keirkner. The dining room and library furniture designed by Saarinen for the Keirkners' previous home were, however, moved there.

top
Dining hall

bottom left
View of the hall with artworks on the walls

bottom right
Turkish room

top left
Section

top right
First-floor and basement plans

bottom
In the library several paintings by Akseli Gallen-Kallela were displayed; on the right is a portrait of Russian writer Maxim Gorky.

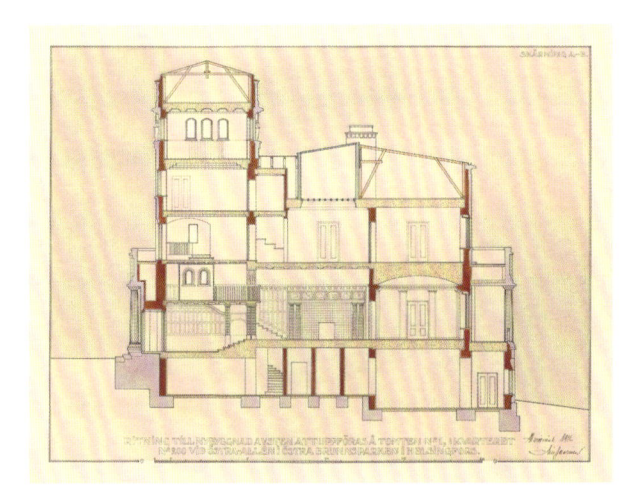

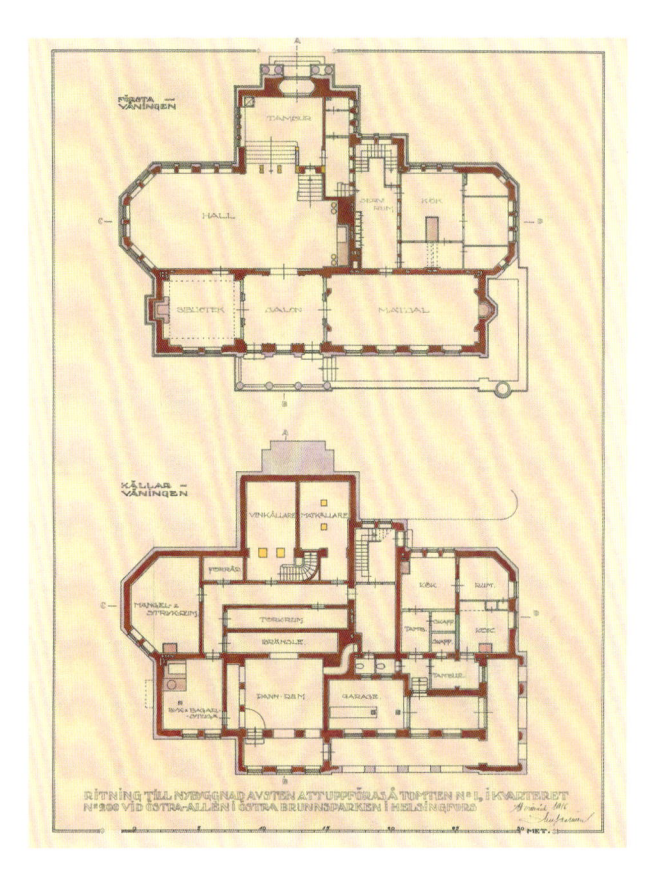

top
Lamp with hunting ornaments, designed by Finne

bottom
Tower room

opposite
The staircase leads to the gallery level with the Turkish room.

overleaf
The side pillars of the main door are decorated with foxes and running rabbits (left). Detail of wooden relief by Finne, depicting the life of August Keirkner (right)

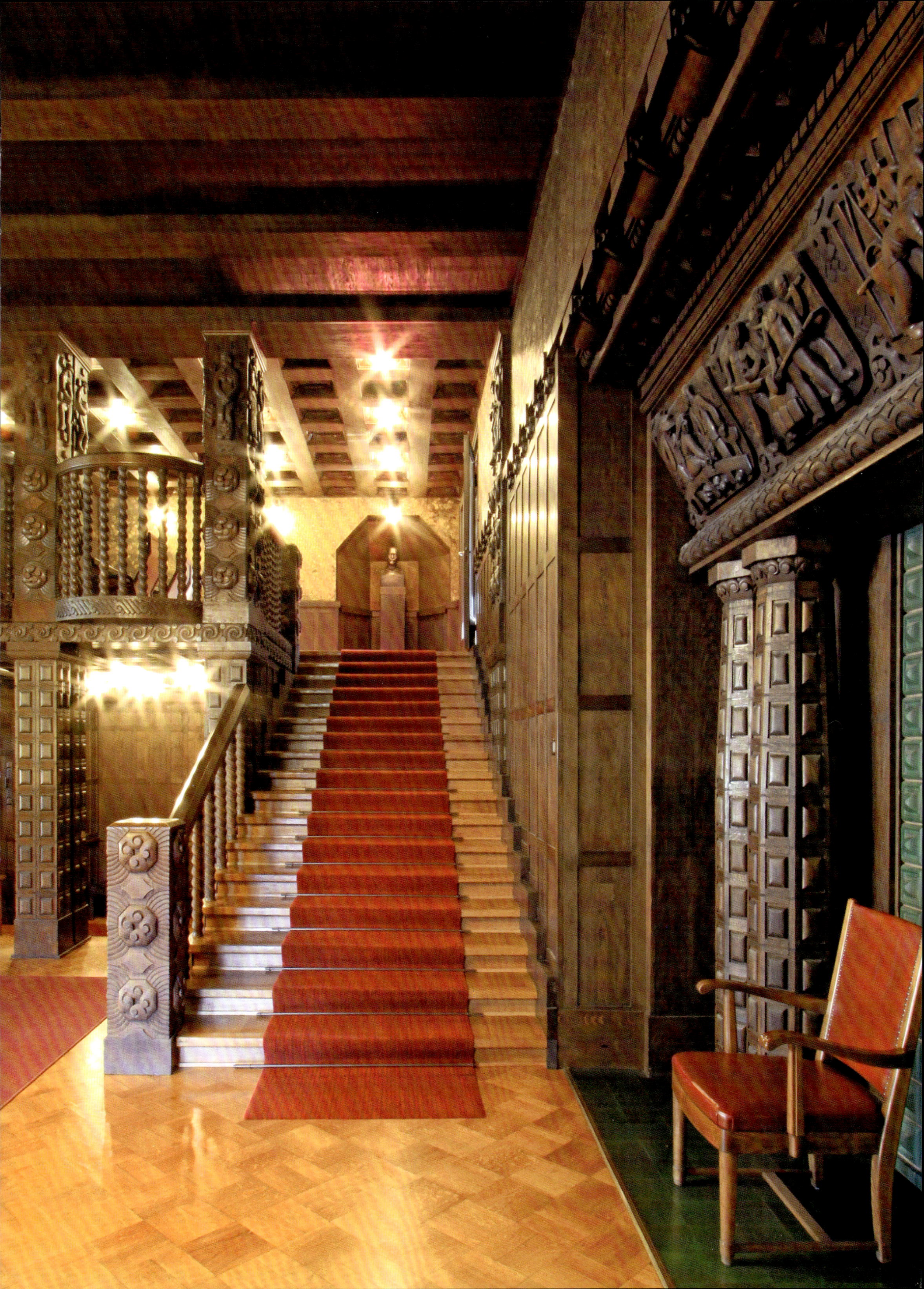

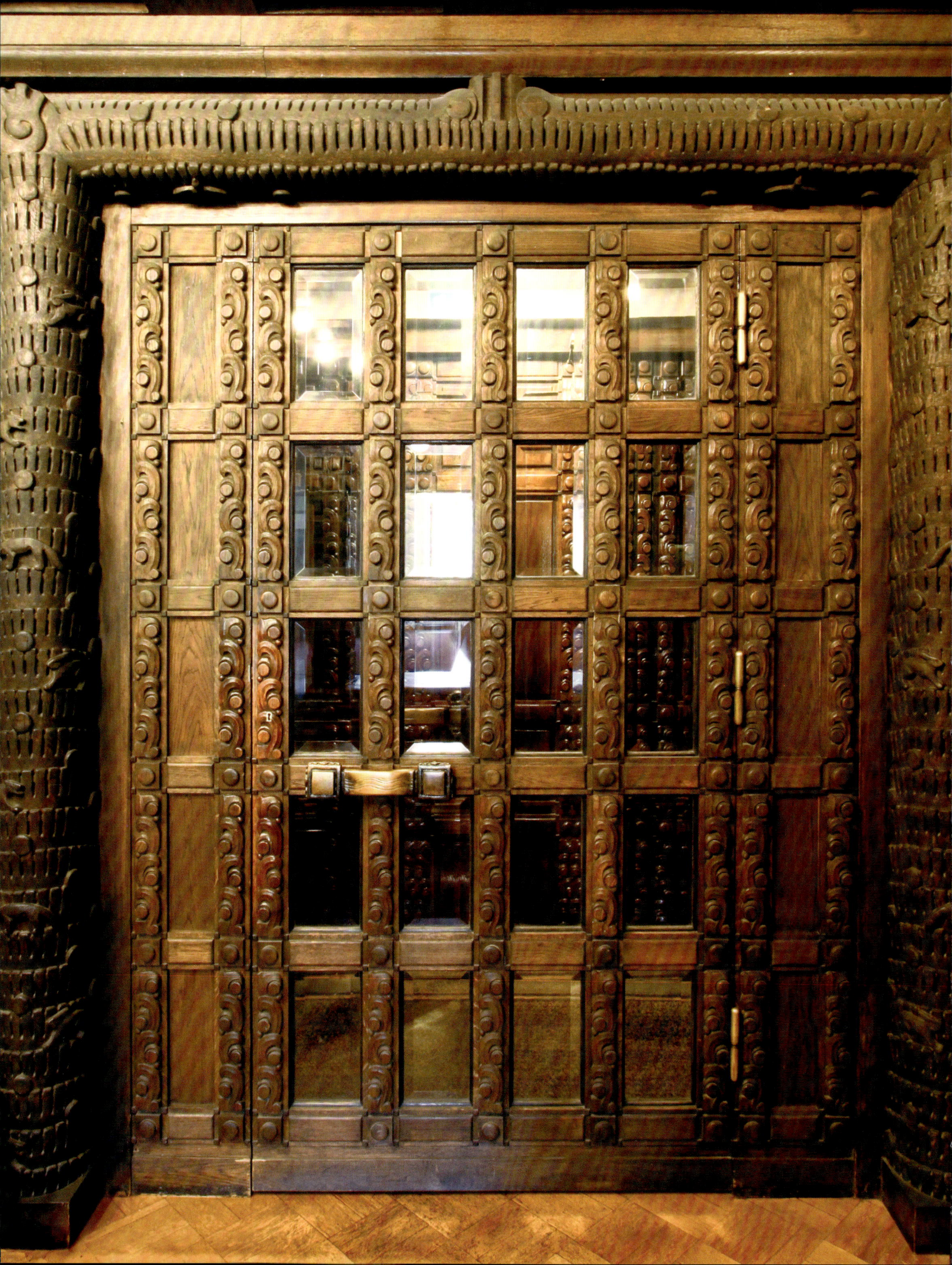

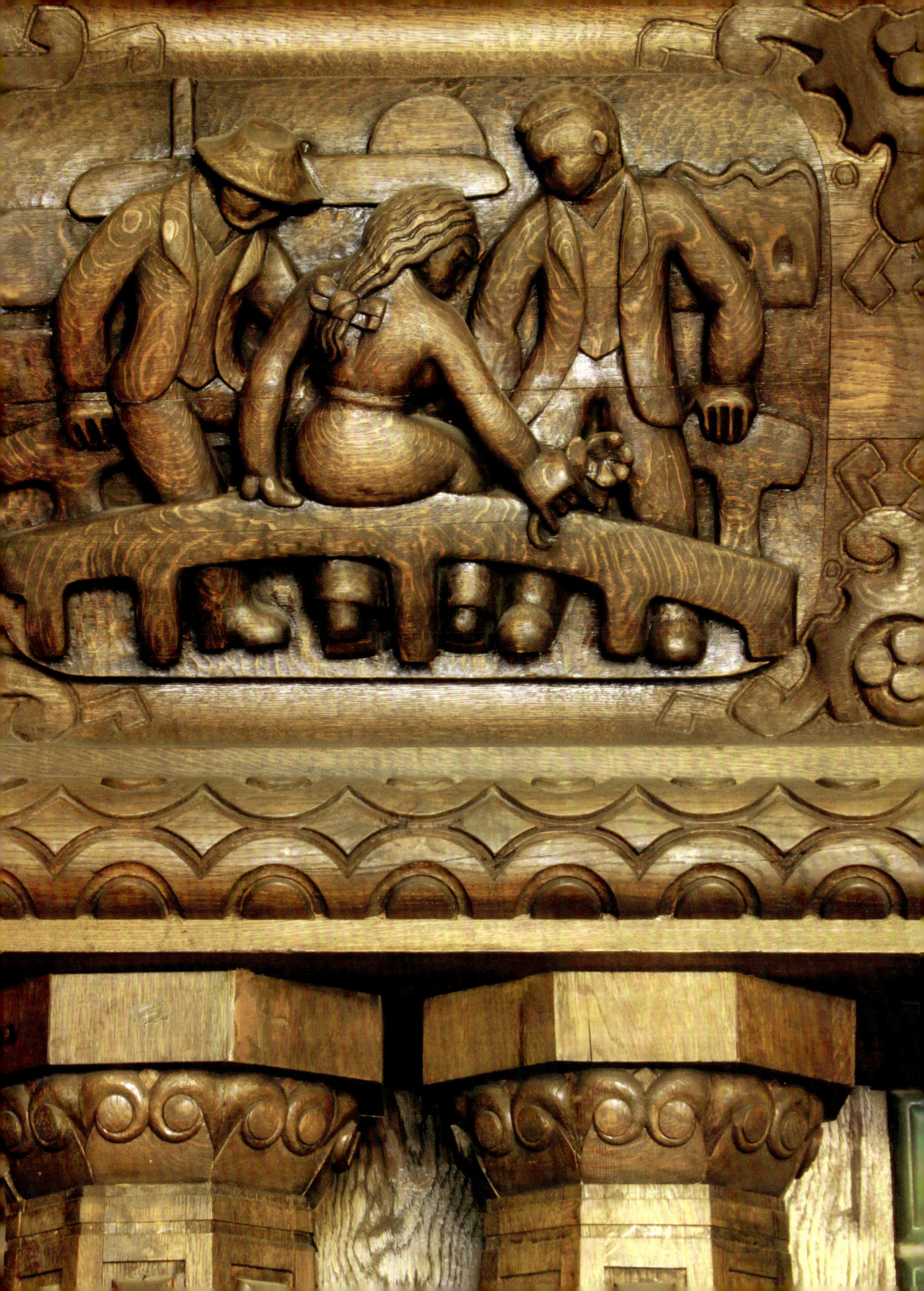

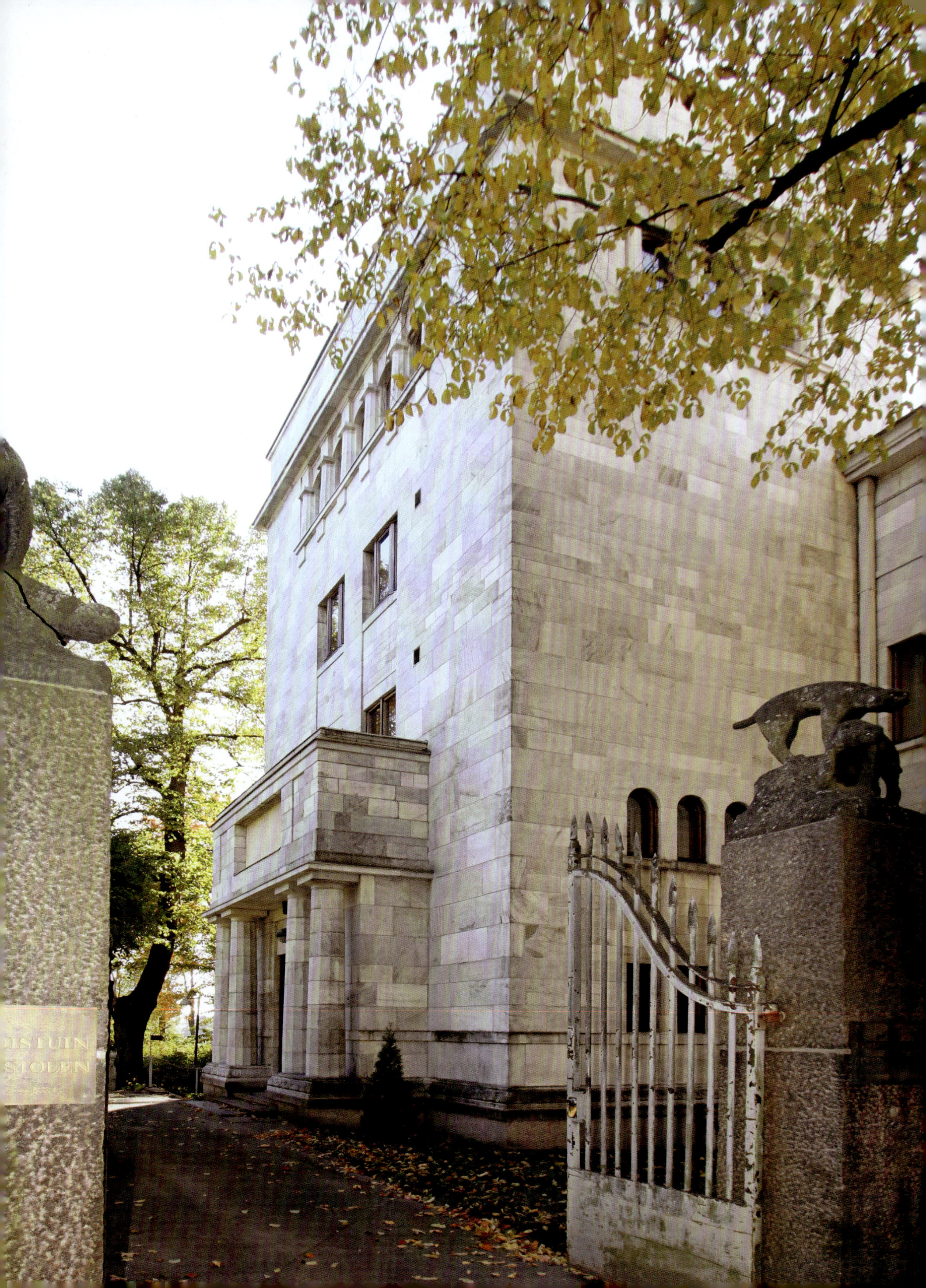

opposite
View of the house from the entrance gate. On the right is Gunnar Finne's lynx sculpture.

top
Dining room with glass-door armoires

bottom
Library with furniture designed by Saarinen

Row House in Hollantilaisentie Street

Helsinki, 1916

Saarinen's ambitious Munkkiniemi-Haaga plan for the northern and western sections of Helsinki, a collaboration between the M. G. Stenius company and the architect in the 1910s, was a grand urban vision to expand the city. Helsinki was then the rapidly growing capital of Finland. Communities of villas had begun to form in neighboring localities outside the city limits. To the west of Helsinki, only a few miles from the city center, was a large area of land extending to the sea shore owned by the M. G. Stenius company, which launched a major project for developing the area. The company's principal owner, Sigurd Stenius, invited Saarinen to participate, and the architect created the large-scale Munkkiniemi-Haaga plan for an area of 2,125 acres. He divided the use of land into four sections: public buildings, residential buildings, parks, and an industrial area. The project was speculative and visionary at the same time, and Saarinen's plan was both efficient and of a human scale. It was the first major expression of the architect's interest in urban architecture and town planning.

Only minor parts of the Munkkiniemi-Haaga plan were realized, due to changes brought about by the Finnish declaration of national independence and the ensuing civil war. Along with arrangements of streets, closed city blocks, and public buildings, there were to be urban villas and row houses of the English type along peaceful residential squares. The plan was the first time that row houses were suggested for Finnish conditions. Saarinen regarded this type of housing to be the most economical way to develop private residential dwellings in towns and suburbs.[6] The architect designed several types of row houses for various income levels, carefully studying the needs of different classes of society and taking them into account in his designs. He paid particular attention to the connections between interior and exterior spaces, becoming a forerunner of modern architectural thinking in his emphasis on yards and gardens.

The row house in Hollantilaisentie Street is one of the few realized parts of the plan. It consists of five originally two-story homes built contiguously with common walls, each of which has its own street entrance and a narrow garden in the back. Angular gable motifs and high-pitched tiled roofs alternate in the buildings' fronts. The houses'

opposite

Entrance from the street

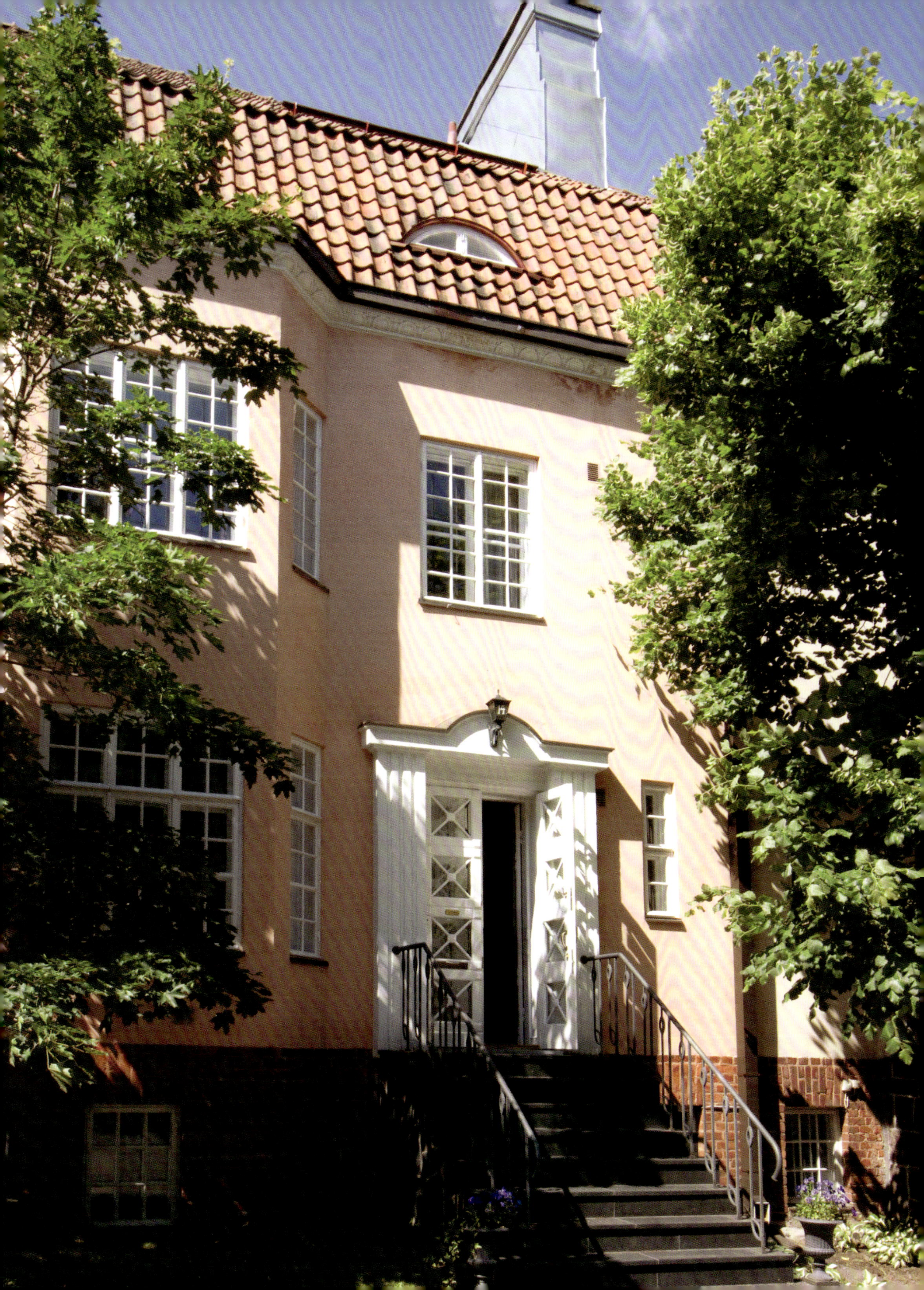

small-paned windows were an integral aspect of the architectural style of the time.

On the first floor a kitchen faces the street, and a dining room and living room look out into the garden. High French doors open onto the yard, making it a part of the lounging area of the house. The well-lit interior exudes Continental elegance. The exteriors of the privately owned houses are preserved quite well today.

top
Row houses, circa 1916

bottom
Row house typology, watercolor and ink drawing by Saarinen, 1915

opposite
Winter view from the garden

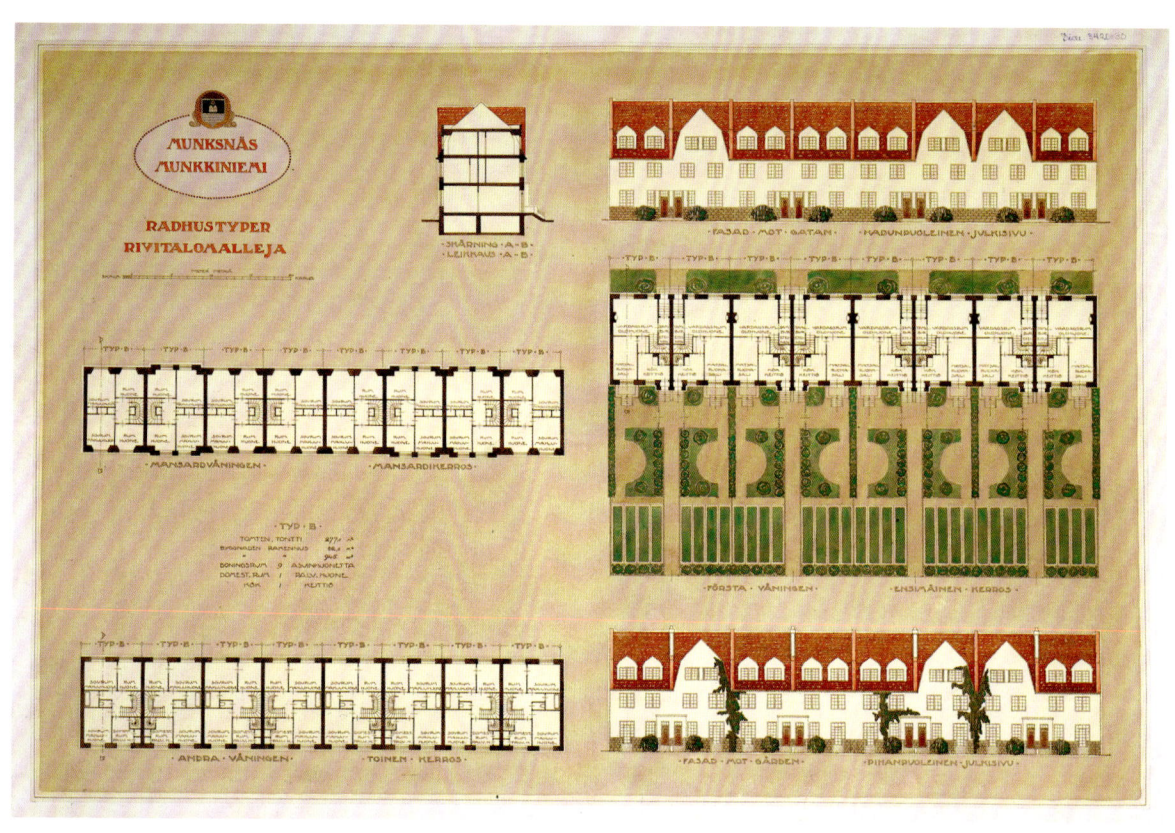

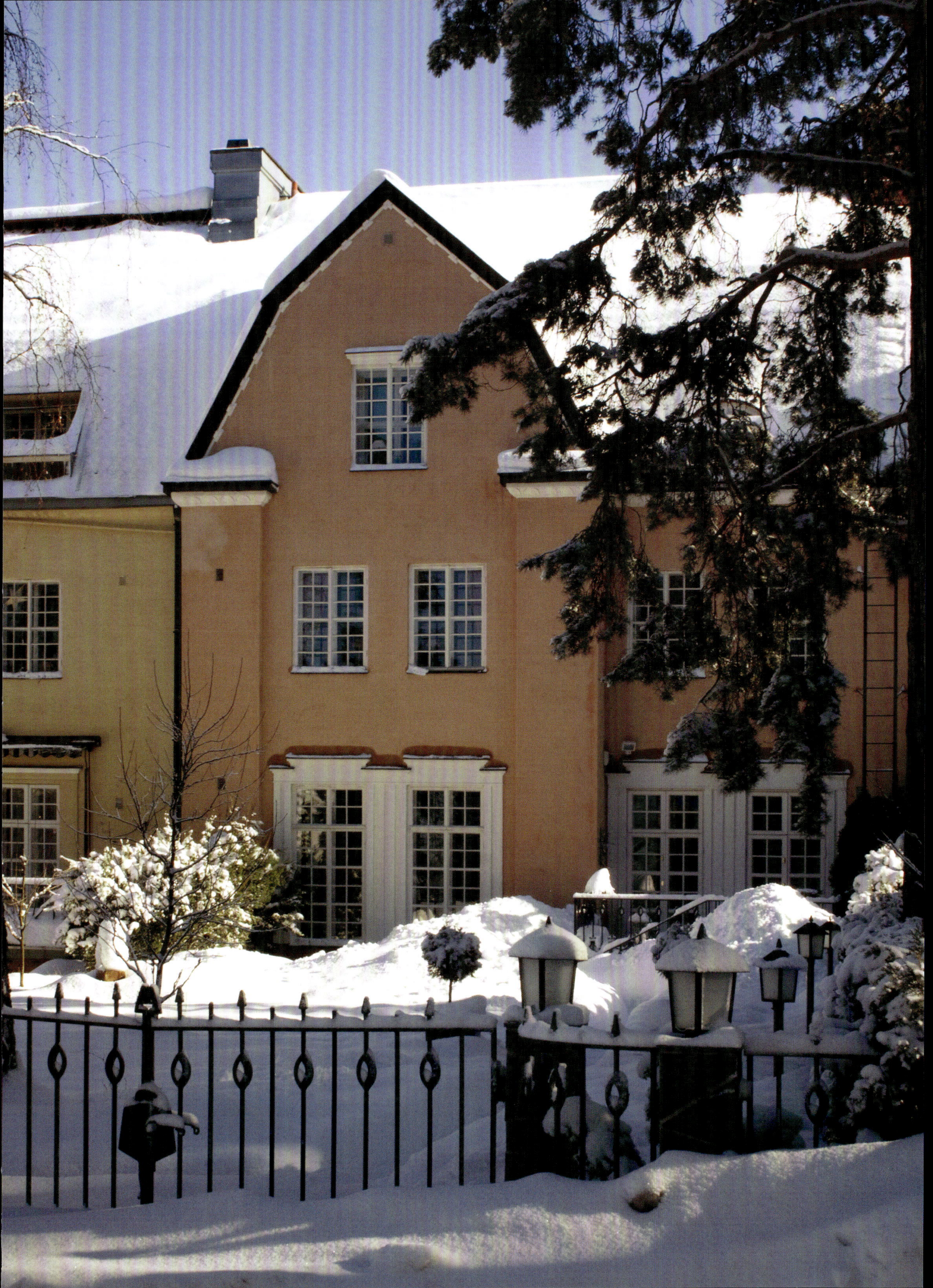

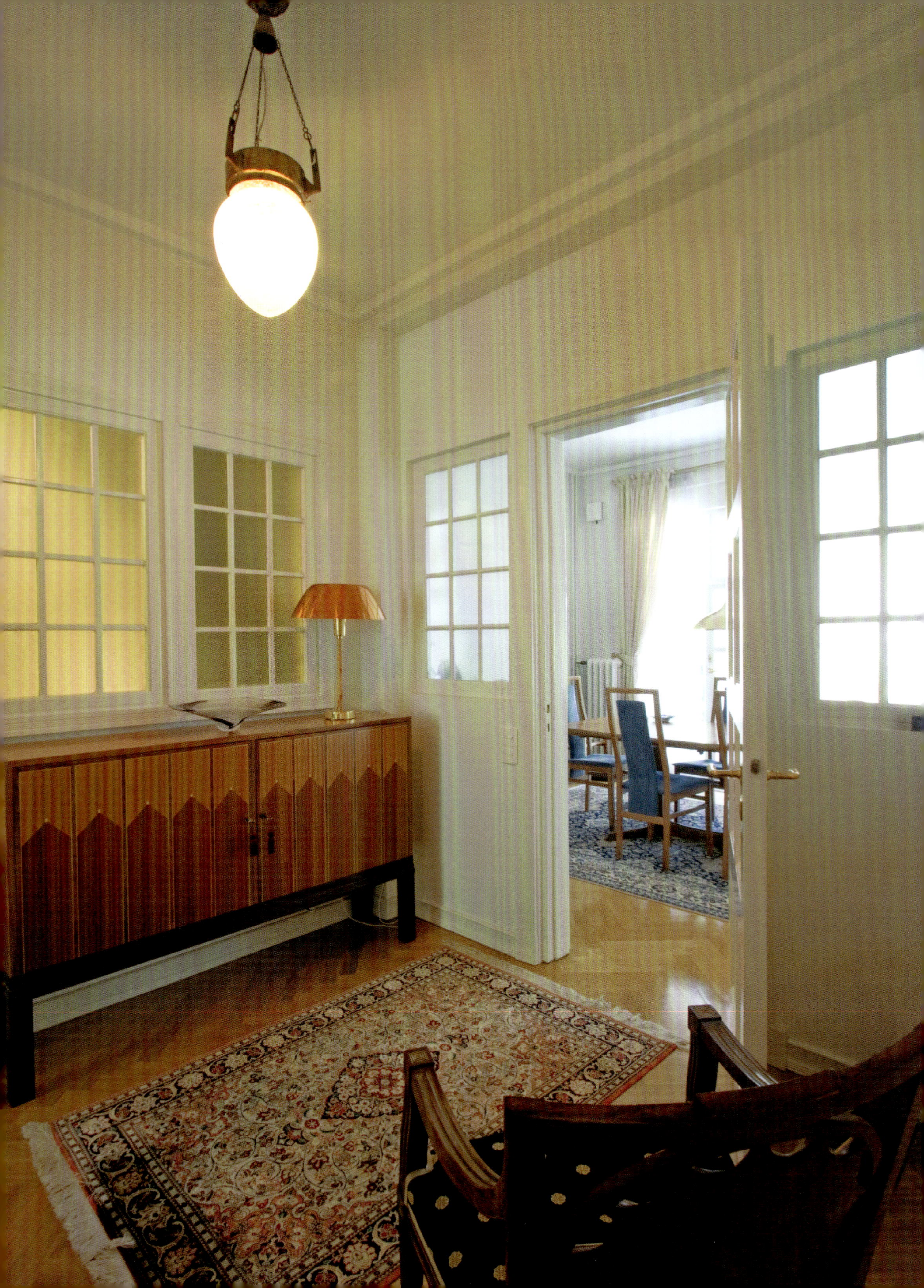

opposite
View from the hall to the dining room. The cabinet was designed by Saarinen for Saarinen House.

below
Second-floor living room

top
French doors lead out to the garden.

bottom
The large windows in the living room open to the garden.

opposite
View of the house from the garden

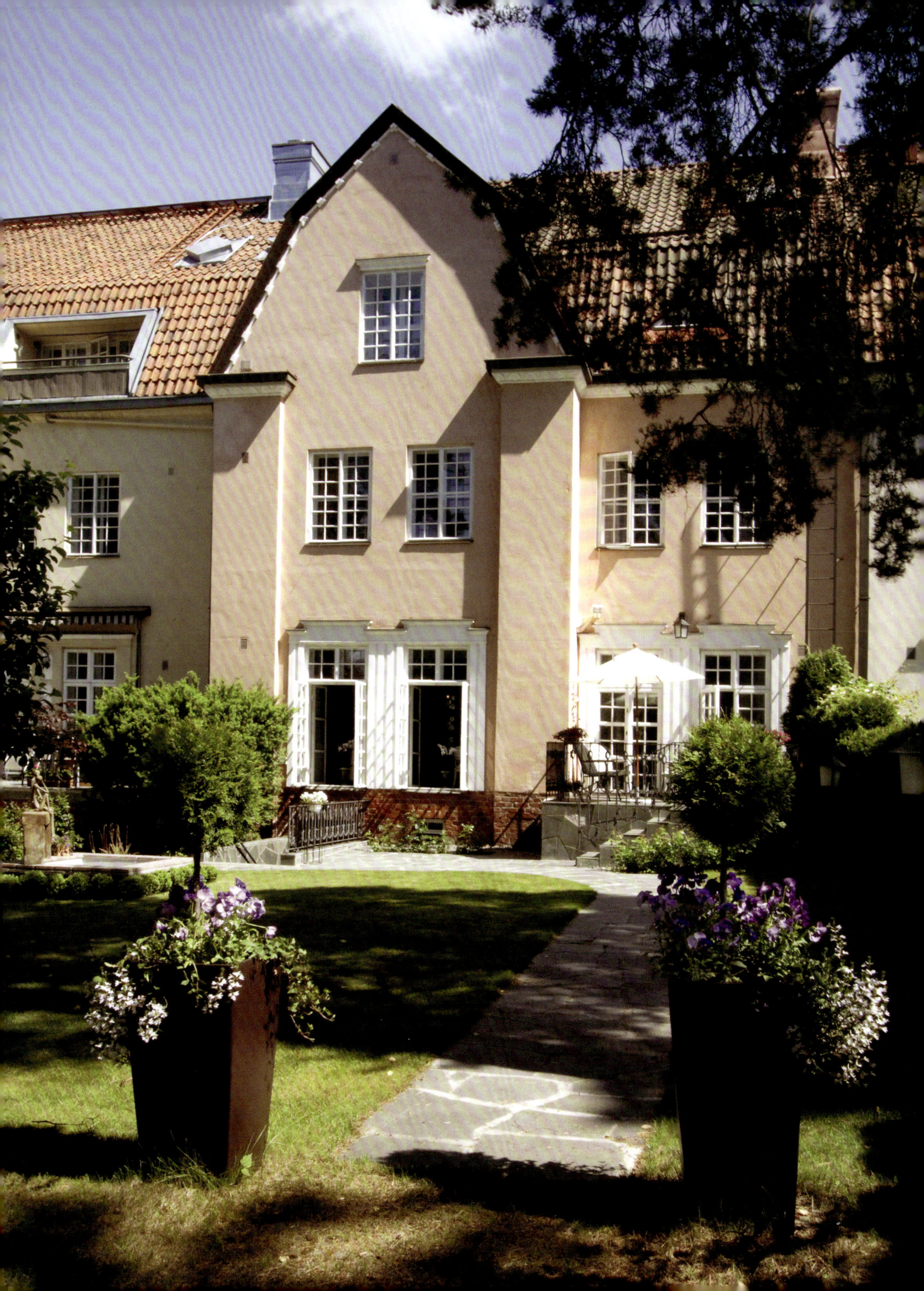

The American Years

Eliel Saarinen, 1923–50
Eero Saarinen, 1936–61

A new phase in the life of Eliel Saarinen and his family began in 1922, when he won second prize in the competition for the Tribune Tower in Chicago. Inspired by this success, he traveled to the United States in 1923, together with his colleague and friend, architect Gustaf Strengell, who was fluent in English and helped him get his bearings. Eliel was soon followed by Loja and their two children, Pipsan (then eighteen) and Eero (then twelve). After working for a few years as a visiting professor at the University of Michigan, Ann Arbor, Saarinen was invited in 1925 by newspaper publisher George G. Booth to create and develop a multidisciplinary art academy and its campus at Cranbrook in Bloomfield Hills, Michigan, which was to play the leading role in the architect's years in the United States. He taught there, became its president when it first opened in 1932, and was responsible for the design of new buildings to serve the growing community.

Saarinen continued to develop his ideal of a total work of art in the United States. The buildings at Cranbrook made extensive use of the art academy's resources, with its faculty's artists and artisans participating in the design work. Loja Saarinen had become the head of the art academy's weaving department and also contributed in this effort.

From the mid-1930s onwards, Saarinen once again had his own architectural office, where he was joined by Eero in 1936. Pipsan's husband, architect J. Robert F. Swanson (1900–1981), was also part of the family business for some years.[1] Eliel's private commissions eventually began to interfere with his work at Cranbrook, and when relations between Booth and Saarinen worsened in the 1940s, Booth asked the architect to move his architectural office off the campus.[2] Saarinen's second career in the United States was defined by his firm's work on public buildings and churches, as well as some residential projects.

Among Eliel and Eero's first collaborative projects were church designs for Columbus, Indiana, and Minneapolis, Minnesota, although Eliel was still the main designer.[3] Eero would later become known for his individual designs for large corporate office buildings that served the client company's needs and reflected its users, location, and setting in a unique way. His first project for a major corporation was the design of the General Motors Technical Center (1946–56), which started as a collaboration with Eliel.

Eero inherited his father's (and mother's) comprehensive attitude to design, considering details and furniture important elements even in large projects. Each client, whether IBM, Bell Telephone, Deere & Co., or Trans World Airlines (TWA), was given a building that was characteristic of it. Eero also developed campus plans and buildings for existing universities, which reflected the heritage of his father's work at Cranbrook.

Eliel and Eero were not only collaborators, however, but at times also competitors. They both submitted designs for the Jefferson National Expansion Memorial competition in 1947/48. When a telegram was received at Cranbrook stating that the competition had been won by Mr. Saarinen, a toast was first raised to Eliel. Later it was revealed that the winner was in fact Eero— and there was cause to celebrate again. This competition was a kind of symbolic watershed between two generations, with Eero launching a new era, while his father stepped aside. As Eero observed: "A better name for architect is form-giver and until his death in 1950, when I started my own form, I worked within the form of my father."[4]

Eero's own career can be summarized as wide-ranging and multi-faceted. The architect died in 1961, at the age of fifty-one, after developing a brain tumor. But in a decade's time he had designed corporate buildings, embassies, airports, and university buildings and dormitories, to mention some of his diverse projects. His enthusiasm and eagerness were apparent even to his contemporaries, as evidenced by a postcard that Frank Lloyd Wright wrote to Eero in 1959: "Build it Eero—build it!"[5] Eero's many ideas and a continuous urge to develop them further led him to find new solutions and technologies. The architect wanted his buildings to convey their purpose and evoke an emotional response. Each use or function, each site required its own solution, its own architectural form and expression. The style of his buildings therefore varies greatly. In Eero's residential projects the architect aimed to design houses that reflected both their settings and the personal identities of his clients.

opposite
Tulip Chair by Eero Saarinen, 1956

Saarinen House

Bloomfield Hills, Michigan, 1928–30

In addition to designing various institutional buildings, including the school of art and design on the Cranbrook campus, Saarinen also developed homes with studios for faculty members. His own residence was a twin house starting the row of houses on Academy Way. The other half was first occupied by the Hungarian sculptor and artist Géza Maróti (1875–1941), followed by the Swedish sculptor Carl Milles (1875–1955), who lived there for several years when he was artist-in-residence and director of the sculpture department of Cranbrook Academy of Art.[6]

In his residential architecture on campus, Saarinen implemented the concepts developed for the urban row houses of his Munkkiniemi-Haaga plan. The houses are situated between the street and the main axis of the park at Cranbrook. In contrast to the spaciousness of the rest of the campus, the street vista is of a condensed and urban character. In front of the red brick houses are small yards enclosed by a low brick wall and plants to provide privacy for the occupants. A larger garden and courtyard are in seclusion behind the houses. The interior spatial and functional layout follows the basic design of an ordinary two-story row house with a living room, dining room, and kitchen on the first floor, and bedrooms and bathrooms upstairs.

The creepers growing on Saarinen's own house's facade, the rose bushes on top of the yard wall, and a magnolia in bloom in the spring are original elements of his design. The two-story wing of the U-shaped house running parallel to the street contains a dining area and a combined living room–library on the first floor and private bedrooms and the housekeeper's room on the second floor. On the first floor, only the library section faces the street, while the other rooms look out into the garden behind the house. The kitchen and an auxiliary space are at the north end of the wing. The dining room, library, and studio were used on a daily basis by the family, while the living room, with its formal character, was mainly a reception and welcoming area for guests.[7] It is connected to Saarinen's studio in the south wing, which has a separate entrance and is only a few steps away from an adjacent studio where students drafted their work. The north wing contained a covered porch, which was used for lounging and spending time outdoors.

Saarinen House forms an elegant entity that is carefully designed down to its details. The layout of the interconnected series of spaces is based on a combination of symmetry and asymmetry. Each room has a distinctive nook or corner for reading

opposite
View of Academy Way with the sculpture Triton with Shell (1916) by Carl Milles in the front and Saarinen House in the back

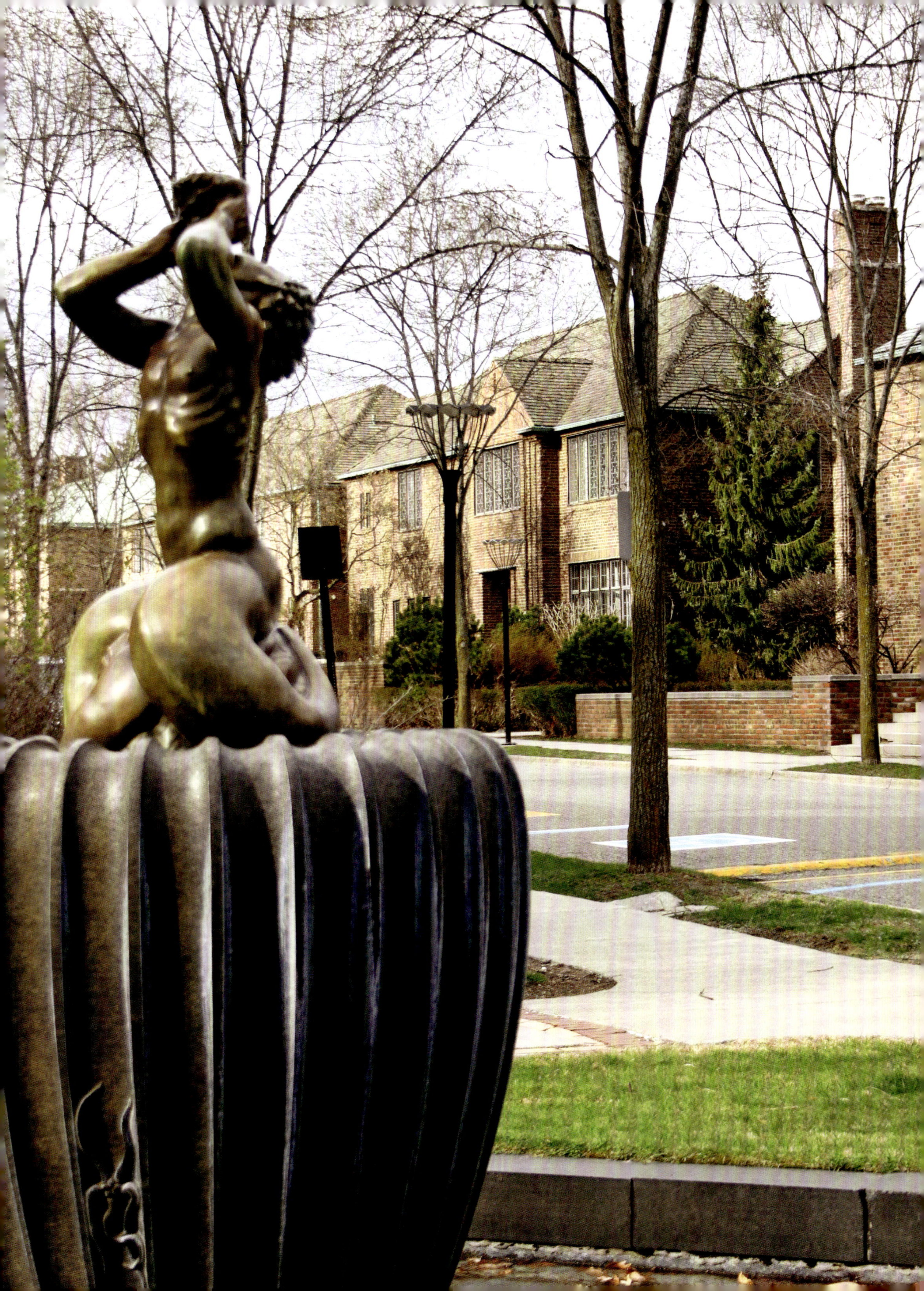

or enjoying the company of others. Variations of the same soft green hues and carefully considered and finished details of furnishings, light fittings, fireplaces, textiles, and objects support each other and express a shared language. Light enters the stained-glass windows through translucent curtains, creating a soothing atmosphere in the rooms. Patterns based on linear geometry are used throughout the house and join the various parts, such as textiles, stained-glass windows, furniture, and even the stone paving of the courtyard.[8] In Saarinen House, the complexity and richness of Hvitträsk was further developed by the architect, who could now build on years of experience.

Saarinen wrote in The Search for Form of the roles of form and color:

> Form is mainly constituted by its proportions, rhythm, volume, and scale. The colors used, therefore, should support and emphasize these form-properties, rather than bring disarray to them. Thus, the more neutral the general color scheme, the more form is apt to appear to its full value, as form.[9]

On form and decoration he stated:

> Ornament represents the spirit of man in an abstract form. It transposes the rhythmic characteristics of time into a significative pattern of line, form, and color. It evolves from the simple toward the rich, from directness toward symbol. In this evolution, ornament assimilates new ideas, new thoughts, and new patterns, until by and by it embodies decorative interpretations of floral and faunal forms and of all that man feels, observes, enjoys, and likes to live with. But no matter how ornament develops, it always is—or should be—a translation of emotions with inner meaning behind the forms; it always is—or should be—an emotional play of forms with sincerity at the bottom; it always is—or should be—a product of true art.[10]

The living room and adjacent library are dominated by a rug designed by Loja Saarinen and a low, tiled art deco fireplace. The square dining area, which forms the core of the house, is, though small, the most carefully finished and luxurious space in the house. Its warm-hued plywood panels are complemented in the corners by recesses painted glowing red and by a golden ceiling with concentric circles. The space is furnished with a round wooden table with inlay, slender chairs, a suspended lamp, and a rug with an octagonal pattern, all designed by Saarinen. A wall-hanging by the textile designer Greta Skogström (1900–1994) shows the branches of a tree with birds, perhaps a reminder of Finland for the Saarinens.

The studio in the one-story south wing receives daylight from three directions. A sofa nook in the corner is set a step higher than the rest of the space and separated by a pair of pillars. Saarinen's family and students regarded this alcove as the heart of the house. It was a place for discussing the work of students and meeting clients, but the family would also sit together there after dinner, and the grandchildren would play there. Loja Saarinen called it the cozy corner.[11]

The courtyard behind the house is sheltered by the main house, the studio wing, and a roofed porch. The courtyard and a garden, which is set on a lower level, are oriented toward the park axis of the campus and descend in stages toward it, thus connecting to the larger landscape of the academy. In the center of an octagonal paving is a sculpture by Finnish artist Wäinö Aaltonen (1894–1966) entitled Kivi's Muse, a reminder of the old country.

The strong bond of Eliel's and Loja's collaboration is particularly evident in the houses he designed in the United States, and Saarinen House is a prime example. In addition to the work of Eliel and Loja, the home also features designs by Pipsan and Eero. The stenciled patterns of the bedroom and closet doors in the second-floor hallway were designed by Pipsan, and the furniture of the master bedroom is by Eero.[12] Eliel died in 1950, and Loja moved out the following year, after which Saarinen House became the residence of the directors of the Cranbrook Academy of Art until the 1980s. The house was carefully restored in the 1990s to its original state and is now open to the public.[13]

top left
Eliel Saarinen standing in front of Saarinen House in 1943

top right
Site plan and first-floor plan

bottom
Section, pencil drawing by Saarinen, 1928

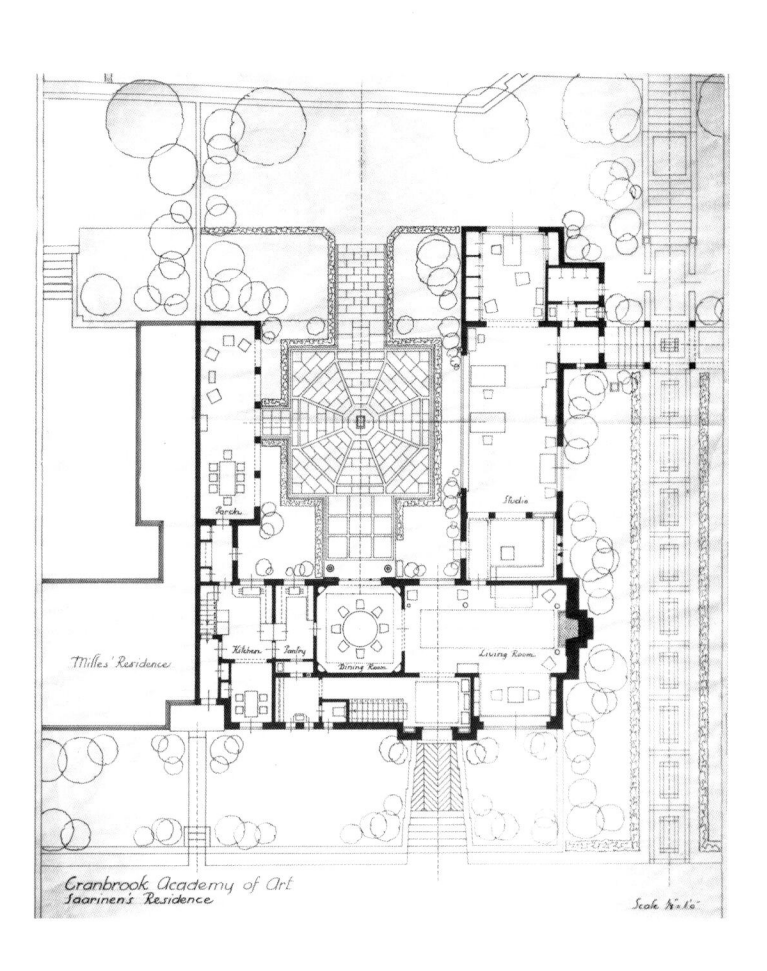

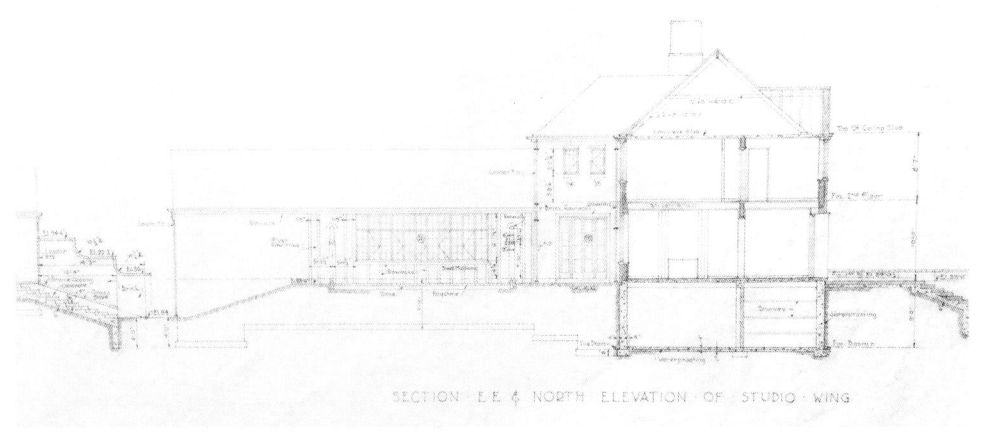

below
View of the house from the garden

top
**Saarinen House plaque,
early 1950s**

bottom
West facade

top
Dining room chair, 1929

bottom
Living room fireplace with peacock andirons designed by Eliel Saarinen, 1928–29

opposite
View through the dining room to the living room

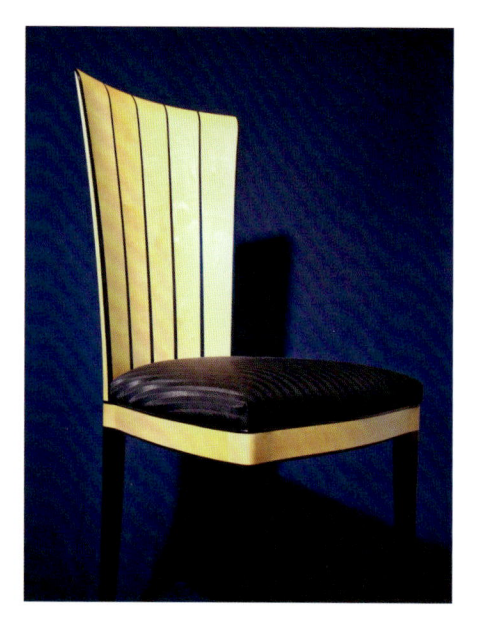

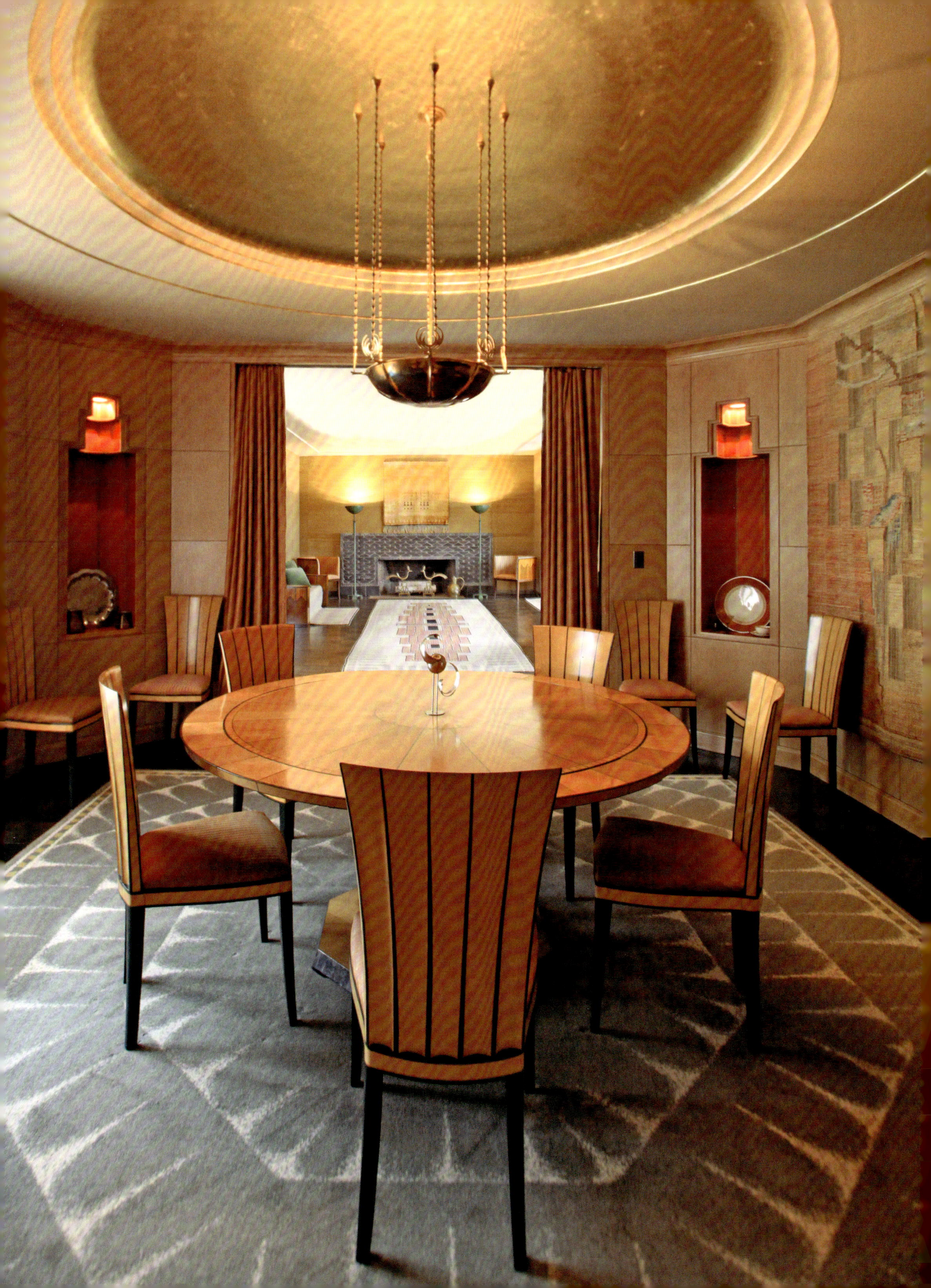

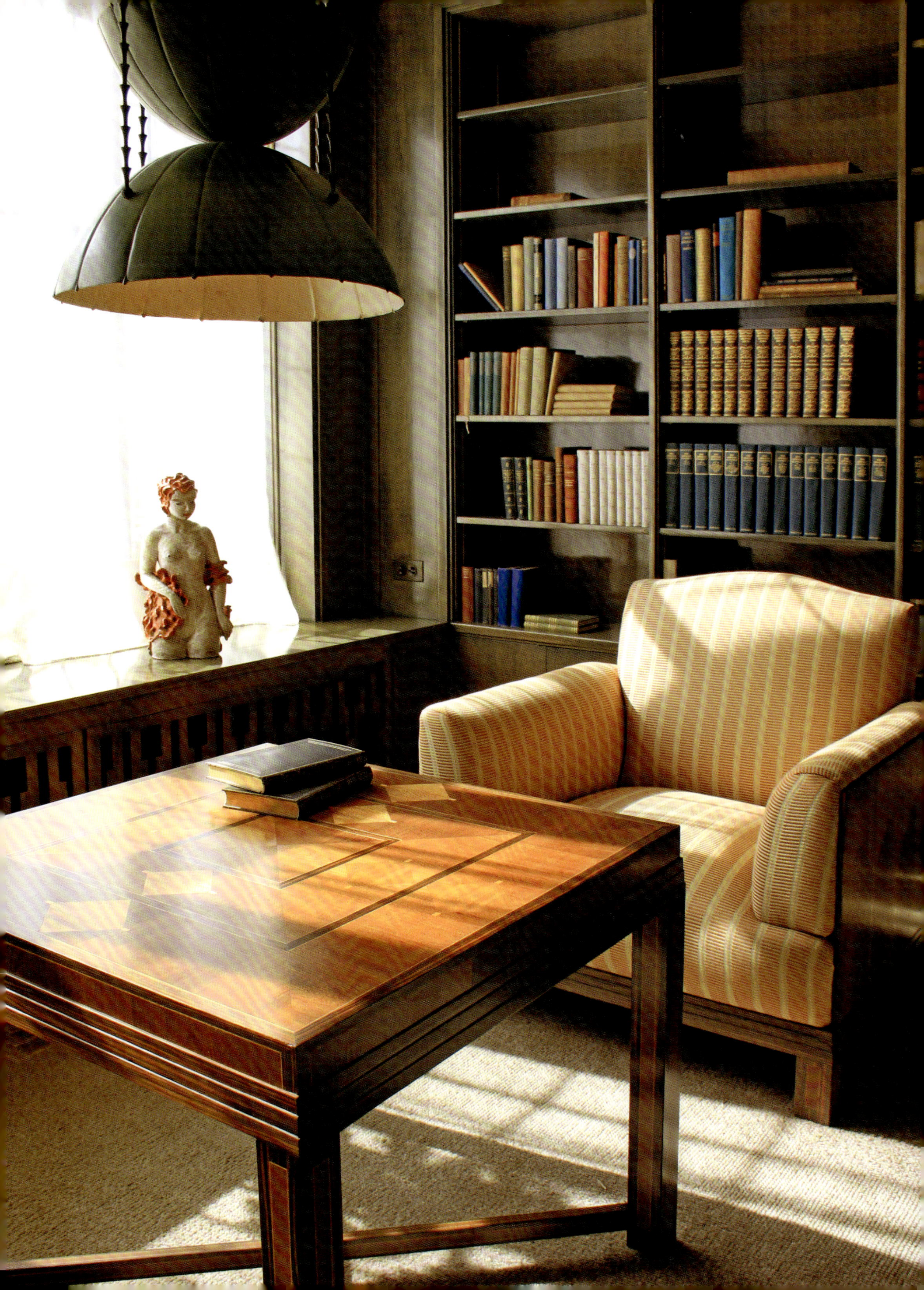

opposite and below
Library with pendant lamp by
Eliel Saarinen, 1930–31

157

top
Second-floor closet doors with stenciled decorations by Pipsan, 1931

bottom
The second floor held both the family's bedrooms and the housekeeper's room. On the side facing the street a well-lit hallway forms a kind of protective zone similar to the entrance hall on the first floor. This corridor is not just a route of access; it also contains a small set of furniture for sitting, designed in 1930.

top
Dressing table, mirror, and lamps by Eero Saarinen, 1930. The dresser set was designed by Eliel Saarinen around 1934.

bottom
Master bedroom with tables and twin beds designed by Eero Saarinen, 1930

top
As at Hvitträsk, the master bathroom is well-appointed, spacious, and receives plenty of daylight.

bottom
Pantry

160

top
Studio alcove with Carl Milles's *Head of a Dancing Girl*, **circa 1917 and Eero Saarinen's bust of Eliel Saarinen, 1930**

bottom
Studio alcove

overleaf
Studio, with Saarinen's desk in the foreground

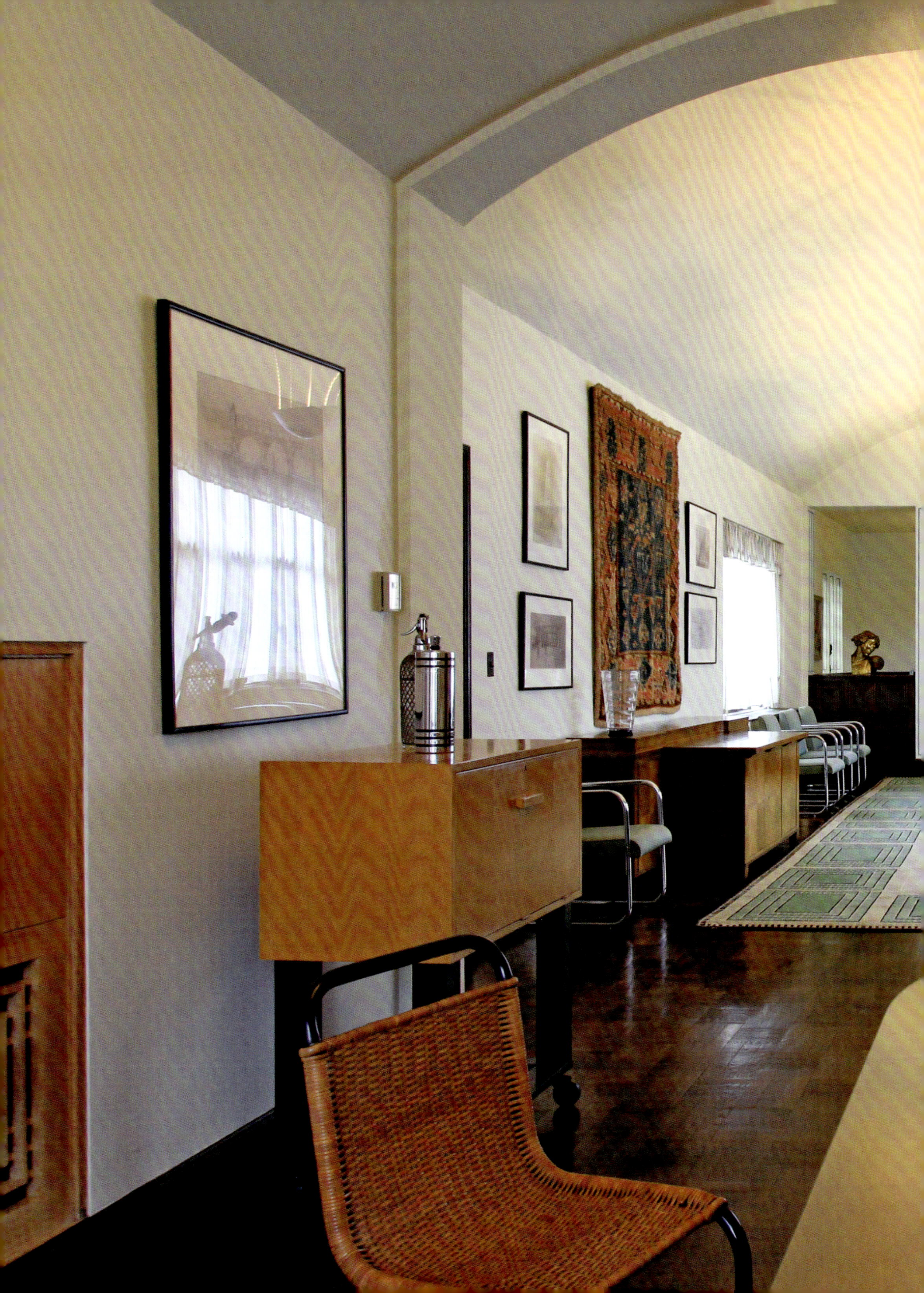

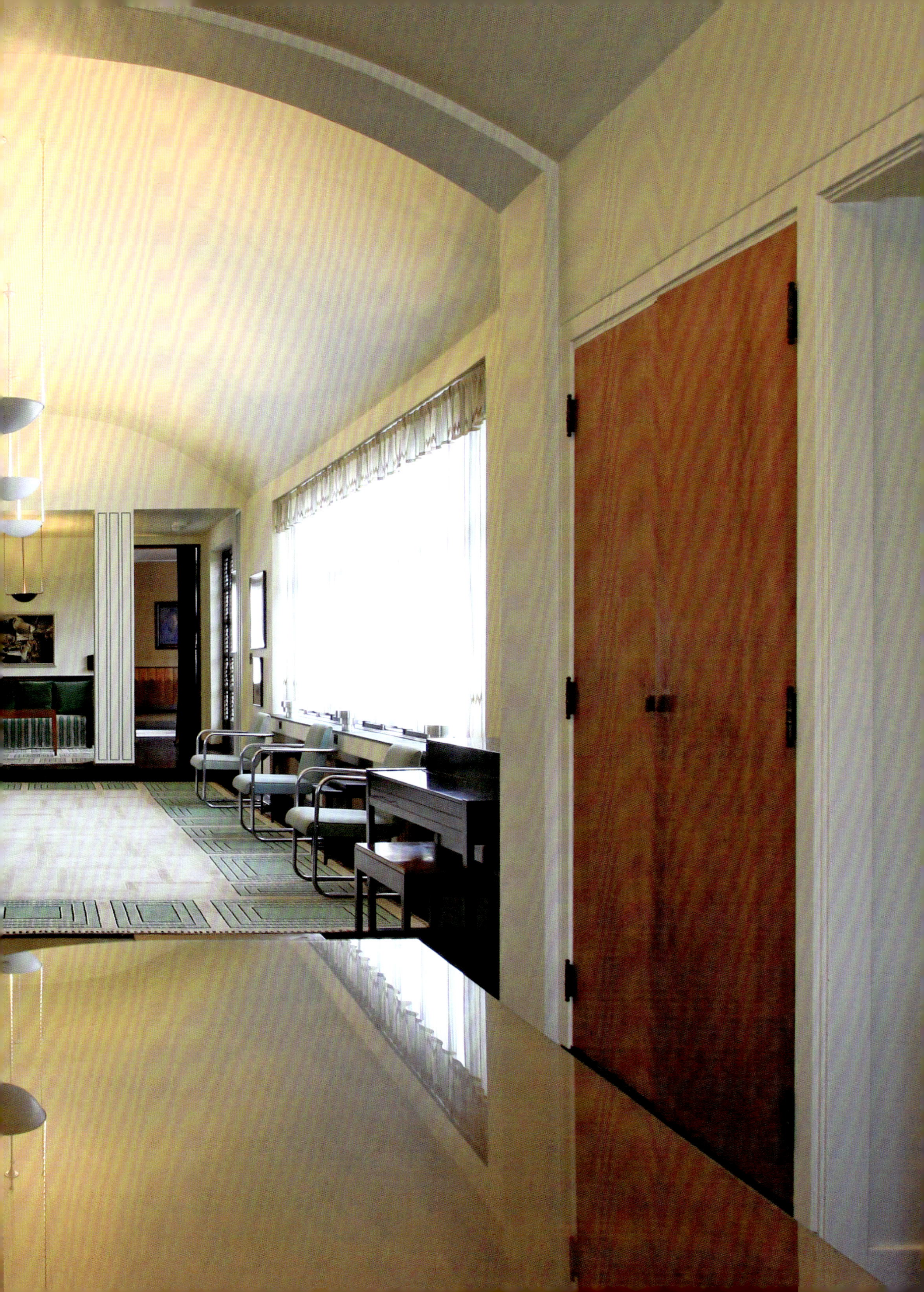

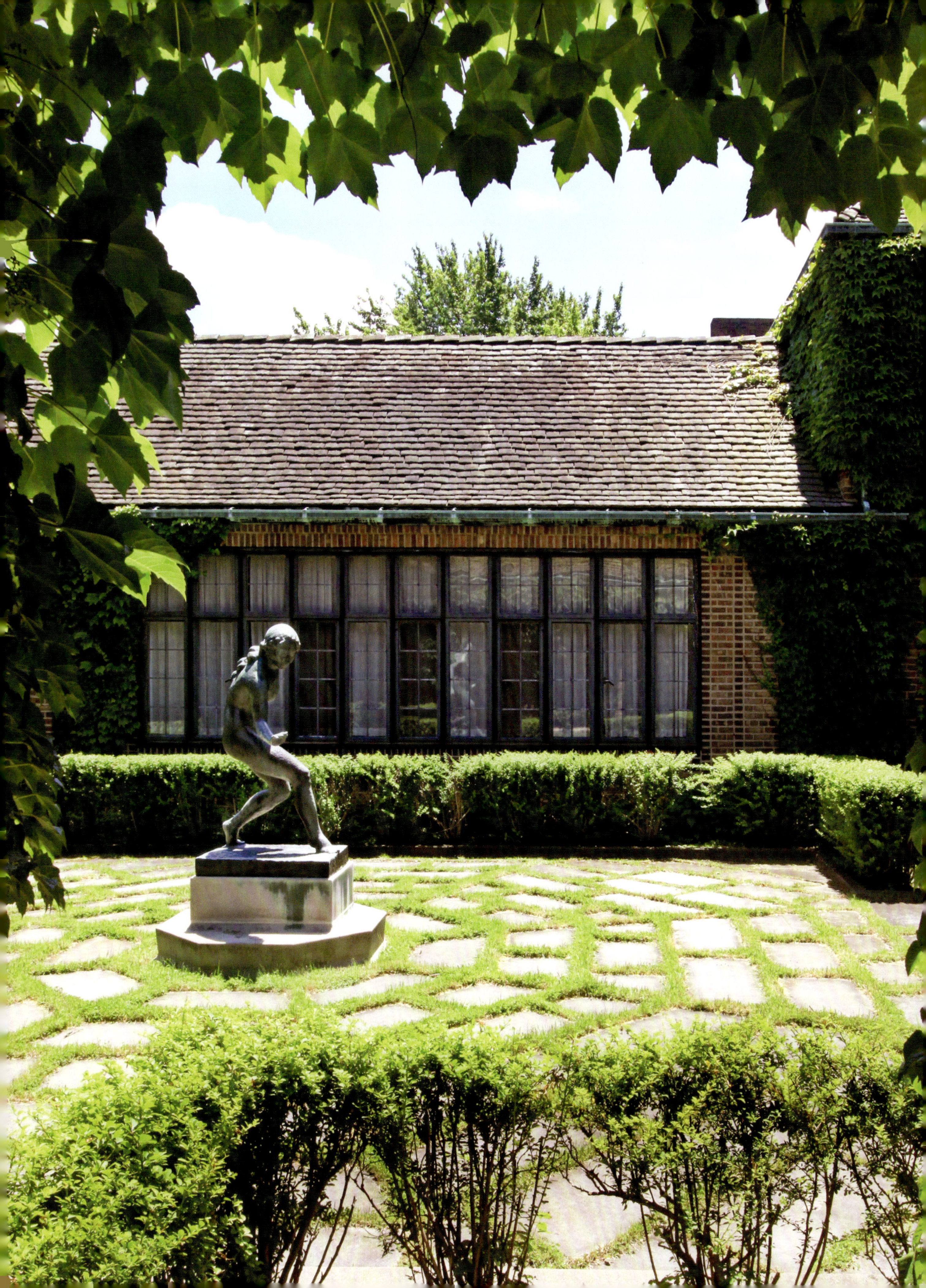

opposite
Courtyard with Wäinö Aaltonen's sculpture *Kivi's Muse*

below
View from the studio to the courtyard

165

Koebel House

Grosse Pointe Farms, Michigan, 1937, 1939–40

Eliel and Loja Saarinen met Charles J. Koebel (1889–1980), of Swedish descent and the owner of the Koebel Diamond Tool Company, and his wife Ingrid, on an ocean voyage from Europe to the United States. When the Koebels wanted to build a house for themselves in an affluent suburb of Detroit on the shores of Lake St. Clair, they commissioned Saarinen to design a residence that had the same refined, distinctly modern appearance as the architect's own home.[14]

The design work, which began in 1937, originally involved both Eliel and Eero, who had just established their architectural firm, Saarinen & Saarinen. The final plans, however, were prepared by J. Robert F. Swanson, Pipsan's husband, in 1939–40. Pipsan herself designed the interior of the house and selected the furniture, and some of the textiles were made at Cranbrook Academy of Art according to designs by Loja. Eliel Saarinen and Swanson also took Koebel House as a starting point for developing a line of furniture that would fit rooms of various types and sizes, produced by the Grand Rapids–based Johnson Furniture Company. All in all, thirty-two different, combinable items of wooden furniture of a light and simple design were eventually taken into production under the name Flexible Home Arrangements.[15]

To the consternation of some of the Koebels' neighbors, the clear-cut building with its rectangular shape and flat roof formed a strong contrast to the surrounding houses of the area, which were of Spanish influence or copied the features of French chateaux.[16] Reflecting the modern architectural style, the design was based on the program of the house, the needs of the family, and the natural setting rather than historical precedents. The contribution of the younger-generation architects Eero Saarinen and Robert Swanson led to an emphasis of modern elements.

Except for the garage and a one-story wing framing the garden, the building has two floors, with common spaces on the first floor and bedrooms upstairs. The entrance facade faces the street with specially made yellowish bricks. The spatial arrangement of Saarinen's own house was slightly modified for Koebel House. The dining area, living room, and library / study are interconnected, and their use can be flexibly modified. They form an almost contiguous space that is structured through furniture. Fixed furnishings and interior decoration play an important role in the main rooms. The combination of a corner sofa and fireplace in the library is reminiscent of the lounging areas at

opposite
View of the house from the driveway

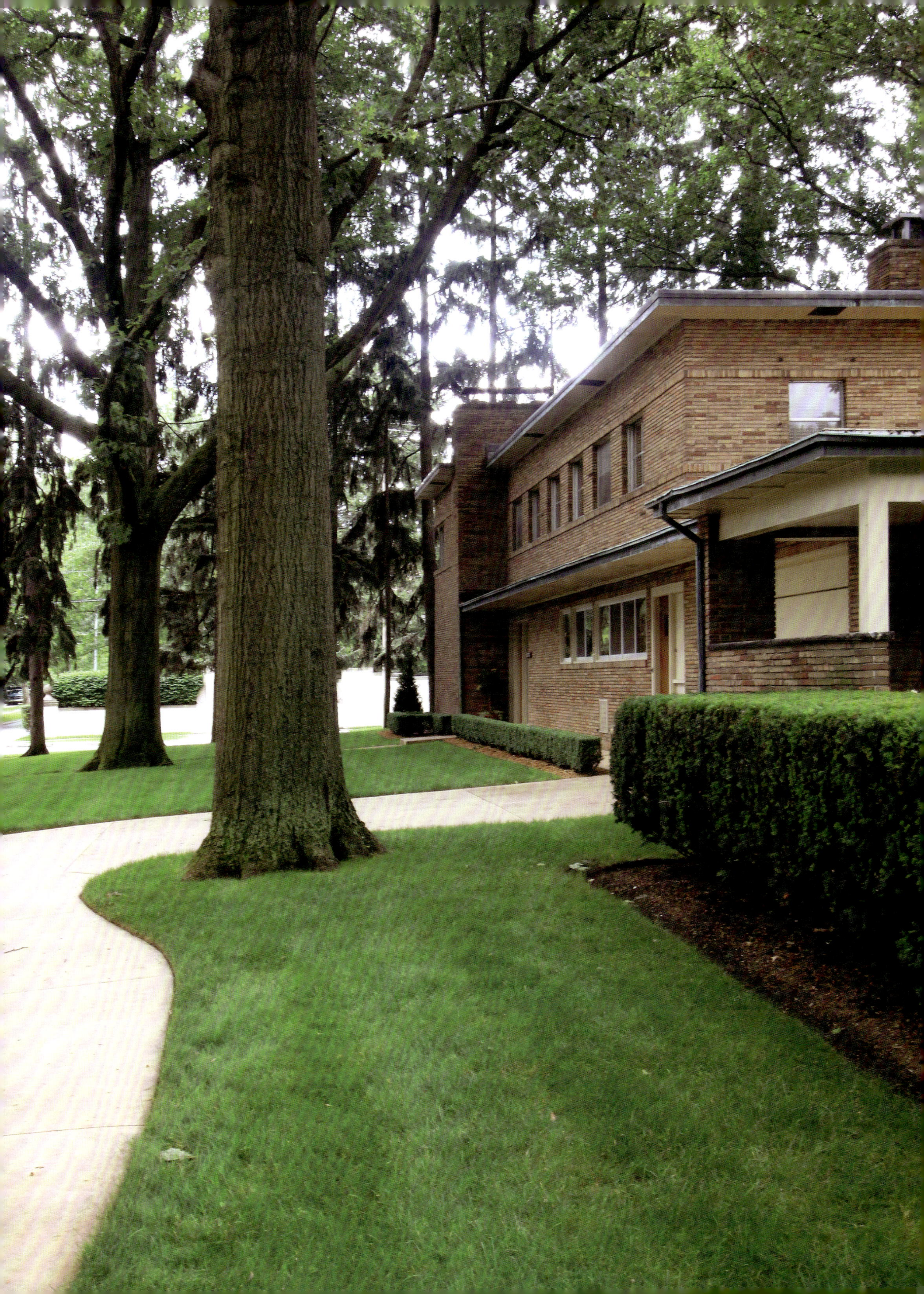

Hvitträsk. In a few places, curving walls steer movement within the house or close off a space in a gentle manner, such as the wall leading to the library and the round mahogany wall of the dining room, orienting the space toward the lounging area with its grand piano and the view of the garden. Above the dining room table, the ceiling features round concentric niches accentuating the intimate nature of the space. Among the many details of Koebel House that derive from Saarinen House are this ceiling and its light fitting, the staircase railings, and the painted door ornaments of the upstairs bedrooms, designed by Pipsan.

The one-story wing containing the winter garden is marked by curving forms in both end walls; the wall adjoining the garage leads inside, and a rounded wall and skylight end the space toward the yard. The unfinished materials of this wing, with its floor of natural stone, brick wall, and bamboo ceiling, underline the close connection of this space with nature. The garden to which it looks out is shielded by conifers lining the spacious site.

The residence demonstrates the importance of the relationship between fine craftsmanship and industrially manufactured parts in the architectural design by the Saarinens. The privately owned house has been carefully restored and has preserved both its atmosphere and many of its original interior details.

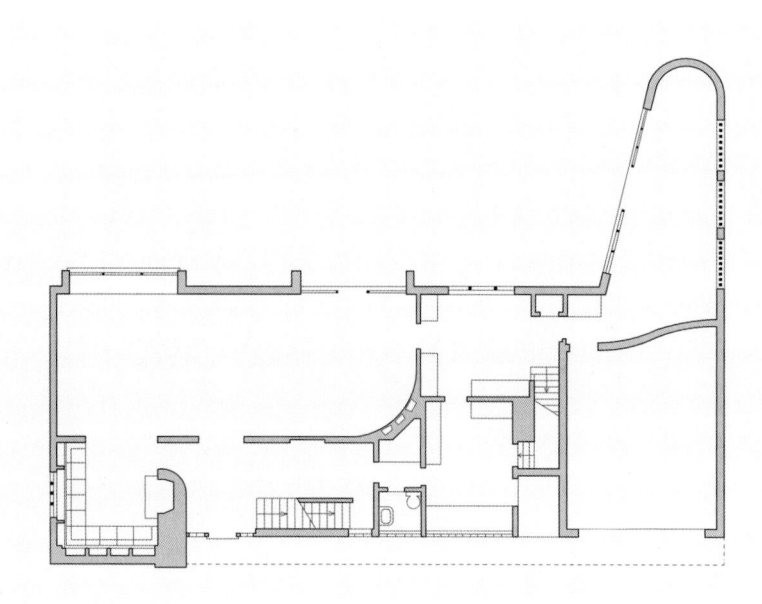

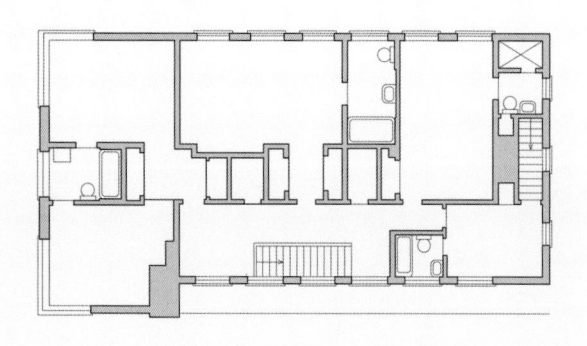

opposite
First- and second-floor plans

top
Perspective for proposed alterations to the residence in the 1940s

bottom
Northeast facade

top
Main entrance

bottom
View of the house from the garden

below
Winter garden

below
Living room

opposite
Dining room

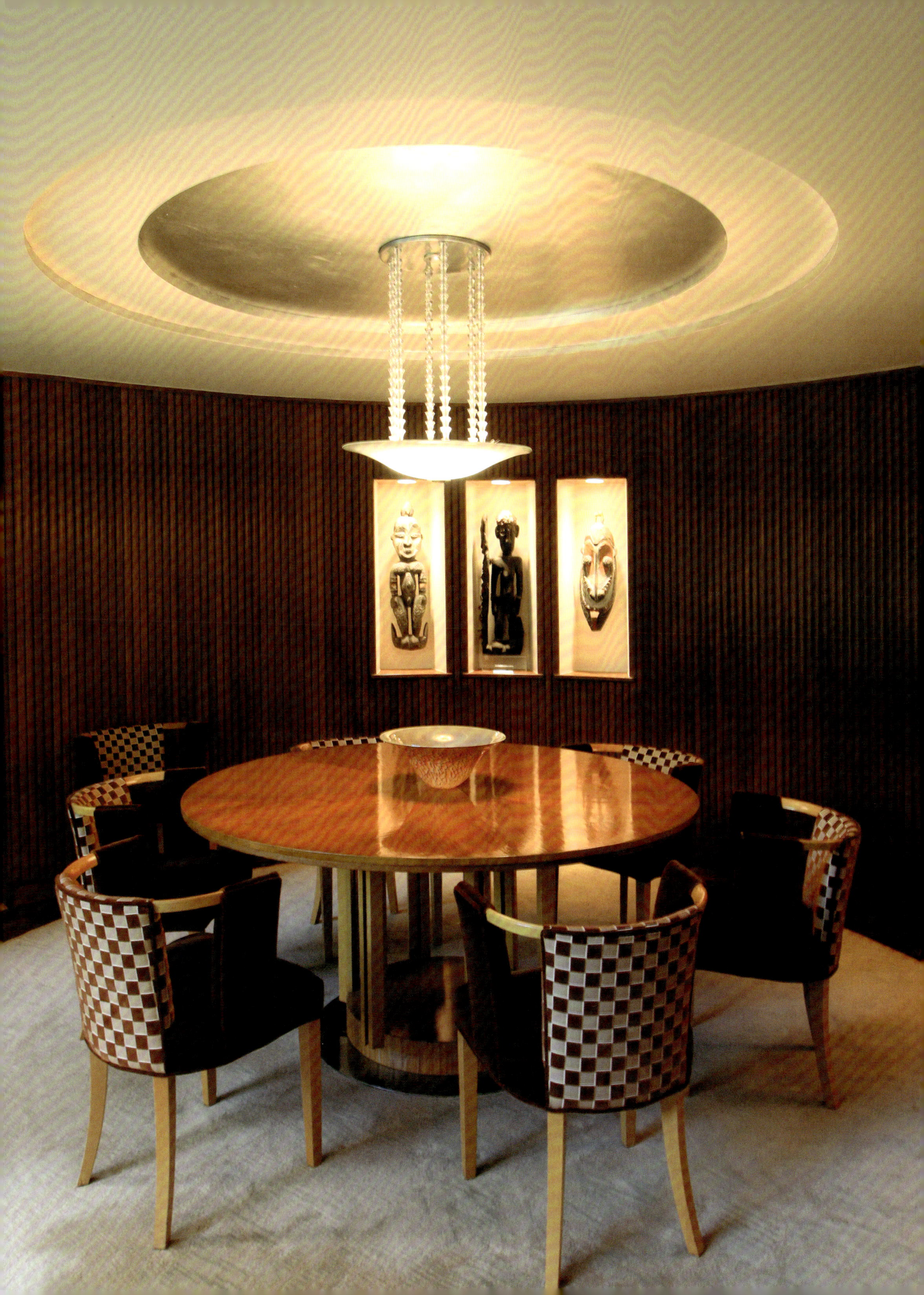

below
Kitchen after modernization

top
Library fireplace with custom-designed andirons

bottom
Library

top
Stencil decoration on the second-floor bedroom door, designed by Pipsan

bottom
Chair designed by Saarinen and produced by Johnson Furniture Company

opposite
Second-floor guest room

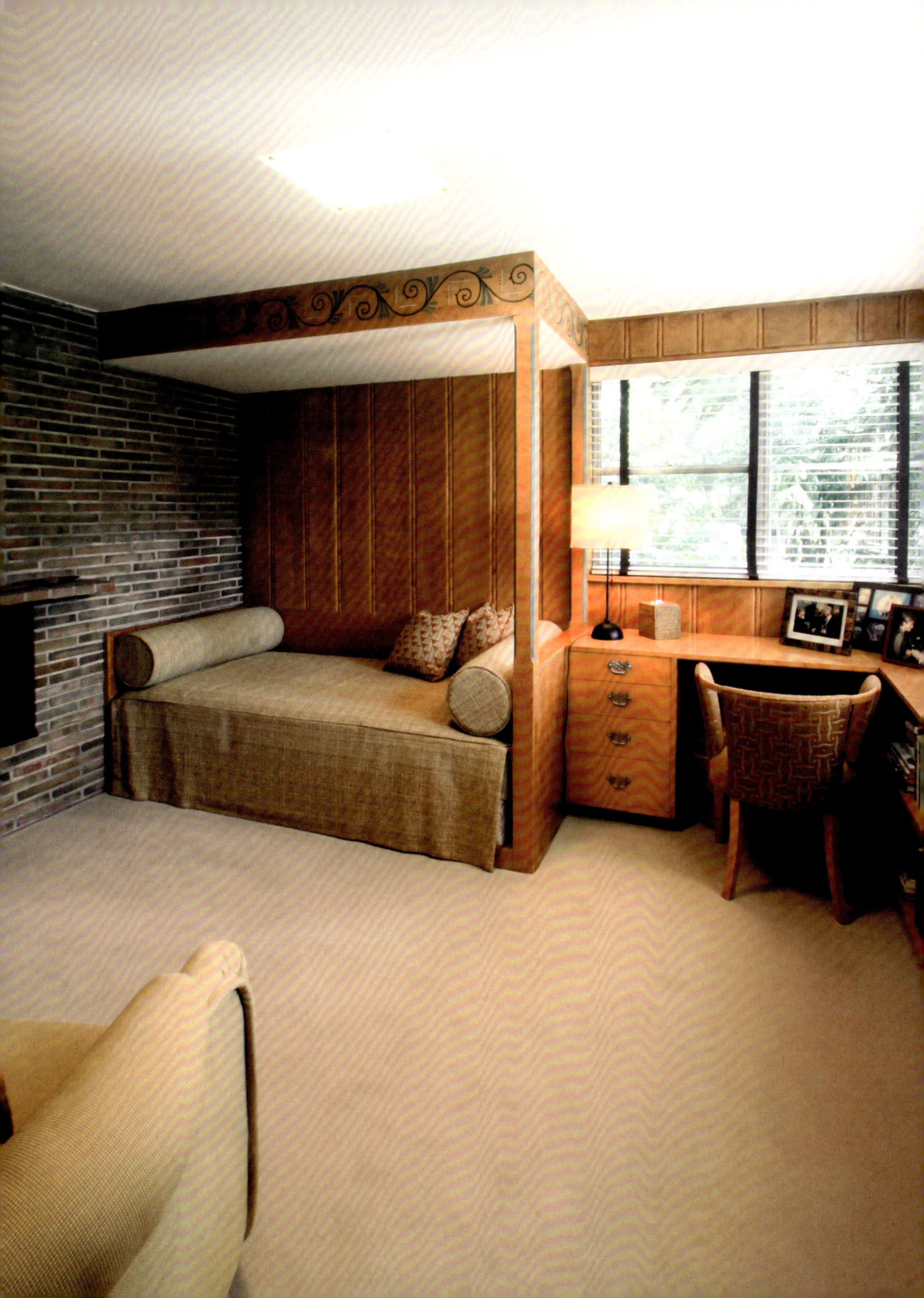

A. C. Wermuth House

Fort Wayne, Indiana, 1941–42

Albert C. Wermuth (1893–1977), a building contractor active in Bloomfield Hills, commissioned the Saarinens to design a home for him in the peace and quiet of Indiana's countryside. Wermuth's company had constructed several buildings on the Cranbrook campus, and Eliel had become friends with Wermuth, who as a German-speaker had been an important contact for him during his first years in the United States, when his knowledge of the English language was poor.[17] Around the time they worked on Wermuth's house, the First Christian Church (1942) by Eliel and Eero was also under construction in Columbus, Indiana.

The house sits in gently rolling terrain near a stand of forest on the edge of a steep ridge leading to a small brook. It consists of two wings meeting at a slight angle, with one wing containing the living room, dining space, kitchen, and auxiliary rooms and the other the family's bedrooms. A tall, rounded chimney faced with stone creates a stark contrast to the otherwise markedly horizontal building. The garage is joined to the house by a long covered walkway.

The different character of the two wings is underscored in their facades: the shared rooms are faced with light-colored local limestone, while the bedroom wing, which is raised on columns, has wooden cladding painted white, giving it a lighter and more vivid appearance. The bedrooms provide views over the treetops, while the space beneath this wing is used as a sheltered patio. The public areas of the main building are open to the green surroundings through a row of glass windows extending the length of the whole wall. Long penticelike eaves shield this room from the midday sun. A stone wall divides the large space, and a part of this wing is set a few steps lower to provide a more intimate space.

The influences of Eliel and Eero meet in an interesting way in this house. The building is mainly based on Eero's concepts, although Eliel had studied the site in 1939 and proposed a modern design due to its special nature. Mrs. Wermuth had originally wanted the house to be of Colonial style with columns.[18] The site on the brink of a steep slope resembles Hvitträsk to some degree, and the

opposite

Covered walkway leading to the main entrance

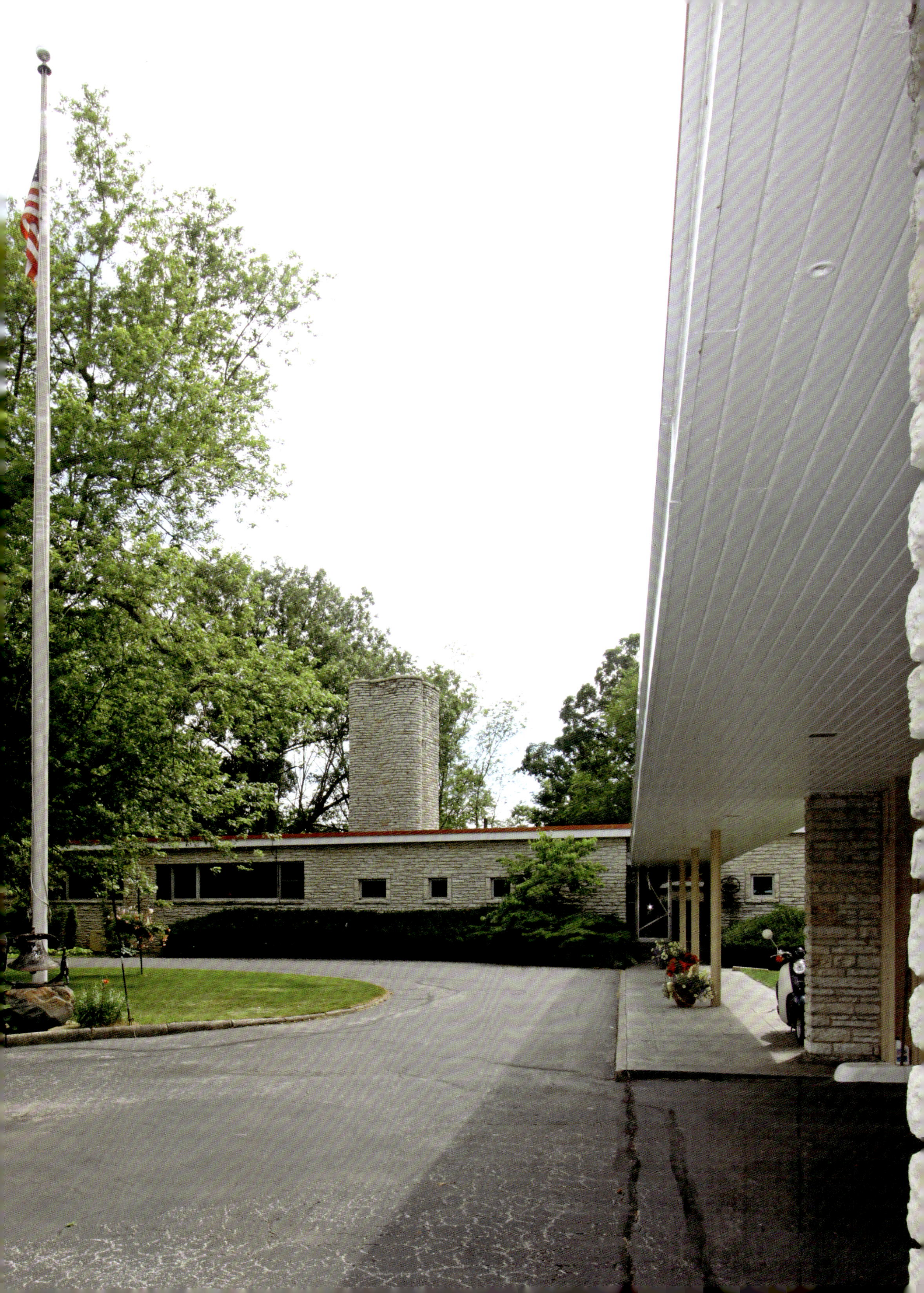

interior contains some of Eliel's favorite themes, such as built-in sofas and wood paneling in the living room. Eero's modern approach is visible in the simplified details and the way the shared spaces are joined to each other in a fluid manner and open up to the surrounding landscape through large windows. Eliel described the interior in the following terms: "I feel it ought to have a neutral quality, so that any sensible furniture that is genuine can fit in."[19] Today the privately owned house is well preserved with many original details.

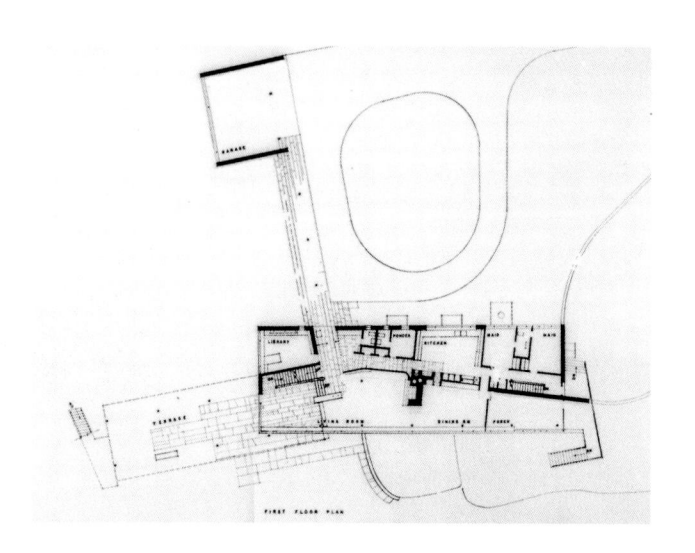

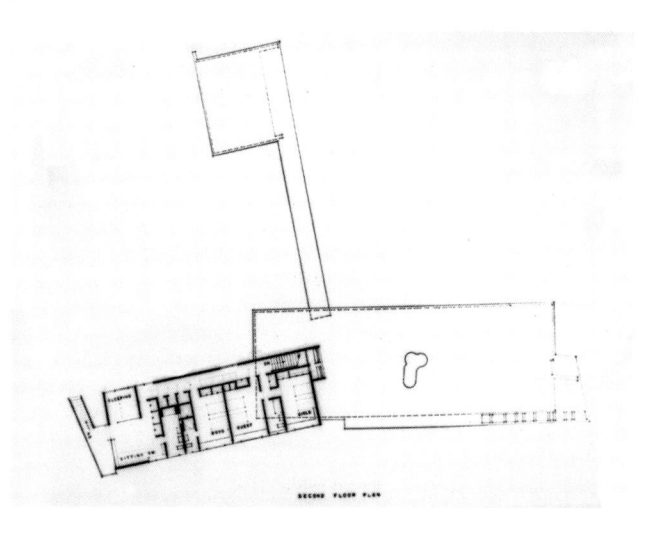

top
First- and second-floor plans

bottom
Wermuth House seen from the gorge

top
Painting of the Wermuth residence by John H. Foreman, 1981

bottom
Living room

below
Lower level of the living room, with armchairs by Alvar Aalto, 1933

below
Custom-designed music cabinet in the living room

overleaf
Dining room

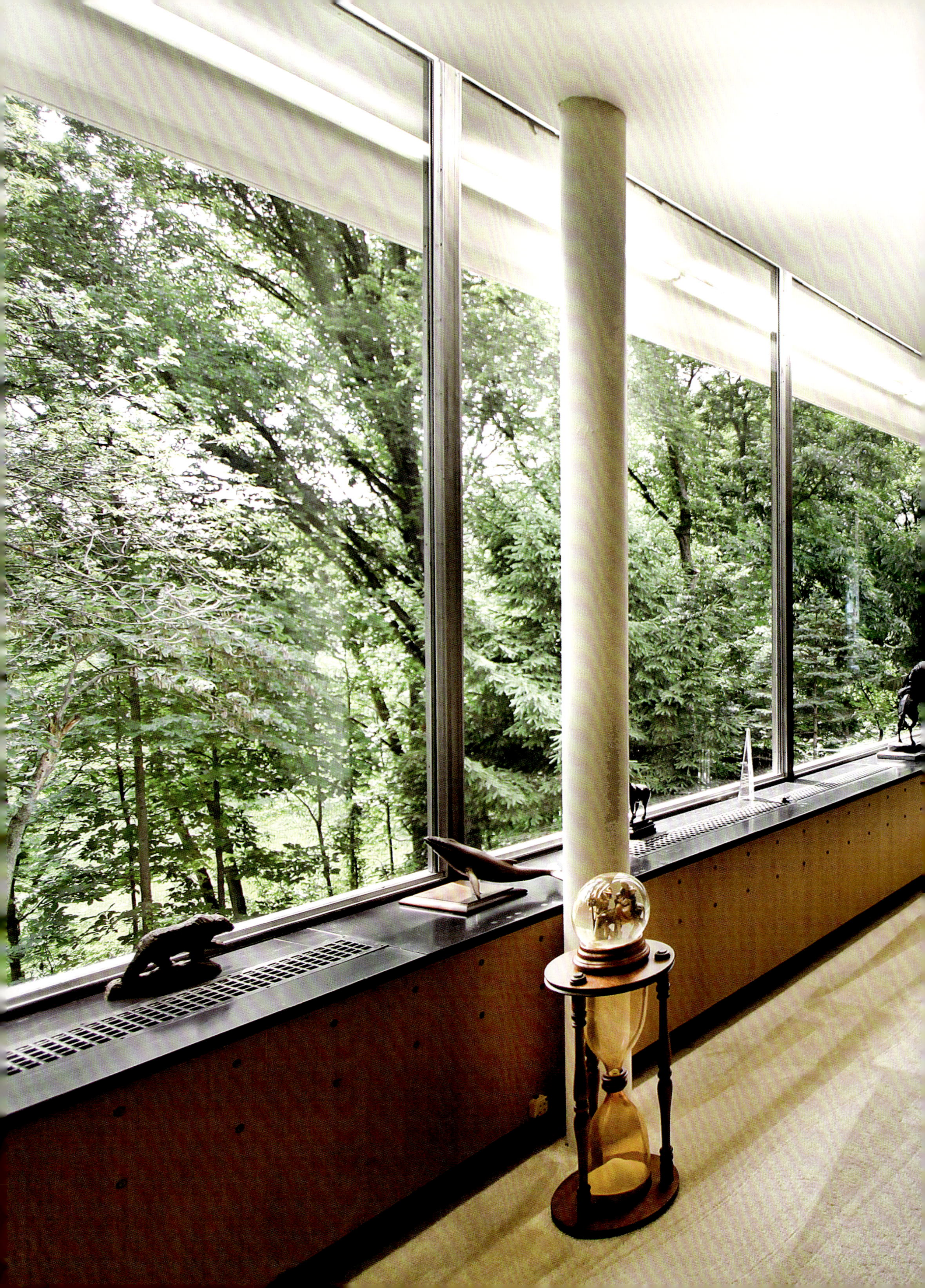

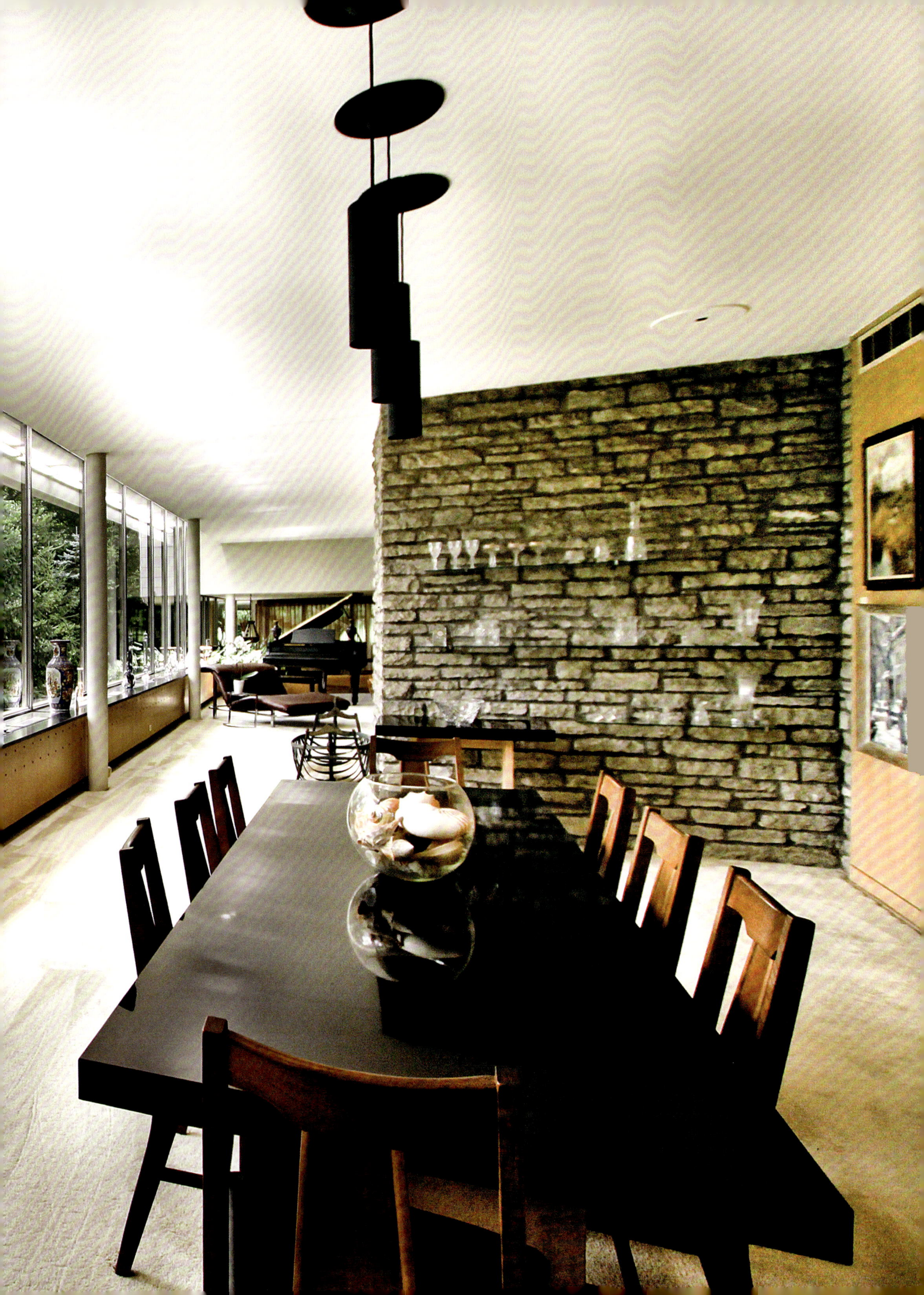

below
Kitchen with table from Eero Saarinen's Pedestal Collection, introduced in 1958, and Tulip Chairs, 1953–58

below
Northeast elevation

Loja Saarinen House

Bloomfield Hills, Michigan, 1950–51

After her husband's death in 1950, Loja had to move out of her home at Cranbrook Academy of Art. Eero lived nearby in a Victorian house, which he had remodeled for his family's needs, and designed a modern dwelling for his mother at the rear end of his site, where she lived until her death in 1968.

The exterior walls of the flat-roofed building are faced with painted vertical boarding, and their few details include wooden ventilation grilles. The house is in three parts, with the public spaces—a living and dining room—in the middle, flanked symmetrically by two bedrooms on one side and the kitchen on the other side. At the south end is a small entrance patio. Eero had experimented with a similar modernist design and layout of space more than a decade ago, when in 1937 he designed "A Combined Living-Dining Room-Study," for *Architectural Forum*.[20] The spaciousness of the combined living and dining room is enhanced by a glass wall facing the garden, with Eero's house partly visible in the back. The size of this space was to some extent dictated by the need to fit the large rug from the studio of Saarinen House there. Loja also brought artworks with her, as well as some objects from Hvitträsk. The latter included metal sconces that were originally on the wall of the main living room.

The three homes that were designed for Loja and her family over the span of some fifty years demonstrate the evolution of Eliel and Eero's architecture through the decades. All of the houses engage in dialogue with the landscape in their own particular manner: Hvitträsk as a castle set in the woods, Saarinen House as a comprehensive academic town house, and Loja Saarinen House as a minimalist suburban home.

opposite

Main entrance

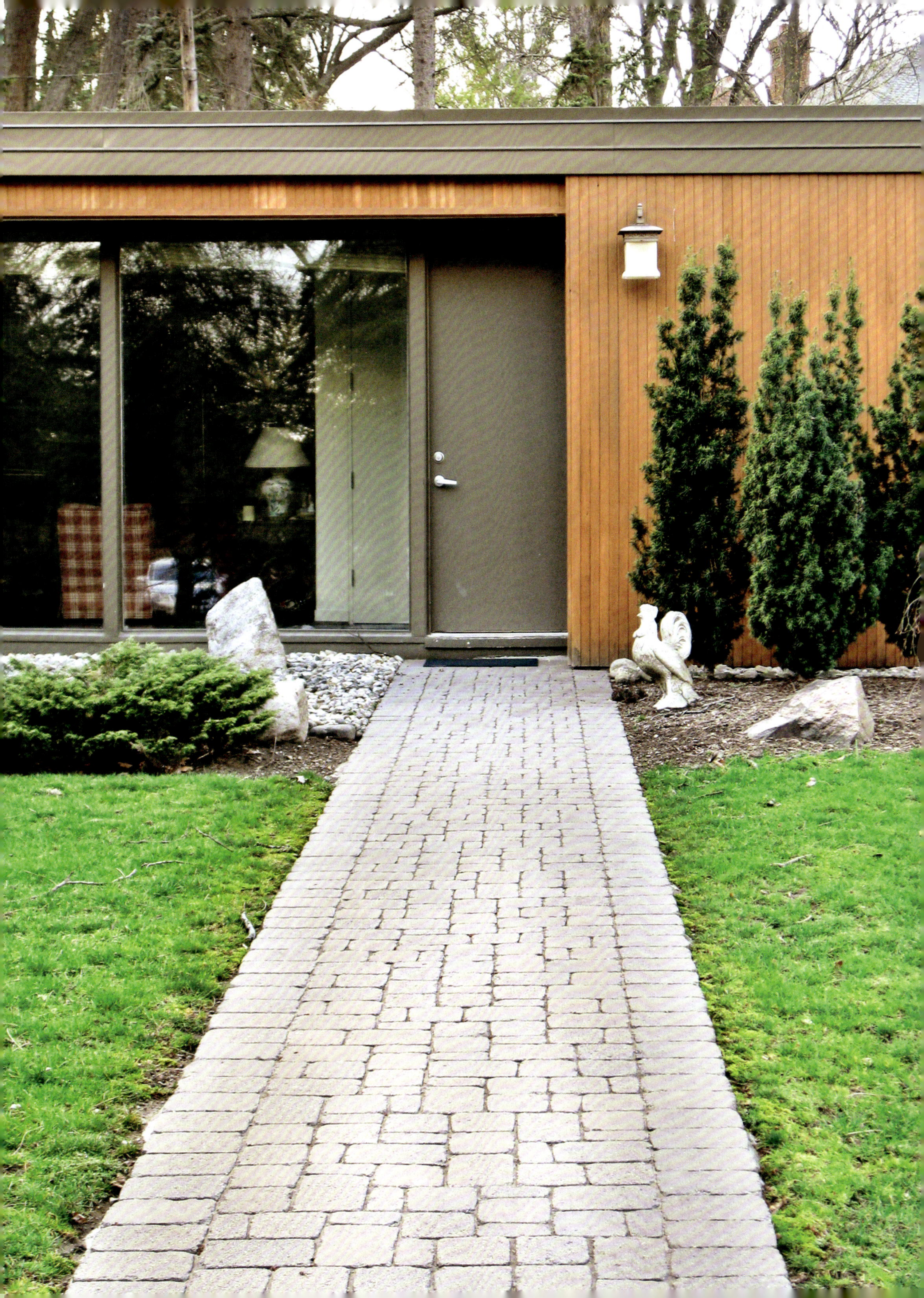

top

Loja Saarinen in the living room, wearing the dress she made for the 1934 Crandemonium Ball (a costume ball held at Cranbrook Academy of Art during Saarinen's tenure there). In the background is a sconce from Hvitträsk and a 1919 painting by Vilho Sjöström of Eliel and Eero. On the right is Eero's sculpture of his father. Other important pieces in the room were Loja's rug from Saarinen House and Eero's womb chair. In this chair Eliel liked to take a nap after dinner, and it was in this chair that he died on July 1, 1950.

bottom

Original floor plan

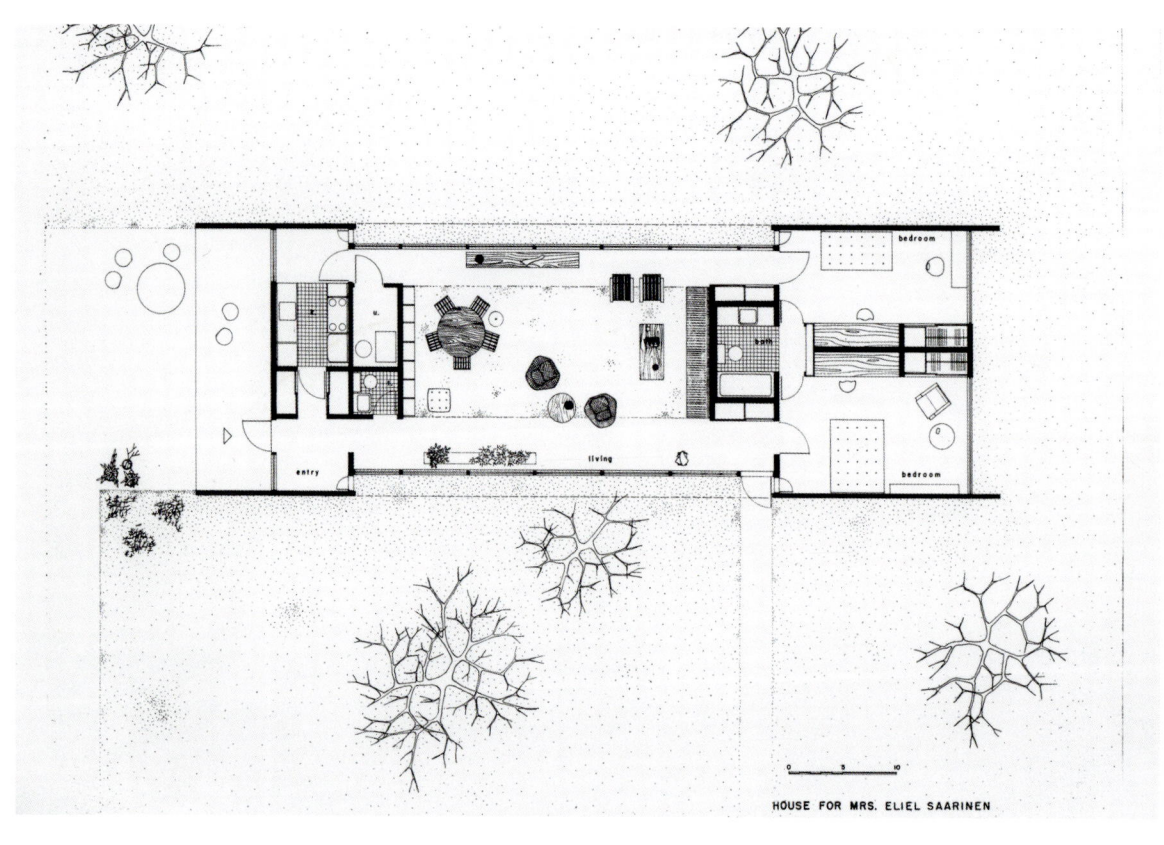

below
View from the driveway

top
The large window opens to a view of Eero's Victorian-style house.

bottom
Living room

below
Kitchen after modernization

below
View of the garden from the living room

opposite
Southeast facade

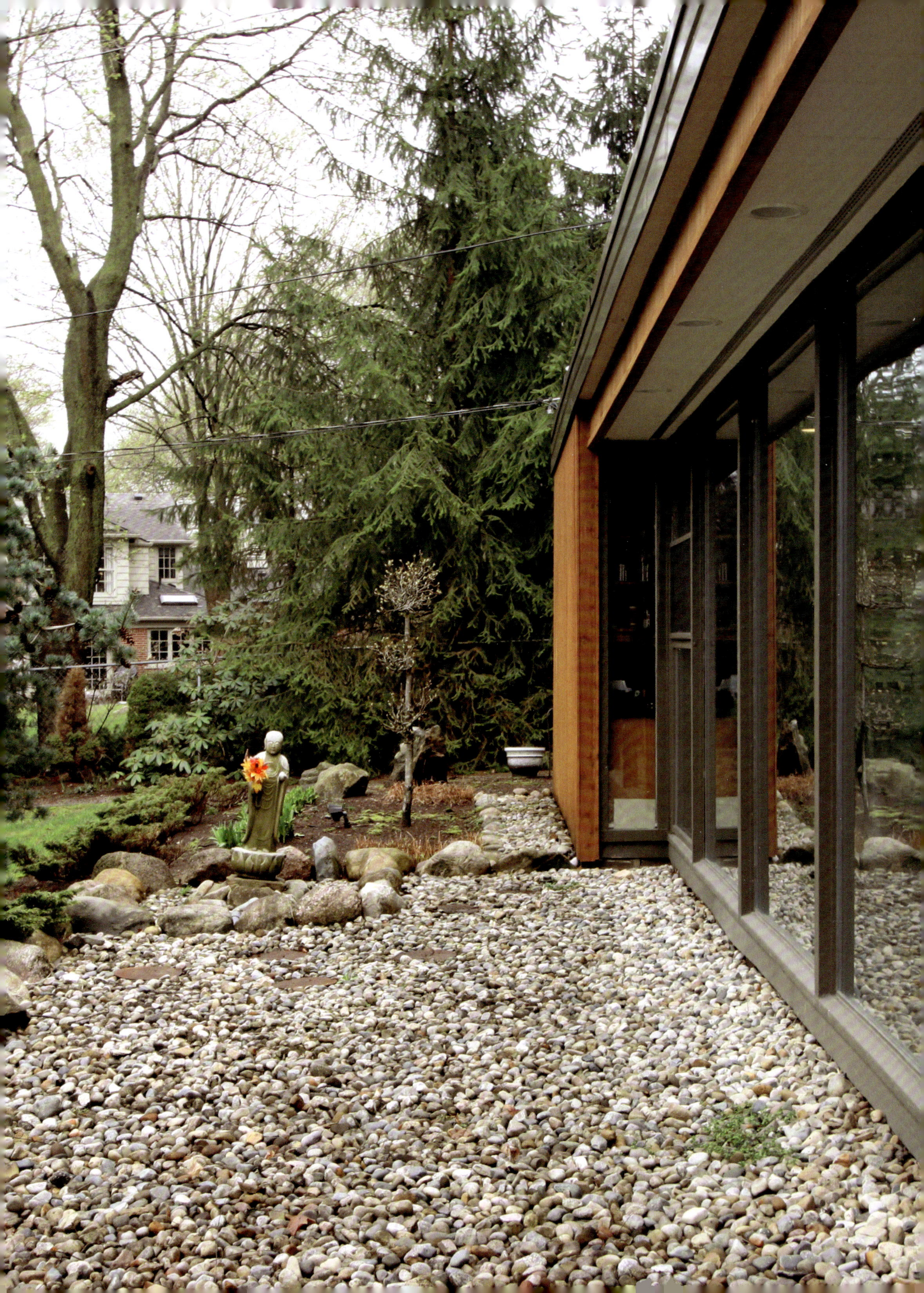

Miller House

Columbus, Indiana, 1953–57

Eero was introduced to J. Irwin Miller, the head of the Cummins Engine Company, a manufacturer of diesel engines, in 1939, when he and Eliel worked on the design of the First Christian Church in Columbus. Miller and his wife, Xenia Simons Miller, were leading philanthropists, cultural figures, and patrons of modern architecture in their hometown. The Saarinens became, in a sense, their trusted architects, and J. Irwin and Eero, who were of the same age, were personal friends for many years. In addition to designing his own projects for Columbus, including a building for the Irwin Union Trust Company (1950–54) and the North Christian Church (1959–64), Eero also served as an advisor when architects were chosen for building projects in the town.

Miller commissioned Eero to design a private residence for his family in 1953. The Millers had bought a large plot on the west edge of Columbus bounded by a river on one side and urban blocks on the other. The house is located on the east part of the site with a view of meadows and a stand of trees by the riverbank. Architect and textile designer Alexander Girard (1907–1993), with whom Saarinen had already collaborated in the design of the Miller family's vacation home in the Muskoka district of Ontario, Canada (1950–52) and previously in the General Motors Technical Center project (1946–56), was involved in the design from the very beginning.[21] He took on a unique role as the supplier of objects for the home and interior designer. The Millers had total confidence in his choices, and Girard continued his work on Miller House after Saarinen's death. Saarinen was also assisted by the lead designer of his firm, architect Kevin Roche (1922–). The result of the three men's collaboration was one of the finest postwar dwellings in the United States.

After a meeting with the clients early in the design process, Saarinen wrote to Girard in 1954:

> I am on my way back from Columbus. The Millers liked the general scheme of the house. They liked the one story concept. They liked the wide overhang and they liked the flat roof with a plenum space in it. In addition to this they liked the general degree of formality-informality inherent in the house. They seem to appreciate the idea of having the earth built up around the house and they also liked the general disposition and grouping of parts. In an overall way I am enthusiastic about their response because I feel there is a genuine feeling on their part that it is for them, and I have a feeling also that nothing is "put over" on them, but simply right for them. The low monumental character they liked.[22]

opposite
Patio

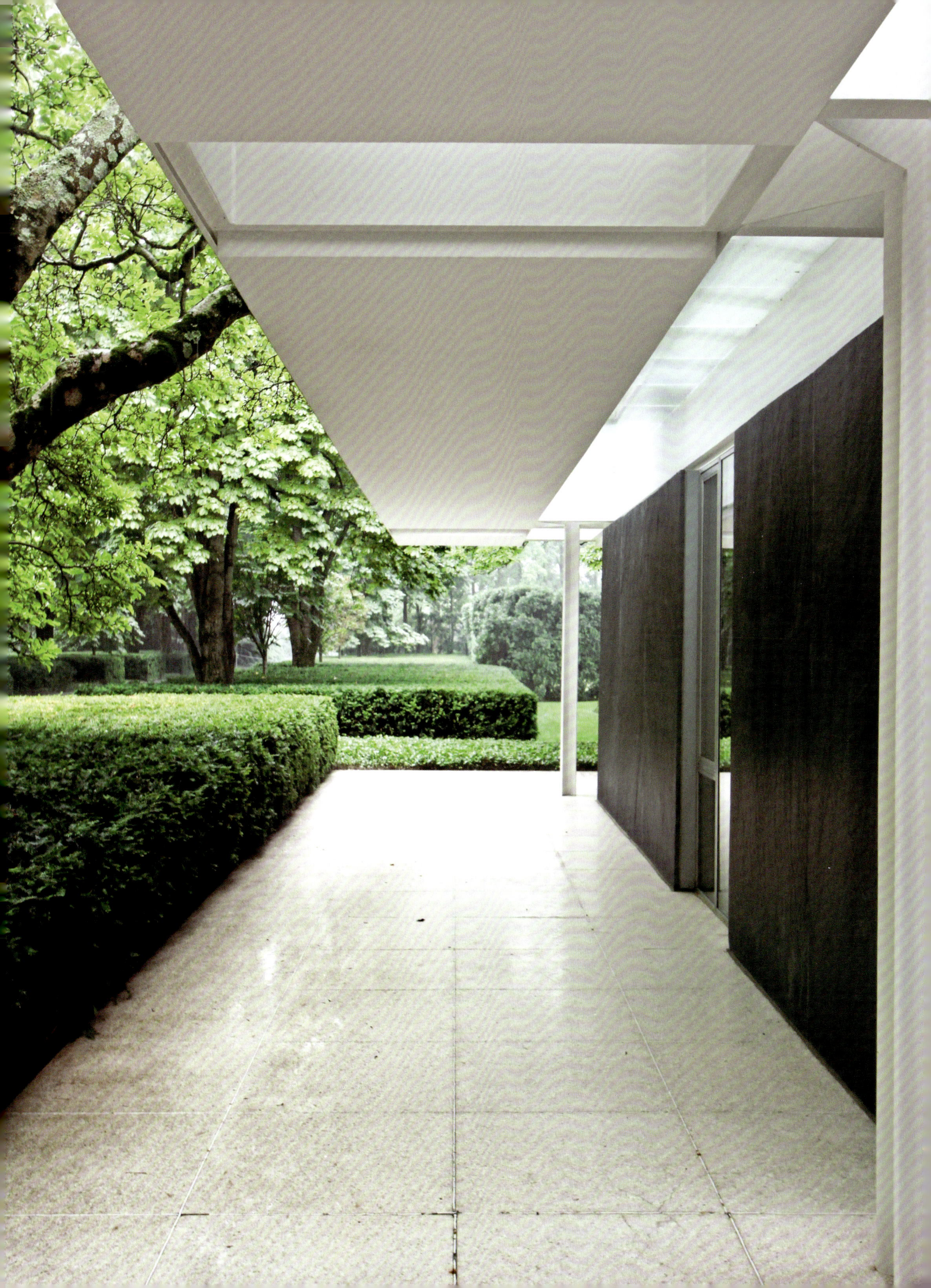

Miller was similarly satisfied and explained to Girard in a letter written a few days later:

> Again let me tell you that you have a couple of very happy clients here who feel that you and Eero have exceeded our expectations in the general conception embodied in this plan.[23]

The Miller House—a contemporary Palladian villa, as it was described in *Architectural Forum* in the late 1950s—is a house of classical balance, like the Villa Rotonda to which it is compared in the article.[24] The almost square building rests on a travertine and terrazzo foundation. Its structural grid of sixteen steel columns and beams is revealed by strip-window skylights, which provide daylight for the core of the house consisting of a large, open living room containing areas for lounging and dining, and a den space. This public space flows freely, in a pinwheel-like arrangement, where each function has its own place and a view of the garden. The other parts of the house are grouped in four volumes according to use: the parents' suite; the children's bedrooms; the guest room, maid's room, and carport; and the kitchen and other auxiliary spaces. The bedrooms are of simple design and quite small, but the children had a shared playroom similar to Eero and Pipsan's playroom at Hvitträsk.

The central focus of the living room is a lounging area with a large square sofa built into the floor, an idea to which Xenia Miller was at first averse.[25] This conversation pit is a modern version of Eliel's lounging nooks, used for the first time by Eero in his Case Study House #9 for John Entenza (1945–49). Because of its low profile, it does not obstruct views of the interior landscape. The sofa cushions were changed according to season, with warm reds used during the winter and cool hues in the summer.[26] A free-standing fireplace and a grand piano in an adjacent part of the room were other elements of the overall design.

The travertine floors and marble walls of the shared spaces are replaced by warm wooden surfaces in the family's private rooms. Girard interspersed the predominantly white interiors with boldly colored curtains, cushions, and rugs of his design, inspired by folk textiles and providing warmth and joy to the spaces. Small decorative objects from Mexico, Asia, or Murano hint at the family's interests but also show the mark of Girard's hand. The designer would inspect lists of different kinds of items together with the Millers, and their correspondence shows that he paid attention to even the smallest details. In one of his letters to Girard, Miller asked, for example, where the designer intended to place a pencil sharpener meant for the table in the master bedroom.[27] Modern art also played an important role in the house. In addition to *Le Bassin aux Nymphéas* by Claude Monet, the Millers displayed works by Pablo Picasso and Henri Matisse in the house, and there was a sculpture by Henry Moore in the garden.

The one-story residence is surrounded by a garden designed by landscape architect Dan Kiley (1912–2004), who alternated regular plantings with wooded lanes, open lawn areas, and forest. Using walls, hedges, and walks, he created a series of verdant rooms corresponding to and continuing the spaces of the interior. Kiley described his concept as follows:

> The house was designed in functional blocks, such as the kitchen, the dining room, the master bedroom, and the living room. So I took this same geometry and made rooms outside using trees in groves and allées. [...] Below to the west we designed a very romantic kind of park in contrast to the geometry near the house.[28]

In the spring the house, which has been open to the public since 2011, is enveloped by a cloud of pink magnolia blossoms. The terrace encircling the building links interior and exterior spaces and is a pleasant and shady place to relax on a hot summer's day. The home and its setting are seamlessly linked.

The Miller House is an exemplary realization of the total concept of design, from the shaping of its landscape down to the smallest decorative objects. As a collaboration of three different designers, it can be viewed in similar terms as the results of the joint work of Gesellius, Lindgren, and Saarinen, who first developed this ideal.

top
Xenia and J. Irwin Miller in the living room

bottom
Floor plan

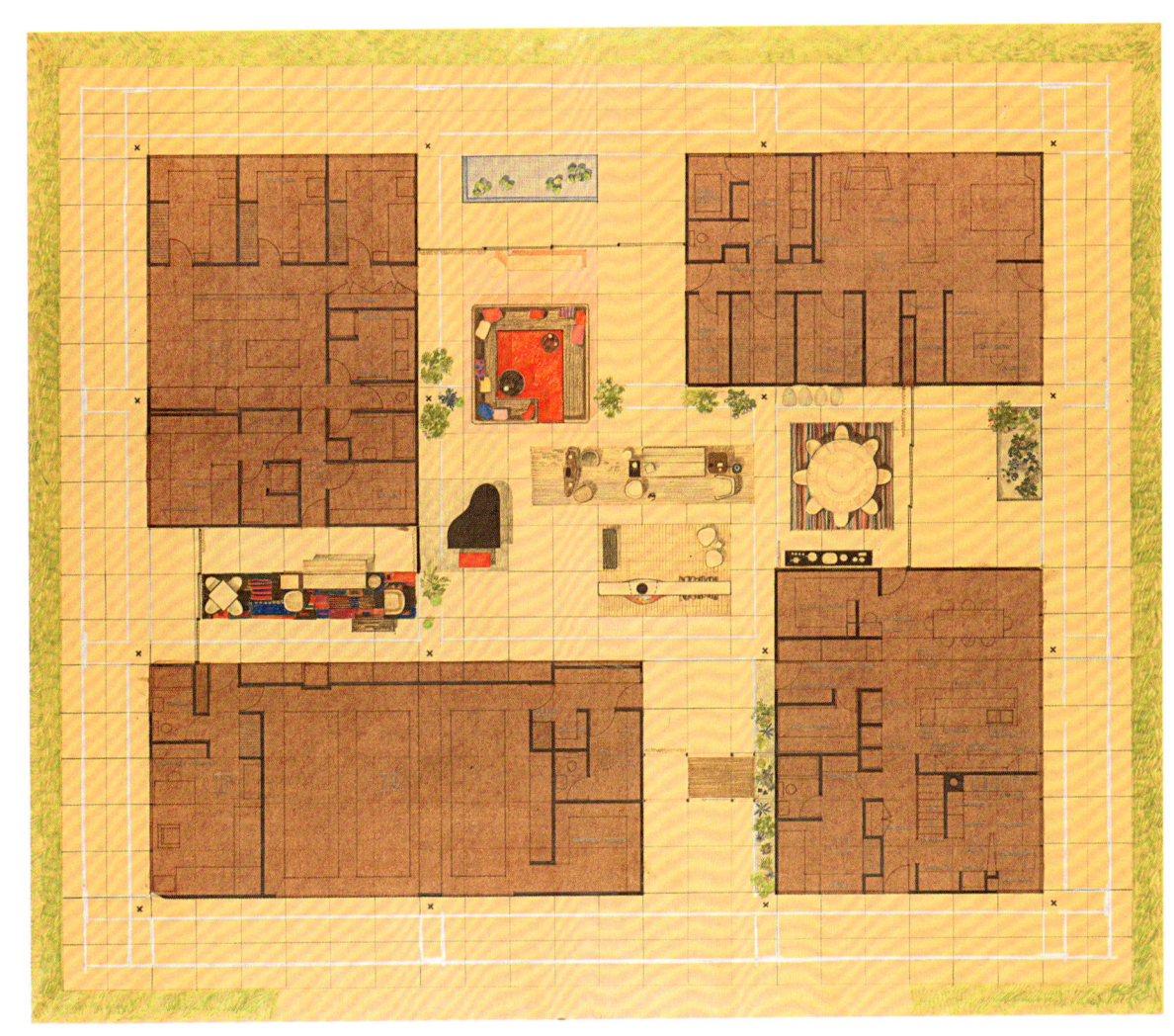

top
Structural pillar and skylights

bottom
View of the garden

below
View of the north facade from the garden

overleaf
South facade, with saucer magnolias flanking the entrance to the children's wing

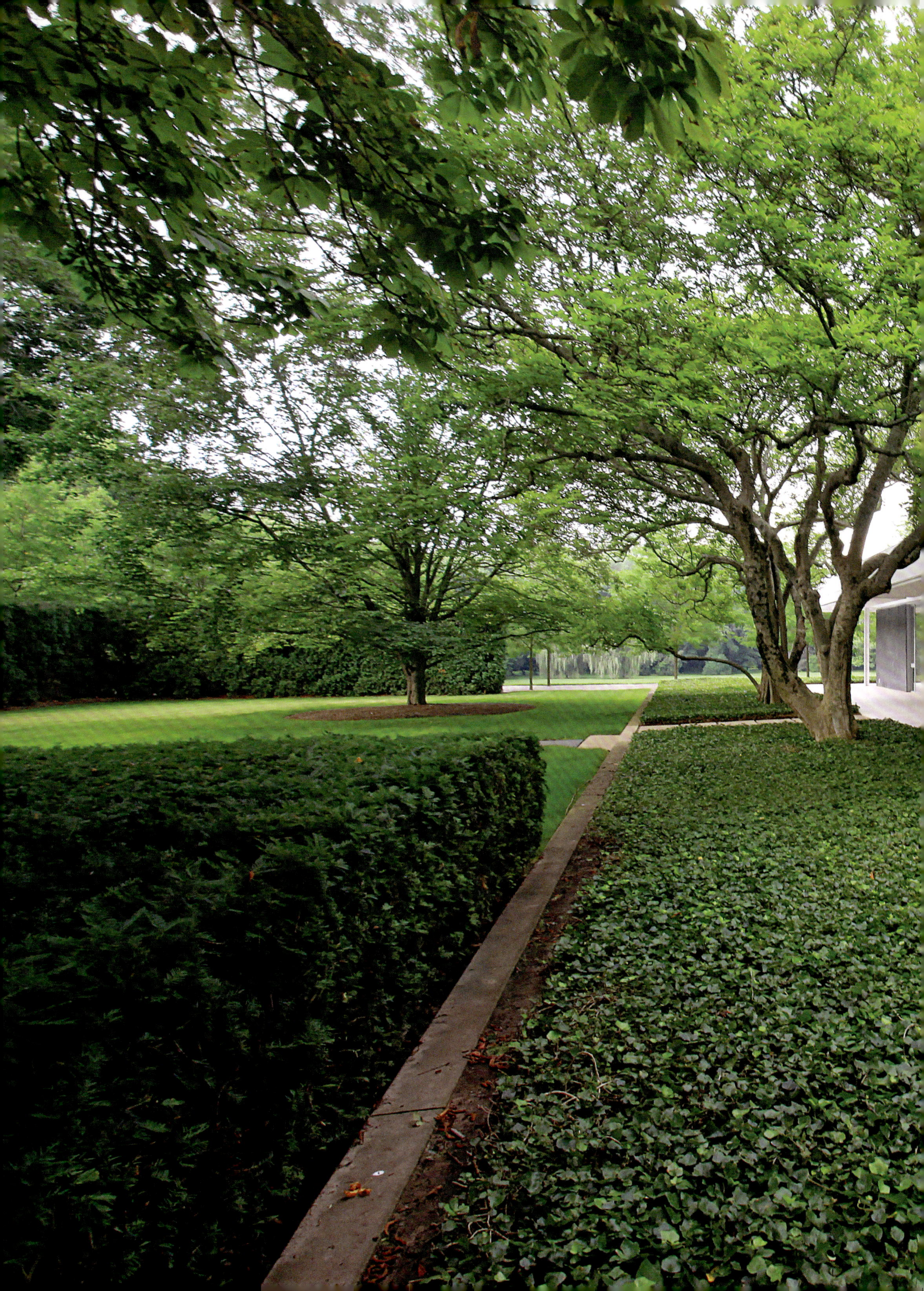

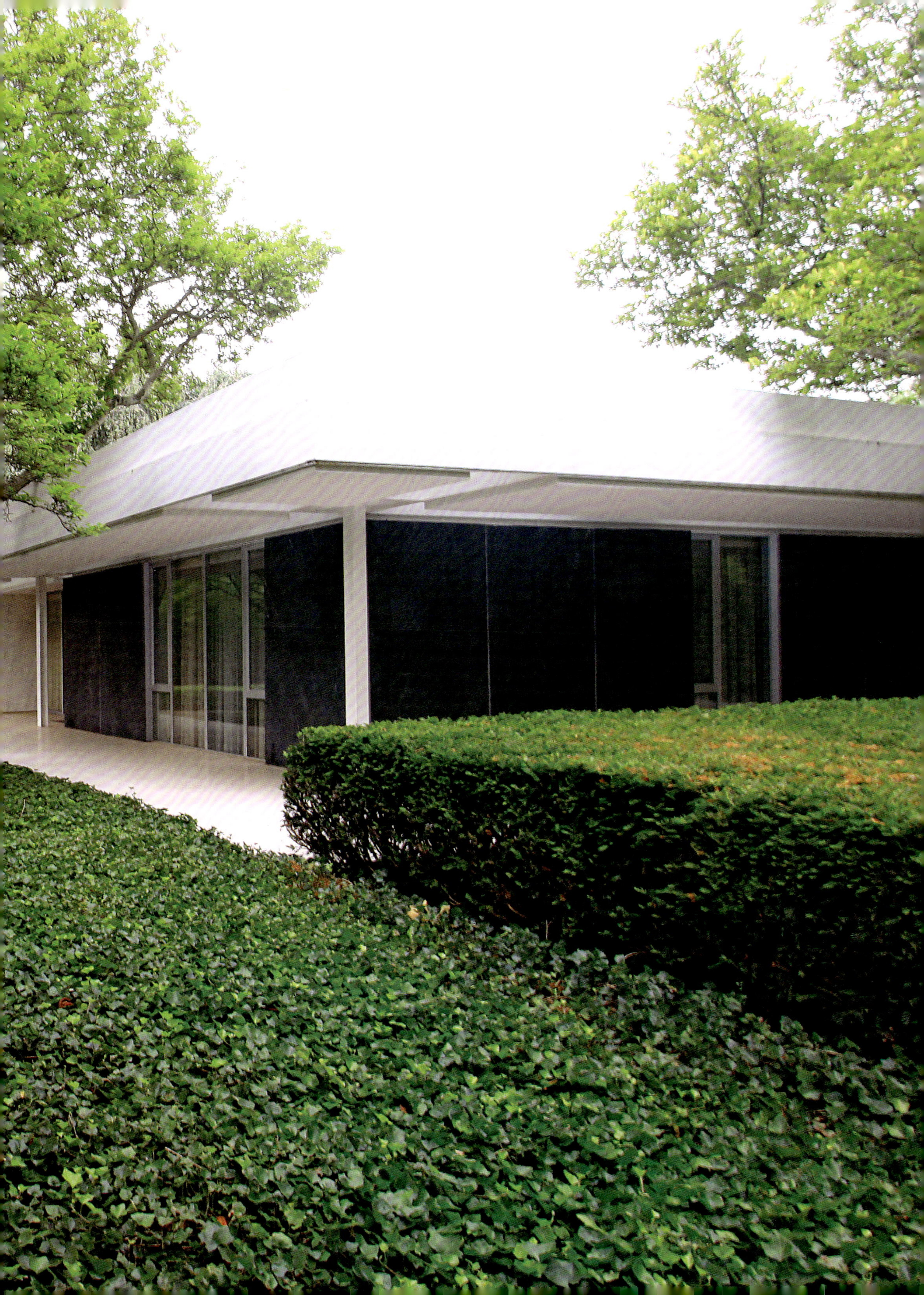

below
Adult Garden

opposite
Main entrance, with a rug designed by Alexander Girard in 1957 and the Eames Sofa Compact, designed by Charles and Ray Eames in 1954

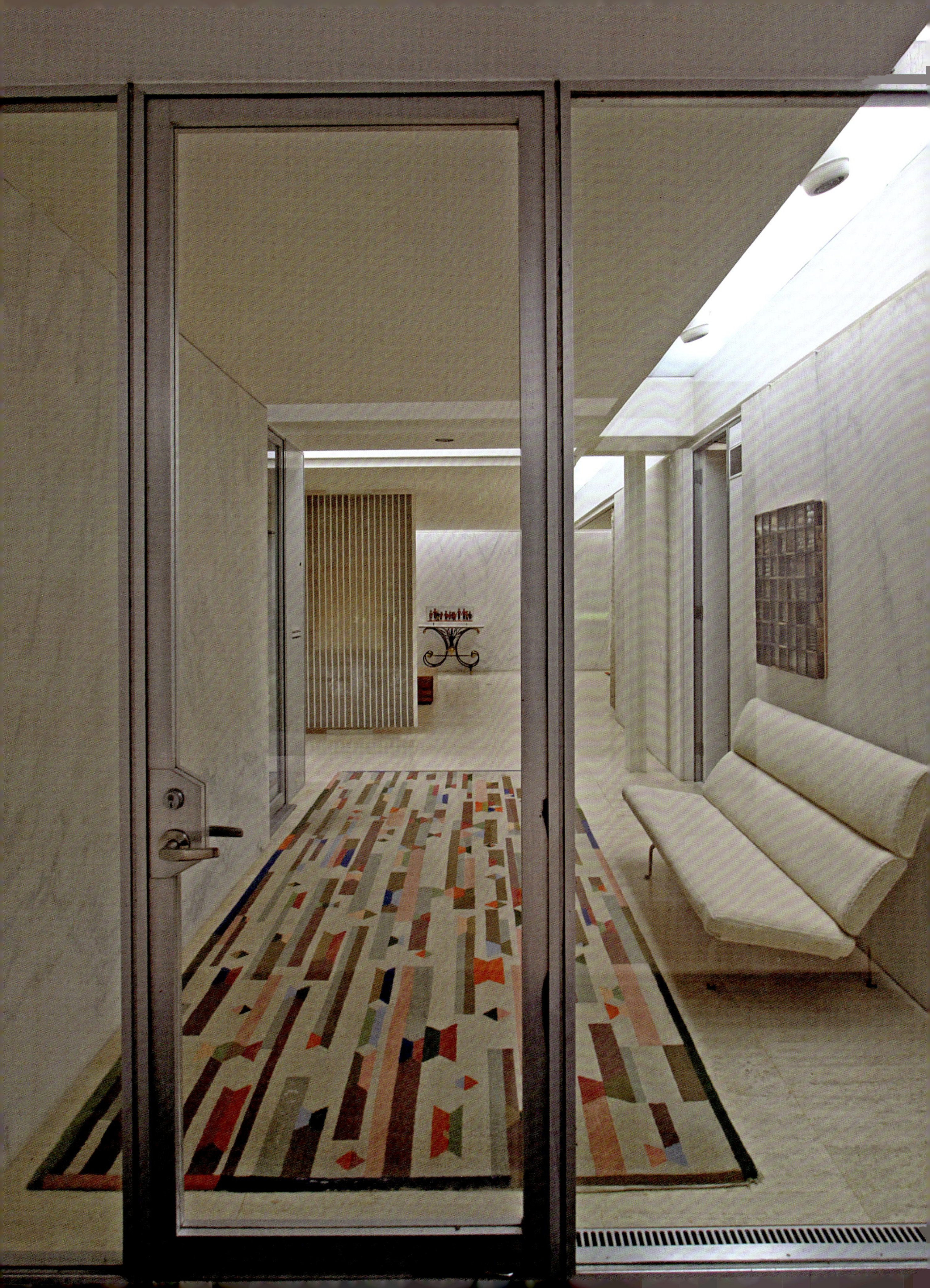

below
Dressing room, with a stool designed by Girard

below
Conversation pit in the living room. Most of the pillow fabrics were designed or selected by Girard or Jack Lenor Larsen.

overleaf
Conversation pit (left) and custom-designed storage wall (right)

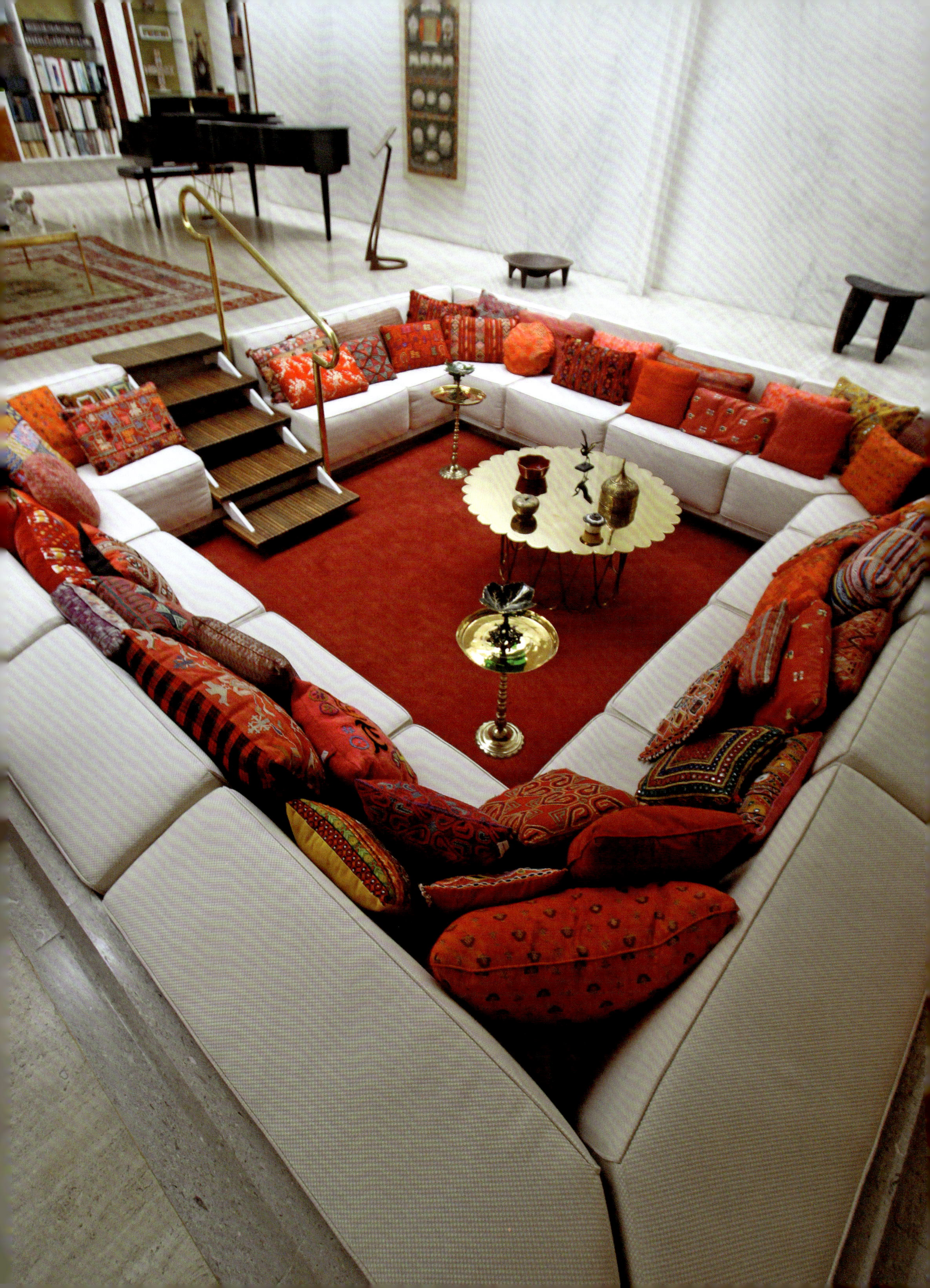

A HISTORY OF ART
CONTEMPORARY SCULPTURE
LE CORBUSIER Creation is a Patient Search
The National Gallery London
Matisse
ACUARELAS DE MARK
Twentieth-Century Architecture
WORLD ARCHITECTURE
TREASURES OF THE VATICAN
AMERICAN PAINTING
ARGONAUTICA
HERMITAGE
Great Private Collections
RENOIR
PICASSO
GAMBERAIA
Tutankhamen
OBJECTS: USA
modern sculpture
ART SINCE 1945

top
Children's playroom

bottom
Storage wall

210

below
Den with a rug designed by Girard and an Eames Lounge Chair and Ottoman

top and bottom
Kitchen

opposite
Dining room with table and Tulip chairs by Saarinen. The rug was designed by Girard, and the light fixture of Murano glass was imported from Italy.

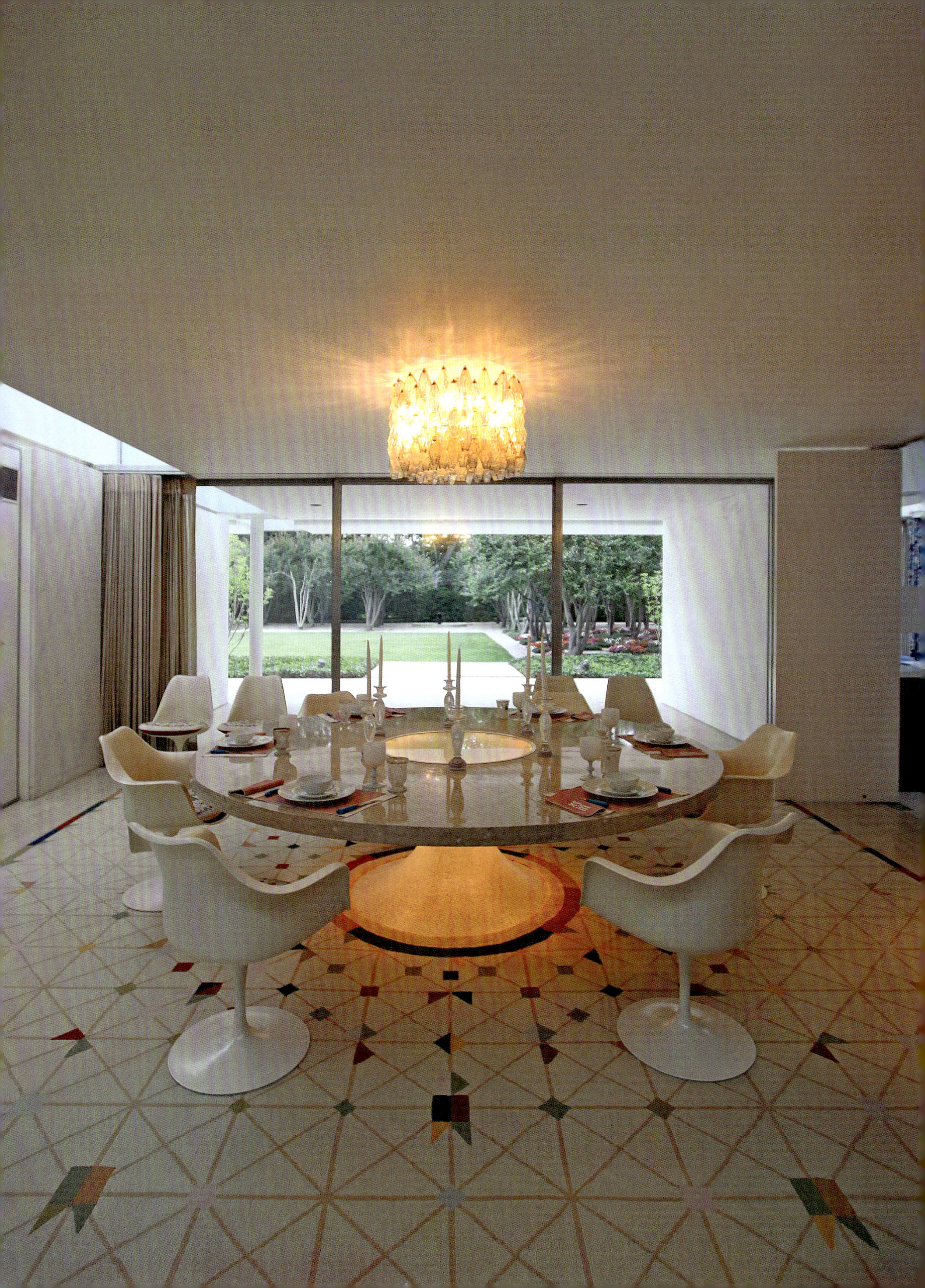

The Dwellings We Inhabit

Susan Saarinen

Class of 1893 at the Polytechnic Institute (from left to right): Armas Lindgren, Eliel Saarinen, Albertina Östman, and Herman Gesellius in 1893

Eero Saarinen visiting Hvitträsk in 1958, with Hal Loucheim, Aline Loucheim Saarinen, and Eric Saarinen sitting on the sofa and Susan Saarinen on the floor

We all grow up experiencing the world influenced by our parents, grandparents, and the places we live. I was born into a family where art and design were common topics of conversation at the dinner table, but I never gave this much thought until I went to Finland with my father, brothers, and stepmother when I was thirteen. I knew that my grandparents came from Finland and that my father and aunt had been born there. I knew that my grandfather and his design partners had created a compound made up of three homes for their respective families and a shared studio west of Helsinki. And I knew that my father and grandfather were both architects and very close, but I only understood what all this meant when we visited my father's ancestral home.

 Built on a bluff above a large lake, standing in the midst of boulders, moss, huge spruce trees, and gleaming white birches, was a huge villa made up of black logs, red shingles, and white masonry with rocks artfully exposed. In its center was a courtyard, and the complex was surrounded by a large garden with different areas. The villa, known as Hvitträsk, was now owned by Anelma and Rainer Vuorio, but they welcomed us, and we stayed with them for almost two weeks. During that time my father showed us around the different parts of the complex and pointed out the spot where my grandfather was buried. The Vuorios invited us quite ceremoniously to use their wood-fired sauna, giving elaborate instructions to those of us who had never had the experience. The sauna house was new, modern, and mostly built of beautiful white birch. While I loved the light-colored wood of this small building, it was the villa itself that fascinated me. It was of another time, made of old materials—grand but cozy. Some of the spaces were designed for entertaining a large number of guests while others were much more intimate. Compared to the sauna, the house was darker but its spaces were filled with playfully painted walls, tapestries, handmade Finnish ryijy rugs, rich-brown glazed brick, intricate iron and metal work, and a variety of elements defined by both modern and medieval form language.

 One of the interesting things about Hvitträsk for me at the time was its mixture of shapes, sizes, and materials, and the resulting juxtapositions. It looked like the master bath had been designed by one person and the living room by another, while repeated motifs, such as medallions with trees or flowers carved into furniture or embroidered on a tablecloth wove a common thread throughout my grandfather's living quarters. It occurred to me that he was experimenting with ideas here. His home was his laboratory, and the natural environment that surrounded the compound provided him with an infinite variety of subjects. Some thirty years later my grandfather's design of the family's residence at the Cranbrook Academy of Art, known today as the Saarinen House, featured the same repeated themes, but they had become modern in character, refined, more derivative, and totally integrated.

When I returned home from Finland after that first visit, I began to pay more attention to family conversations about art and design, and I became conscious for the first time of the differences between Hvitträsk and Saarinen House, my grandparents' home in Michigan. I began to listen to other families' dinner conversations and realized that they rarely talked about design at home, focusing instead on what they had done during the day, on regional or global news, or perhaps some aspect of finance or business. Their houses also looked different: comfortable and pretty but considerably less individual.

I hadn't been to Saarinen House since my grandfather's death eight years before, but I clearly remembered the beautifully crafted dining room chairs that we sat in for Christmas dinner, around a round table that had been magically expanded into a larger one and covered with a custom-made tablecloth. I remembered the many kinds of different woods that were inlayed in clever, nature-inspired designs in various elements on the ground floor, and the rugs that my grandmother designed for each room. Every item in every room seemed to fit together, as if it were made especially for that room. It was then that I realized for the first time that my father, aunt, and grandparents were designers and what that meant. They had created all of the things in Saarinen House *for* Saarinen House, and everything *did* fit together. They didn't go to the store and buy a chair that went with something else. They went ahead and designed it!

Loja Saarinen in the dining room of Saarinen House, ca. 1942

My family's conversations about art and design began to stir my interest. I remember a discussion about the difference between the rounded sculptural forms of a piece by Hans Arp and the more stylized and mechanistic forms of one by Constantin Brancusi. Another exchange was about all the aspects to consider when designing the perfect door handle or the perfect teapot. When my father married my stepmother, Aline, then an art critic for the *New York Times*, the history of art and design became another topic, alongside design theory and the practicalities of manufacturing.

To share his work with us, my father also took my brother and me on a tour through the office from time to time and showed us the firm's current projects. Large models of buildings sat surrounded by rolls and rolls of drawings; the walls were covered with myriad sketches in many different styles of hand. I came to understand that while every member of the team had his or her own workspace, they all worked together to determine what the best ideas were, how to improve them, and what the priorities were. This collaboration reminded me of our discussions at home.

I didn't realize how much I had learned from those conversations and the tours through the studio until I started to study landscape architecture, first at Radcliffe College and later at the University of Colorado at Denver. I brought with me an understanding of process that my fellow students only began to learn in college or in graduate school. But, accustomed as I was to the richness of materials and colors found in Eliel and Eero's architecture, I had to study the development and history of modernism to understand and appreciate modernist architecture with its stark white walls and empty spaces. I found my father's Womb Chair and Pedestal furniture beautiful, but considered Le Corbusier's La Tourette ugly and Dan Kiley's landscape for the Miller House in Columbus, Indiana, unnatural. Only gradually did I comprehend the thinking

left
Chairs designed by Eero Saarinen for Knoll International, with the Womb Chair (1946–48) seen in front

right
Miller House (1953–57), west terrace and living room

behind these new forms and approaches. The Industrial Revolution had given designers and artists new possibilities through advanced building technologies and manufacturing techniques. They had new materials to work with and were eager to experiment with a different kind of architecture.

My father had learned a great deal from the many years of working together with my grandfather, but he was part of a new generation and loved the new technologies. He incorporated them into his designs, such as the Gateway Arch in St. Louis. The stunningly simple-looking memorial to Jefferson's Louisiana Purchase and the opening up of the western part of the North American continent was made of concrete and titanium sandwiched between plates

Eero Saarinen, TWA Terminal (1956–62)

Eero Saarinen working on the design of the Jefferson National Expansion Memorial (1947–65). Working models were an important design tool for Saarinen, who believed that the three-dimensionality of architecture required three-dimensional media to study it. The memorial was one of Saarinen's favorite projects.

of steel. Eero adapted a freight elevator to carry people and designed a machine that could bring materials up the outside of the arch to build it. He often used technology for inspiration. The former Trans World Airlines (TWA) building at New York's John F. Kennedy Airport, a complex sculptural hall conceived to generate a feeling of joy and upward movement, was created before computers were design tools in architectural offices. Drawings were created from large-scale models in the traditional way, but the form the building took was a new kind of architecture.

Today designers have even more materials and processes at their disposal, but they also face more regulations and the ever-present crush of financial realities. Our everyday life has changed as well. We spend much of our time in the digital world, working and socializing via computers, tablets, and mobile phones, or watching television for hours, leaving little time to dream, to enjoy family dinners, or to take pleasure in the living spaces we inhabit. The houses presented in this book remind us of how important the design of the real world surrounding us is for our well-being. They show how much the dwellings we inhabit influence our thinking, our comfort, our happiness, and even our health. Just as I was inspired by our family dinner conversations, these houses will leave their mark in the minds of anyone seeing or experiencing them.

Biographies

The Saarinen family in Hvitträsk (left to right): Pipsan, Loja, Eliel, Eero, and Eliel's father, Juho Saarinen in 1919

ELIEL SAARINEN

1873
Born as Gottlieb Eliel Saarinen in Rantasalmi, Finland, on August 20

1897
Graduates from the department of architecture at the Polytechnic Institute, Helsinki

1896–1905
Founding partner of the architectural office of Gesellius, Lindgren, and Saarinen in Helsinki and Kirkkonummi

1898
Marries Mathilda Tony Charlotta Gyldén (1877–1921)

1903
Divorces Gyldén

1904
Marries Minna Carolina Mathilda Louise (Loja) Gesellius (1894–1949)

1905–7
Continues collaboration with Herman Gesellius in Kirkkonummi, after Armas Lindgren leaves the firm

1907–23
Establishes independent architectural office in Kirkkonummi

1915
Publishes Munkkiniemi-Haaga and Suur-Helsinki plan

1922
Wins second prize in the Chicago Tribune Tower competition

1923
Emigrates to the United States

1923–24
Teaches at the University of Michigan, Ann Arbor

1924–50
Establishes independent practices, first in Ann Arbor, then in Bloomfield Hills, Michigan (Saarinen and Saarinen, collaboration from 1936; Saarinen and Swanson, 1939–44; Saarinen, Swanson, Saarinen, 1945–47; and Saarinen and Saarinen, 1947–50)

1925
Receives commission to design the campus of the Cranbrook Educational Community

1932–46
Serves as president of the Cranbrook Academy of Art

1932
Awarded Dr. h.c. of the University of Helsinki

1933
Awarded Dr. h.c. of the University of Karlsruhe, Germany, and Dr. h.c. of the University of Michigan

1934
Awarded Dr. h.c. of the Helsinki University of Technology

1940
Awarded Dr. h.c. of Harvard University and Dr. h.c. of the University of Cambridge

1941
Royal Institute of British Architects Gold Medal winner

1943
Publishes *The City: Its Growth, Its Decay, Its Future*

1945
Becomes citizen of the United States

1946–50
Serves as director of the Department of Architecture and Urban Design at the Cranbrook Academy of Art

1947
American Institute of Architects (AIA) Gold Medal winner

1948
Awarded Dr. h.c. of Drake University, Des Moines, Iowa, and Dr. h.c. of the University of Iowa

1948
Publishes *Search for Form: A Fundamental Approach to Art*

1950
Dies in Bloomfield Hills, Michigan, on July 1

EERO SAARINEN

1910
Born in Kirkkonummi, Finland, on August 20

1929–30
Studies sculpture at the Académie de la Grande Chaumière, Paris

1934
Receives bachelor of fine arts from Yale School of Architecture

1936–50
Practices with Eliel Saarinen, in different combinations (Saarinen and Saarinen, collaboration from 1936; Saarinen and Swanson, 1939–44; Saarinen, Swanson, Saarinen, 1945–47; and Saarinen and Saarinen, 1947–50)

1939–41
Teaches at Cranbrook Academy of Art

1939
Marries sculptor Lilian Swann (1912–1995)

1940
Becomes citizen of the United States

1942–45
Works for the Office of Strategic Services, Washington, D.C.

1950
Establishes the architectural office Eero Saarinen and Associates

1952
Divorces Swann

1954
Marries art critic Aline Bernstein Loucheim (1914–1972)

1961
Dies in Ann Arbor, Michigan, on September 1

1962
AIA Gold Medal winner (posthumous)

Eero Saarinen's family (left to right): standing, Hal and Don Louchheim, Eric Saarinen; sitting, Susan Saarinen, Eero Saarinen, Loja Saarinen, Aline Louchheim Saarinen, and Eames Saarinen.

PARTNERS AND COLLABORATORS

Herman Gesellius, 1874–1916
Finnish architect; partner in the office Gesellius, Lindgren, and Saarinen (1896–1905); partner in the office Gesellius and Saarinen (1905–7); independent architectural office (1907–16)

Loja (Minna Carolina Louise) Saarinen (neé Gesellius), 1879–1968
Finnish sculptor and textile artist, Studio Loja Saarinen (1928–42); head of the weaving department at Cranbrook Academy of Art (1929–42)

Armas Lindgren, 1874–1929
Finnish architect; partner in the office Gesellius, Lindgren, and Saarinen (1896–1905); independent architectural office (1905–29); director of the Central School of Applied / Industrial Arts, Helsinki (1902–12); professor of architecture at the University of Technology, Helsinki (1921–29)

Pipsan (Eva Lisa) Saarinen Swanson, 1905–1979
Finnish-American interior and textile designer, daughter of Eliel and Loja Saarinen

J. Robert F. Swanson, 1900–1981
American architect, husband of Pipsan Saarinen, partner in the architectural offices Saarinen and Swanson and Saarinen, Swanson, Saarinen

Selected Works

ELIEL SAARINEN

Tallberg Apartment Building
Helsinki, Finland, 1896–98
(Gesellius, Lindgren, and
Saarinen)

**Finnish Pavilion at
the Exposition Universelle**
Paris, France, 1898–1900
(demolished) (Gesellius,
Lindgren, and Saarinen)

**Pohjola Insurance
Company building**
Helsinki, 1899–1901 (Gesellius,
Lindgren, and Saarinen)

Olofsborg Apartment Building
Helsinki, 1900–2 (Gesellius,
Lindgren, and Saarinen)

Hvitträsk
Kirkkonummi, Finland,
1901–3 (Gesellius, Lindgren,
and Saarinen)

Manor house of Suur-Merijoki
Viipurin maalaiskunta,
Finland (now Russia), 1901–3
(demolished) (Gesellius,
Lindgren, and Saarinen)

National Museum of Finland
Helsinki, 1902–11 (Gesellius,
Lindgren, and Saarinen)

Helsinki Railway Station
Helsinki, 1904–19

Vyborg Railway Station
Vyborg, Finland (now Russia),
1904–13 (mostly demolished)

Haus Molchow (Haus Remer)
Alt-Ruppin, Germany, 1905–7
(demolished)

Joensuu Town Hall
Joensuu, Finland, 1909–14

Lahti Town Hall
Lahti, Finland, 1911–12

**Cranbrook Educational
Community**
Bloomfield Hills, Michigan,
1924–42 (Cranbrook School for
Boys, 1925–31; Saarinen House,
1928–30; Kingswood School
for Girls, 1929–31; Cranbrook
Academy of Art Museum and
Library, 1942)

ELIEL SAARINEN IN COLLABORATION WITH EERO SAARINEN

Cranbrook Institute of Science
Bloomfield Hills, Michigan,
1935–38

Kleinhans Music Hall
Buffalo, New York, 1938–40

**Berkshire Music Center,
(Tanglewood Shed)**
Lenox, Massachusetts, 1938–40

**Tabernacle Church of Christ
(now First Christian Church)**
Columbus, Indiana, 1939–42

Crow Island School
Winnetka, Illinois, 1938–42

Des Moines Art Center
Des Moines, Iowa, 1945–48

Christ Church Lutheran
Minneapolis, Minnesota,
1947–49, 1962

Eliel and Eero Saarinen in 1938
with a model of the Berkshire
Music Center opera house

EERO SAARINEN

Case Study House #9, the John Entenza House
Pacific Heights, California, (Eero Saarinen in collaboration with Charles Eames), 1945–49

General Motors Technical Center
Warren, Michigan, 1946–56 (mainly carried out and completed by Eero Saarinen)

The Womb chair and ottoman
1946–48

The United States Jefferson National Expansion Memorial (Gateway Arch)
St. Louis, Missouri, 1947–48 (competition), 1963–65 (construction)

Medbury, Fitch, and Harvey Ingham halls, Quadrangle Dormitories, Hubbell Dining Hall, and Oreon E. Scott Chapel at Drake University
Des Moines, Iowa, 1945–57 (mainly carried out and completed by Eero Saarinen)

Irwin Union Trust Company
Columbus, Indiana, 1950–54

Kresge Auditorium at the Massachusetts Institute of Technology
Cambridge, Massachusetts, 1950–55

Kresge Chapel at the Massachusetts Institute of Technology
Cambridge, Massachusetts, 1950–55

Milwaukee County War Memorial
Milwaukee, Wisconsin, 1952–57

Concordia Senior College, now Concordia Theological Seminary
Fort Wayne, Indiana, 1953–58

Pedestal furniture series
1954–57

United States Chancellery Building
Oslo, Norway, 1955–59

United States Chancellery Building
London, Great Britain, 1955–60

David S. Ingalls Hockey Rink
Yale University, New Haven, Connecticut, 1956–58

IBM Manufacturing and Training Facility
Rochester, Minnesota, 1956–58

Trans World Airlines Terminal at John F. Kennedy International Airport
New York, New York, 1956–62

IBM Thomas J. Watson Research Center
Yorktown Heights, New York, 1957–61

Bell Telephone Laboratories
Holmdel, New Jersey, 1957–62

John Deere and Company Administrative Center
Moline, Illinois, 1957–63

Samuel F. B. Morse and Ezra Stiles Colleges at Yale University
New Haven, Connecticut, 1958–62

Dulles International Airport Terminal
Chantilly, Virginia, 1958–63

Vivian Beaumont Repertory Theater in Lincoln Center
New York, New York, 1958–65

North Christian Church
Columbus, Indiana, 1959–64

Notes

The Home as a Work of Art

1. Eero Saarinen quoting Eliel Saarinen, "The Maturing Modern," in *Time*, July 2, 1956: 51.
2. Eliel Saarinen, *The Search for Form in Art and Architecture* (1948: New York; repr., Dover Publications, 1985), 139–40.
3. Aline B. Saarinen, ed., *Eero Saarinen on His Work* (New Haven and London: Yale University Press, 1962), 6.

Years of Collaboration

1. Marika Hausen, Kirmo Mikkola, Anna-Lisa Amberg, and Tytti Valto, *Eliel Saarinen: Suomen aika* (Helsinki: Suomen rakennustaiteen museo, 1990), 66.
2. Riitta Nikula, *Armas Lindgren 1874–1929: arkkitehti architect* (Helsinki: Suomen rakennustaiteen museo, 1988), 31.
3. Hilla Tarjanne, *S. Wuorio: helsinkiläinen koristemaalausliike* [S. Wuorio, Decoration Painting Firm in Helsinki] (Helsinki: Helsingin kaupunginmuseo, 2007), 136–41.
4. Hausen et al., *Eliel Saarinen*, 16, 38.
5. Marika Hausen, "Hvitträsk: The Home as a Work of Art" in *Hvitträsk: koti taideteoksena* [Hvitträsk: The Home as a Work of Art], ed. Juhani Pallasmaa (Helsinki: Suomen rakennustaiteen museo, 1987), 24.
6. Hausen et al., *Eliel Saarinen*, 29.
7. Tarjanne, *S. Wuorio*, 127.
8. Ibid., 127–28.
9. Letter to Hannes Saarinen, June 22, 1901. In *Kirjeitä Inkerinmaalta: Pietarista ja Suomesta* [Letters from Ingria, St. Petersburg, and Finland], ed. Pentti Voipio (Helsinki: Juho Saarisen sukutoimikunta, 1996), 42.
10. Hausen et al., *Eliel Saarinen*, 39.
11. Riitta Salastie and Raisa Kiljunen-Siirola, *Vuosaari: Uutelan Rakennetun ympäristön arvot* [Vuosaari: Values of Uutela Built Environment] (Helsinki: Helsingin kaupunkisuunnitteluvirasto, 2003), 37.
12. Minna Piispanen, *Villa Miniaton historia* [History of Villa Miniato] (Helsinki: Suunnittelutoimisto Molino Oy, 2002), 9–26.
13. Hausen et al., *Eliel Saarinen*, 127–28; Päivi Hovi-Wasastjerna, *Hvittorp: arkkitehtuuria ja kulttuurihistoriaa.* [Hvittorp: Architecture and Cultural History] (Hämeenlinna: self-published: 2011), 10.
14. Hovi-Wasastjerna, *Hvittorp*, 88–91, 97–99.
15. Hovi-Wasastjerna, *Hvittorp*, 23–25.
16. Hovi-Wasastjerna, *Hvittorp*, 28, 44–50, 70.
17. Hovi-Wasastjerna, *Hvittorp*, 30–33.
18. Hovi-Wasastjerna, *Hvittorp*, 40–43.
19. Hovi-Wasastjerna, *Hvittorp*, 53.
20. According to the terms of the interim peace agreement between Finland and the Soviet Union in 1944, the Soviets leased the Porkkala area west of Helsinki as a military base. The area remains in Soviet control and closed to Finns from 1944 until 1956.
21. Hovi-Wasastjerna, *Hvittorp*, 101-105, 109.
22. Albert Christ-Janer, *Eliel Saarinen* (Chicago: The University of Chicago Press, 1948), 21.
23. Frans Nyberg, *Minnen från Hvitträsk* [Memories from Hvitträsk manuscript] (Helsinki: Suomen rakennustaiteen museo, 1950), 3, 6.
24. Otto-I. Meurman, "Vanha Hvitträsk: luovan hengen monumentti ja arkkitehtien koti [Old Hvitträsk: the Monument of Creative Spirit and Architects' Home]," *Arkkitehti (Finnish Architectural Review)* 8 (1971): 58–59.
25. Eino Ketola, *Suomen sydäntä kuullen. Päivölä 1905–95* (Helsinki: Päivölän Virkistyskoti, 1997), 35–37.

Eliel Saarinen in Finland

1. Marika Hausen, Kirmo Mikkola, Anna-Lisa Amberg, and Tytti Valto, *Eliel Saarinen, Suomen aika* (Helsinki: Suomen rakennustaiteen museo, 1990), 66.
2. *Sortavala-projekti: Winterin huvila* [Sortavala Project: Villa Winter] Report of the engineering office Aaro Kohonen Oy (Espoo, Aaro Kohonen Oy: 1991), 1.
3. Lars och Bernt Paqvalén, *Villa Granagård: 100 år* [Villa Granagård: 100 Years] (Helsinki, self-published: 2011), 20.
4. Ibid., 25, 50, 57.
5. "Taidetta eleganteille naisille ja silinterihattuherroille [Art for Elegant Ladies and Top Hat Gentlemen]" in *Helsingin Sanomat*, June 30, 2001.
6. Eliel Saarinen, *Munkkiniemi-Haaga ja Suur-Helsinki* (Helsinki: M. G. Stenius Osakeyhtiö, 1915), 91.

The American Years

1. Saarinen and Saarinen collaboration, 1936–50; Saarinen and Swanson, 1939–44; Saarinen, Swanson, Saarinen, 1945–47; and Saarinen and Saarinen, 1947–50.
2. George Booth's letter to Eliel Saarinen, 29 December, 1941. George G. Booth Archives; Cranbrook Archives.
3. Tabernacle Church of Christ, later First Christian Church, Columbus, Indiana (1942) and Christ Church Lutheran, Minneapolis, Minnesota (1949).

4   Aline B. Saarinen, ed., *Eero Saarinen on His Work* (New Haven and London: Yale University Press, 1962), 14.

5   Frank Lloyd Wright's note to Eero Saarinen, January 27, 1959. Manuscripts and Archives, Yale University Library.

6   The apartments were named residence #1 and #2.

7   Gregory Wittkopp, "Saarinen House: An Architectural History," in *Saarinen House and Garden* (Cranbrook Academy of Art Museum; New York: Harry N. Abrams, Inc., 1995), 31.

8   Ibid., 30–31, 35, 39.

9   Eliel Saarinen, *The Search for Form in Art and Architecture* (1948: New York: repr., Dover Publications, 1985), 231.

10 Ibid., 242.

11 Wittkopp, "Saarinen House," 38.

12 Wittkopp, "Saarinen House," 42–43.

13 Gregory Wittkopp's book describes in detail the restoration work.

14 Marsha Miro, "A House Ahead of its Time" in *Free Press*, January 21, 1982: 1C.

15 Grand Rapids Historical Commission, "Johnson Furniture Co.," *Furniture City History*, www.furniturecityhistory.org/article/3645/johnson-furniture-co.

16 Miro, "A House Ahead of its Time," 1C.

17 Phyllis G. Brockmyer, *The A. C. Wermuth House, Fort Wayne, Indiana Designed by Eliel and Eero Saarinen, 1939* (Manuscript, Architectural Historic Survey, College of Architecture and Planning, Ball State University, 1989), 1.

18 Ibid., 1.

19 Albert Christ-Janer, *Eliel Saarinen* (Chicago: The University of Chicago Press, 1948), 93.

20 Eero Saarinen, "A Combined Living-Dining Room-Study Designed for the *Architectural Forum*," in *Architectural Forum*, October 1937: 303–5.

21 Letters from J. Irwin Miller to Eero Saarinen and Alexander Girard, May 2 in 1953. Miller House and Garden Collection, IMA Archives, Indianapolis Museum of Art.

22 Eero Saarinen's letter to Alexander Girard, March 10 in 1954. Miller House and Garden Collection, IMA Archives, Indianapolis Museum of Art.

23 J. Irwin Miller's letter to Alexander Girard, March 19 in 1954. Miller House and Garden Collection, IMA Archives, Indianapolis Museum of Art.

24 "A Contemporary Palladian Villa," in *Architectural Forum*, September 1958: 126–31.

25 J. Irwin Miller's letter to Alexander Girard, March 19 in 1954. Miller House and Garden Collection, IMA Archives, Indianapolis Museum of Art.

26 "H&G's Hallmark House No. 3: A New Concept," in *House & Garden*, February 1959: 67.

27 J. Irwin Miller's letter to Alexander Girard, 10 August 1955. Miller House and Garden Collection, IMA Archives, Indianapolis Museum of Art.

28 Dan Kiley, "Lecture," in *Dan Kiley Landscapes: The Poetry of Space*, eds. Reuben M. Rainey, Marc Treib (Richmond, Virginia: William Stout Publishers, 2009), 26.

Illustration Credits

All images are by Jari Jetsonen unless credited otherwise.

7, 216 (right), 217 (bottom), 218, 219: unknown photographer, Yale University Library Manuscripts and Archives
18, 168 (top and bottom): Daishi Sakaguchi, 2013
19 (top): Eric Sundström, Wuorio Foundation
19 (middle left): C. Grünberg, Helsinki City Museum's Picture Archives (HCM)
19 (middle right): unknown photographer, Wuorio Foundation
19 (bottom), 28 (left and right), 45 (top), 59 (top), 60 (top and bottom right), 76 (top), 94 (top and bottom), 104 (top and bottom right), 120 (middle), 140 (bottom): Eliel Saarinen, MFA
29 (top left and right): Hannes Saarinen, Martti Saarinen photo album
29 (bottom): Einar Saarinen, Martti Saarinen photo album
36, 110 (middle): Simo Rista, MFA
37, 93 (top right and bottom): Gesellius, Lindgren, Saarinen, MFA
44 (left and right): measuring drawing, architectural history students at Helsinki University of Technology, MFA
45 (bottom), 73 (middle and bottom), 74 (top), 75 (top): unknown photographer, MFA
58 (left and right): unknown draftsman, Evangelical Lutheran Parishes of Espoo
59 (bottom): Artur Faltin, NBA
60 (top left): Eric Sundström, HCM
60 (bottom left), 140 (top): unknown photographer, HCM
73 (top left and top right), 104 (middle and bottom left), 131 (bottom): unknown photographer, National Board of Antiquities in Finland, picture collections (NBA)
81 (top): Lars-Bertil Paqvalén
93 (top right): unknown photographer, Martti Mäkelä photo album
110 (top): Tytti Valto, MFA
110 (bottom): unknown photographer, Bernt Paqvalén photo album
111 (top): Eliel Saarinen, Bernt Paqvalén photo album
120 (top): Alvar Cawén, NBA
120 (bottom): building permission document 1929, Helsinki City Archives
130: Eric Sundström, MFA
131 (top left and right): Eliel Saarinen, The National Archives
151 (top left), 190 (top): unknown photographer, Cranbrook Archives
151 (top right and bottom): Eliel Saarinen, Cranbrook Archives
169 (top): Saarinen, Swanson, Saarinen, private collection (James A. Kelly)
180 (top left and right): Saarinen, Saarinen, Cranbrook Archives
180 (bottom): Askew, Cranbrook Archives
181 (top): John H. Foreman, 1981, private collection (Barbara and J. Paul Gentile)
190 (bottom), 199 (bottom): Eero Saarinen, Yale University Library Manuscripts and Archives
199 (top): unknown photographer, Miller family album, American Decorative Arts, Indianapolis Museum of Art (IMA)
214 (top): C. P. Dyrendahl, MFA
214 (bottom): Jussi Pohjakallio, Finnish Press Agency
215: unknown photographer, Cranbrook Archives
216 (left): Harvey Croze, Cranbrook, Yale University Library Manuscripts and Archives
217 (top): Sirkkaliisa Jetsonen, 2011
220: unknown photographer, Susan Saarinen photo album

Published by
Princeton Architectural Press
37 East 7th Street
New York, New York 10003
www.papress.com

© 2014 Princeton Architectural Press,
Jari Jetsonen, Sirkkaliisa Jetsonen
All rights reserved
Printed and bound in China by C&C Offset Printing Co., Ltd.
17 16 15 14   4 3 2 1 First edition

No part of this book may be used or reproduced in any manner without written permission from the publisher, except in the context of reviews. Every reasonable attempt has been made to identify owners of copyright. Errors or omissions will be corrected in subsequent editions.

Editor: Nicola Brower
Designer: Benjamin English

Special thanks to: Meredith Baber, Sara Bader, Janet Behning, Megan Carey, Carina Cha, Andrea Chlad, Russell Fernandez, Will Foster, Jan Hartman, Jan Haux, Diane Levinson, Jennifer Lippert, Katharine Myers, Jaime Nelson, Rob Shaeffer, Andrew Stepanian, Sara Stemen, Marielle Suba, Paul Wagner, and Joseph Weston of Princeton Architectural Press —Kevin C. Lippert, publisher

Library of Congress Cataloging-in-Publication Data:
Jetsonen, Jari, 1958– author.
Saarinen houses / Jari Jetsonen and Sirkkaliisa Jetsonen. — First edition.
  pages cm
Includes bibliographical references.
ISBN 978-1-61689-265-4 (hardback)
1. Saarinen, Eliel, 1873–1950—Criticism and interpretation. 2. Saarinen, Eero, 1910–1961—Criticism and interpretation. 3. Architecture, Domestic—History—19th century. 4. Architecture, Domestic—History—20th century. I. Jetsonen, Sirkkaliisa, author. II. Title.
NA1455.F53S24435 2014
728'.370922—dc23   2014013758